YOUR CHINESE HOROSCOPE 2006

NEIL SOMERVILLE

What the Year of the Dog Holds in Store for You

BARNES & NOBLE

NEW YORK

TO ROS, RICHARD AND EMILY

This edition published by Barnes & Noble Publishing, Inc.,
by arrangement with HarperElement,
An Imprint of HarperCollins*Publishers*

2005 Barnes & Noble Books

M 10 9 8 7 6 5 4 3 2 1

ISBN 0-7607-7404-8

A catalogue record for this book is
available from the British Library

Printed and bound in China by
Imago

CONTENTS

ABOUT THE AUTHOR

Neil Somerville is one of the leading writers in the West on Chinese horoscopes. He has been interested in Eastern forms of divination for many years and believes that much can be learned from the ancient wisdom of the East. His annual book on Chinese horoscopes has built up an international following and he is also the author of *What's your Chinese Love Sign?* (Thorsons, 2000), *Chinese Success Signs* (Thorsons, 2001) and *The Answers* (Element, 2004).

Neil Somerville was born in the year of the Water Snake. His wife was born under the sign of the Monkey, his son is an Ox and his daughter a Horse.

ACKNOWLEDGEMENTS

In writing *Your Chinese Horoscope 2006* I am grateful for the assistance and support that those around me have given.

I wish to acknowledge Theodora Lau's *The Handbook of Chinese Horoscopes* (Harper & Row, 1979; Arrow, 1981), which was particularly useful to me in my research.

In addition to Ms Lau's work, I commend the following books to those who wish to find out more about Chinese horoscopes: Kristyna Arcarti, *Chinese Horoscopes for Beginners* (Headway, 1995); Catherine Aubier, *Chinese Zodiac Signs* (Arrow, 1984), series of 12 books; E. A. Crawford and Teresa Kennedy, *Chinese Elemental Astrology* (Piatkus Books, 1992); Paula Delsol, *Chinese Horoscopes* (Pan, 1973); Barry Fantoni, *Barry Fantoni's Chinese Horoscopes* (Warner, 1994); Bridget Giles and the Diagram Group, *Chinese Astrology* (HarperCollins*Publishers*, 1996); Kwok Man-Ho, *Authentic Chinese Horoscopes* (Arrow, 1987), series of 12 books; Lori Reid, *The Complete Book of Chinese Horoscopes* (Element Books, 1997); Paul Rigby and Harvey Bean, *Chinese Astrologics* (Publications Division, South China Morning Post Ltd, 1981); Ruth Q. Sun, *The Asian Animal Zodiac* (Charles E. Tuttle Company, Inc., 1996); Derek Walters, *Ming Shu* (Pagoda Books, 1987) and *The Chinese Astrology Workbook* (The Aquarian Press,

1988); Suzanne White, *Suzanne White's Book of Chinese Chance* (Fontana/Collins, 1978) and *The New Astrology* (Pan, 1987) and *The New Chinese Astrology* (Pan, 1994).

————◆◆————

As we march into a new year
we each have our hopes, our ambitions and our dreams.

Sometimes fate and circumstance will assist us,
sometimes we will struggle and despair,
but march we must.

For it is those who keep going,
and who keep their aspirations alive,
who stand the greatest chance of securing what they want.

March determinedly,
and your determination will, in some way, be rewarded.

Neil Somerville

————◆◆————

INTRODUCTION

The origins of Chinese horoscopes have been lost in the mists of time. It is known that Oriental astrologers practised their art many thousands of years ago and even today Chinese astrology continues to fascinate and intrigue.

In Chinese astrology there are 12 signs named after 12 different animals. No one quite knows how the signs acquired their names, but there is one legend that offers an explanation.

According to this legend, one Chinese New Year the Buddha invited all the animals in his kingdom to come before him. Unfortunately, for reasons best known to the animals, only 12 turned up. The first to arrive was the Rat, followed by the Ox, Tiger, Rabbit, Dragon, Snake, Horse, Goat, Monkey, Rooster, Dog and finally Pig.

In gratitude, the Buddha decided to name a year after each of the animals and that those born during that year would inherit some of the personality of that animal. Therefore those born in the year of the Ox would be hardworking, resolute and stubborn, just like the Ox, while those born in the year of the Dog would be loyal and faithful, just like the Dog. While not everyone can possibly share all the characteristics of a sign, it is incredible what similarities do occur and this is partly where the fascination of Chinese horoscopes lies.

In addition to the 12 signs of the Chinese zodiac there are five elements, and these have a strengthening or moderating influence upon the sign. Details about the effects of the elements are given in each of the chapters on the 12 signs.

To find out which sign you were born under, refer to the tables on the following pages. As the Chinese year is based on the lunar year and does not start until late January or early February, it is particularly important for anyone born in those two months to check carefully the dates of the Chinese year in which they were born.

Also included, in the Appendix, are two charts showing the compatibility between the signs for personal and business relationships, and details about the signs ruling the different hours of the day. From this it is possible to locate your ascendant and, as in Western astrology, this has a significant influence on your personality.

In writing this book, I have taken the unusual step of combining the intriguing nature of Chinese horoscopes with the Western desire to know what the future holds and have based my interpretations upon various factors relating to each of the signs. Over the years in which *Your Chinese Horoscope* has been published I have been pleased that so many have found the sections on the forthcoming year of interest, and hope that the horoscope has been constructive and useful. Remember, though, that at all times you are the master of your own destiny. I sincerely hope that *Your Chinese Horoscope 2006* will prove interesting and helpful for the year ahead.

THE CHINESE YEARS

Horse	25 January	1906	to	12 February	1907
Goat	13 February	1907	to	1 February	1908
Monkey	2 February	1908	to	21 January	1909
Rooster	22 January	1909	to	9 February	1910
Dog	10 February	1910	to	29 January	1911
Pig	30 January	1911	to	17 February	1912
Rat	18 February	1912	to	5 February	1913
Ox	6 February	1913	to	25 January	1914
Tiger	26 January	1914	to	13 February	1915
Rabbit	14 February	1915	to	2 February	1916
Dragon	3 February	1916	to	22 January	1917
Snake	23 January	1917	to	10 February	1918
Horse	11 February	1918	to	31 January	1919
Goat	1 February	1919	to	19 February	1920
Monkey	20 February	1920	to	7 February	1921
Rooster	8 February	1921	to	27 January	1922
Dog	28 January	1922	to	15 February	1923
Pig	16 February	1923	to	4 February	1924
Rat	5 February	1924	to	23 January	1925
Ox	24 January	1925	to	12 February	1926
Tiger	13 February	1926	to	1 February	1927
Rabbit	2 February	1927	to	22 January	1928
Dragon	23 January	1928	to	9 February	1929
Snake	10 February	1929	to	29 January	1930

Horse	30 January	1930	to	16 February	1931
Goat	17 February	1931	to	5 February	1932
Monkey	6 February	1932	to	25 January	1933
Rooster	26 January	1933	to	13 February	1934
Dog	14 February	1934	to	3 February	1935
Pig	4 February	1935	to	23 January	1936
Rat	24 January	1936	to	10 February	1937
Ox	11 February	1937	to	30 January	1938
Tiger	31 January	1938	to	18 February	1939
Rabbit	19 February	1939	to	7 February	1940
Dragon	8 February	1940	to	26 January	1941
Snake	27 January	1941	to	14 February	1942
Horse	15 February	1942	to	4 February	1943
Goat	5 February	1943	to	24 January	1944
Monkey	25 January	1944	to	12 February	1945
Rooster	13 February	1945	to	1 February	1946
Dog	2 February	1946	to	21 January	1947
Pig	22 January	1947	to	9 February	1948
Rat	10 February	1948	to	28 January	1949
Ox	29 January	1949	to	16 February	1950
Tiger	17 February	1950	to	5 February	1951
Rabbit	6 February	1951	to	26 January	1952
Dragon	27 January	1952	to	13 February	1953
Snake	14 February	1953	to	2 February	1954
Horse	3 February	1954	to	23 January	1955
Goat	24 January	1955	to	11 February	1956
Monkey	12 February	1956	to	30 January	1957
Rooster	31 January	1957	to	17 February	1958
Dog	18 February	1958	to	7 February	1959
Pig	8 February	1959	to	27 January	1960
Rat	28 January	1960	to	14 February	1961

Ox	15 February	1961	to	4 February	1962
Tiger	5 February	1962	to	24 January	1963
Rabbit	25 January	1963	to	12 February	1964
Dragon	13 February	1964	to	1 February	1965
Snake	2 February	1965	to	20 January	1966
Horse	21 January	1966	to	8 February	1967
Goat	9 February	1967	to	29 January	1968
Monkey	30 January	1968	to	16 February	1969
Rooster	17 February	1969	to	5 February	1970
Dog	6 February	1970	to	26 January	1971
Pig	27 January	1971	to	14 February	1972
Rat	15 February	1972	to	2 February	1973
Ox	3 February	1973	to	22 January	1974
Tiger	23 January	1974	to	10 February	1975
Rabbit	11 February	1975	to	30 January	1976
Dragon	31 January	1976	to	17 February	1977
Snake	18 February	1977	to	6 February	1978
Horse	7 February	1978	to	27 January	1979
Goat	28 January	1979	to	15 February	1980
Monkey	16 February	1980	to	4 February	1981
Rooster	5 February	1981	to	24 January	1982
Dog	25 January	1982	to	12 February	1983
Pig	13 February	1983	to	1 February	1984
Rat	2 February	1984	to	19 February	1985
Ox	20 February	1985	to	8 February	1986
Tiger	9 February	1986	to	28 January	1987
Rabbit	29 January	1987	to	16 February	1988
Dragon	17 February	1988	to	5 February	1989
Snake	6 February	1989	to	26 January	1990
Horse	27 January	1990	to	14 February	1991
Goat	15 February	1991	to	3 February	1992

Monkey	4 February	1992	to	22 January	1993
Rooster	23 January	1993	to	9 February	1994
Dog	10 February	1994	to	30 January	1995
Pig	31 January	1995	to	18 February	1996
Rat	19 February	1996	to	6 February	1997
Ox	7 February	1997	to	27 January	1998
Tiger	28 January	1998	to	15 February	1999
Rabbit	16 February	1999	to	4 February	2000
Dragon	5 February	2000	to	23 January	2001
Snake	24 January	2001	to	11 February	2002
Horse	12 February	2002	to	31 January	2003
Goat	1 February	2003	to	21 January	2004
Monkey	22 January	2004	to	8 February	2005
Rooster	9 February	2005	to	28 January	2006
Dog	29 January	2006	to	17 February	2007

NOTE

The names of the signs in the Chinese zodiac occasionally differ in the various books on Chinese astrology, although the characteristics of the signs remain the same. In some books the Ox is referred to as the Buffalo or Bull, the Rabbit as the Hare or Cat, the Goat as the Sheep and the Pig as the Boar.

For the sake of convenience, the male gender is used throughout this book. Unless otherwise stated, the characteristics of the signs apply to both sexes.

WELCOME TO THE
YEAR OF THE DOG

The dog has often been called man's best friend and whether as a mountain rescuer, a farm worker, a protector of property or a faithful and loyal pet, he certainly does a great deal for humanity. And some of his qualities will be evident in his own special year.

The Year of the Dog begins on 29 January and a key feature will be an emphasis on defence. The dog is very much a protector of property and rights, and over the year attention will be focused on matters of security and the maintenance of law and order. As a result, many countries will introduce further measures to tighten defence and security systems and protect borders as well as take action against the threat of terrorism. During the year there will also be some key summits on global security, with further agreements being reached, particularly on the sharing of resources.

Bodies such as the United Nations will also play a pivotal role, especially in trying to stabilize troubled areas and bring order to areas of conflict. Often the conflicts that do occur over the year will have their origins in a rise of nationalist and ethnic fervour, with certain groups laying claim to land they consider their own. It was a Dog year when Argentina invaded the Falkland Islands, territory they had long laid claim to, and it was in the last Dog year that there was such bloodshed between factions in Rwanda. Unfortunately this pattern is likely to continue in 2006, with authorities often having to act with considerable force to reimpose order and restore rights as well as to protect any threat to territory. The Dog year is a strict and stout defender of both land *and* property.

Another feature of the year is that interest groups will be active in bringing their causes to the attention of governments. It was in a Dog year that Lord Russell launched the Campaign for Nuclear Disarmament, which resulted in so many protests and culminated in the circling of Greenham Common Airbase by 30,000 women in another Dog year. This Dog year will again see groups actively campaigning, with some historic rallies and protests taking place.

Politically, Dog years have generally favoured the Left and it is likely that several countries will see socialists and liberal-thinking politicians winning increased support for their policies. A number of countries will also see significant changes in their constitutions over the year. It was in Dog years that Portugal and Italy became republics, that the fifth French Republic was formed, that Egypt became independent and that the new South African constitution came into force, with Nelson Mandela being elected President shortly afterwards. In addition several countries are likely to see important changes in their leadership over the year, and those who come to power in Dog years often go on to play an important and historic role in world affairs.

Another issue which will feature prominently will be the environment. It was in a Dog year that the world's first

Earth Day was held, and with further research being released on the effects of global warming and some dramatic weather patterns (and unfortunately some natural disasters too), there will be increased pressure for more to be done to protect the environment and to conserve the world's resources. As a result, some landmark agreements will be reached and many governments will be instrumental in encouraging greater conservation and a more economic use of resources.

Humanitarian matters also feature prominently in Dog years, and this year again initiatives will be launched to help areas affected by drought, disease and disaster. In addition to aid and monetary assistance, attention will be focused on ways of preventing future suffering. Whether through the introduction of new farming methods, greater education, improved medical facilities or the treatment of certain diseases, the year will see many practical improvements. This humanitarian strand will also see many individual governments introducing measures to help the underprivileged, the suffering and those in need of support. The Dog year does have both a practical and a caring element to it.

As far as economic matters are concerned, the year will see slow but steady growth in many countries around the world, accompanied by a levelling off and fall in unemployment figures. In view of the emphasis given to defence and security over the year, industries in these areas could fare particularly well. However, the Dog year does provide some salutary warnings for companies tempted to over-expand in competitive areas or to borrow too heavily. Laker Airways and the De Lorean Car Company both failed in

Dog years and 2006 could see further casualties or some major companies being taken over. For the individual investor, too, this is a year for caution. Many will tend to opt for safer and surer investments rather than riskier speculations.

Another feature of the year will be a lessening in the more materialistic culture seen in recent times. Many will begin to value their existing assets and what is personally important to them, rather than seeking to acquire more. As a result, family bonds will often grow stronger, with many people making more effort to spend quality time with their loved ones as well as on improving their home. Indeed, the Chinese have often held that the Dog year brings harmony and peace to home life, and this will be true for many. This is also considered a favourable year for marriage.

For the individual the year will often see a reappraisal of values and lifestyles and many will benefit from the supportive influence that characterizes the Dog year. However, it should be mentioned that this is not a year for the slacker. It requires effort, discipline and focus, and improvements will need to be worked for.

For us all, the Dog year holds both hope and potential. Use it well, and, while some signs will fare better than others, may this be a good year for you and may the chances that the year will bring go in your favour.

I wish you good fortune and happiness in the year ahead.

YOUR CHINESE
HOROSCOPE 2006

18 FEBRUARY 1912 ～ 5 FEBRUARY 1913	*Water Rat*
5 FEBRUARY 1924 ～ 23 JANUARY 1925	*Wood Rat*
24 JANUARY 1936 ～ 10 FEBRUARY 1937	*Fire Rat*
10 FEBRUARY 1948 ～ 28 JANUARY 1949	*Earth Rat*
28 JANUARY 1960 ～ 14 FEBRUARY 1961	*Metal Rat*
15 FEBRUARY 1972 ～ 2 FEBRUARY 1973	*Water Rat*
2 FEBRUARY 1984 ～ 19 FEBRUARY 1985	*Wood Rat*
19 FEBRUARY 1996 ～ 6 FEBRUARY 1997	*Fire Rat*

THE
RAT

THE PERSONALITY OF THE RAT

I want to be all that I am capable of becoming.

Katherine Mansfield, a Rat

The Rat is born under the sign of charm. He is intelligent, popular and loves attending parties and large social gatherings. He is able to establish friendships with remarkable ease and people generally feel relaxed in his company. He is a very social creature and is genuinely interested in the welfare and activities of others. He has a good understanding of human nature and his advice and opinions are often sought.

The Rat is a hard and diligent worker. He is also very imaginative and is never short of ideas. However, he does sometimes lack the confidence to promote his ideas and this can often prevent him from securing the recognition he deserves.

The Rat is very observant and many Rats have made excellent writers and journalists. The Rat also excels at personnel and PR work and any job which brings him into contact with people and the media. His skills are particularly appreciated in times of crisis, for the Rat has an incredibly strong sense of self-preservation. When it comes to finding a way out of an awkward situation, the Rat is certain to be the one who comes up with a solution.

The Rat loves to be where there is a lot of action, but should he ever find himself in a very bureaucratic or restrictive environment he can become a stickler for discipline and routine.

He is also something of an opportunist and is constantly on the lookout for ways in which he can improve his wealth and lifestyle. He rarely lets an opportunity go by and can become involved in so many plans and schemes that he sometimes squanders his energies and achieves very little as a result. He is also rather gullible and can be taken in by those less scrupulous than himself.

Another characteristic of the Rat is his attitude towards money. He is very thrifty and to some he may appear a little mean. The reason for this is purely that he likes to keep his money within his family. He can be most generous to his partner, his children and close friends and relatives. He can also be generous to himself, for he often finds it impossible to deprive himself of any luxury or object he fancies. He is very acquisitive and can be a notorious hoarder. He also hates waste and is rarely prepared to throw anything away. He can be rather greedy and will rarely refuse an invitation for a free meal or a complimentary ticket to some lavish function.

The Rat is a good conversationalist, although he can occasionally be a little indiscreet. He can be highly critical of others – for an honest and unbiased opinion, the Rat is a superb critic – and sometimes will use confidential information to his own advantage. However, as he has such a bright and irresistible nature, most people are prepared to forgive him his slight indiscretions.

Throughout his long and eventful life the Rat will make many friends and will find that he is especially well suited to those born under his own sign and those of the Ox, Dragon and Monkey. He can also get on well with those born under the signs of the Tiger, Snake, Rooster, Dog and

Pig, but the rather sensitive Rabbit and Goat will find the Rat a little too critical and blunt for their liking. The Horse and Rat will also find it difficult to get on with each other – the Rat craves security and will find the Horse's changeable moods and independent nature a little unsettling.

The Rat is very family-orientated and will do anything to please his nearest and dearest. He is exceptionally loyal to his parents and can himself be a very caring and loving parent. He will take an interest in all his children's activities and will see that they want for nothing. The Rat usually has a large family.

The female Rat has a kindly, outgoing nature and involves herself in a multitude of different activities. She has a wide circle of friends, enjoys entertaining and is an attentive hostess. She is also conscientious about the upkeep of her home and has good taste in home furnishings. She is most supportive to the other members of her family and, due to her resourceful, friendly and persevering nature, can do well in practically any career.

Although the Rat is essentially outgoing, he is also a very private individual. He tends to keep his feelings to himself and while he is not averse to learning what other people are doing, he resents anyone prying too closely into his own affairs. He also does not like solitude and if he is alone for any length of time he can easily get depressed.

The Rat is undoubtedly very talented, but he does sometimes fail to capitalize on his many abilities. He has a tendency to become involved in too many schemes and chase after too many opportunities all at once. If he can slow down and concentrate on one thing at a time, he can become very successful. If not, success and wealth can elude him. But, with his tremendous ability to charm, the Rat will rarely, if ever, be without friends.

THE FIVE DIFFERENT TYPES OF RAT

In addition to the 12 signs of the Chinese zodiac there are five elements and these have a strengthening or moderating influence on the sign. The effects of the five elements on the Rat are described below, together with the years in which the elements were exercising their influence. Therefore those Rats born in 1960 are Metal Rats, those born in 1912 and 1972 are Water Rats, and so on.

Metal Rat: 1960

This Rat has excellent taste and certainly knows how to appreciate the finer things in life. His home is comfortable and nicely decorated and he likes to entertain and mix in fashionable circles. He has considerable financial acumen and invests his money well. On the surface the Metal Rat appears cheerful and confident, but deep down he can be troubled by worries that are quite often of his own making. He is exceptionally loyal to his family and friends.

Water Rat: 1912, 1972

The Water Rat is intelligent and very astute. He is a deep thinker and can express his thoughts clearly and persuasively. He is always eager to learn and is talented in many different areas. He is usually very popular, but his fear of

YOUR CHINESE HOROSCOPE 2006

loneliness can sometimes lead him into mixing with the wrong sort of company. He is a particularly skilful writer, but he can get side-tracked very easily and should try to concentrate on just one thing at a time.

Wood Rat: 1924, 1984

The Wood Rat has a friendly, outgoing personality and is popular with his colleagues and friends. He has a quick, agile brain and likes to turn his hand to anything he thinks may be useful. His one fear is insecurity, but given his intelligence and capabilities, this fear is usually unfounded. He has a good sense of humour, enjoys travel and, due to his highly imaginative nature, can be a gifted writer or artist.

Fire Rat: 1936, 1996

The Fire Rat is rarely still and seems to have a never-ending supply of energy and enthusiasm. He loves being involved in the action – be it travel, following up new ideas or campaigning for a cause in which he fervently believes. He is an original thinker and hates being bound by petty restrictions or the dictates of others. He can be forthright in his views, but can sometimes get carried away in the excitement of the moment and commit himself to various undertakings without thinking through all the implications. Yet he has a resilient nature and with the right support can often go far in life.

Earth Rat: 1948

This Rat is astute and very level-headed. He rarely takes unnecessary chances and while he is constantly trying to improve his financial status, he is prepared to proceed slowly and leave nothing to chance. The Earth Rat is probably not as adventurous as the other types of Rat and prefers to remain in familiar territory rather than rush headlong into something he knows little about. He is talented, conscientious and caring towards his loved ones, but at the same time can be self-conscious and worry a little too much about the image he is trying to project.

PROSPECTS FOR THE RAT IN 2006

The Year of the Rooster (9 February 2005 to 28 January 2006) will have been a busy one for the Rat and the remaining months will see little let up in the activity. However, while the Rat may sometimes despair over the number of things he has to do, he has a resourceful nature and this will serve him well.

In his work there will be chances for him to make good use of his skills and for those Rats who are keen on furthering their career or are looking for work, September and November could bring some interesting openings. Overall, though, this is a time to be bold and alert and to act quickly when opportunities arise.

The Rat's domestic and social life will also become busier as the Rooster year draws to a close. As well as the many activities he is already involved in, there will also be chances to travel and to meet friends and relations he does not often get to see as well as invitations to various social gatherings. The Rat will certainly find himself in demand at this time, with August, September and the weeks leading up to and just following Christmas being busy and often enjoyable. Also, romantic prospects are favourable and for those Rats enjoying newfound romance, the closing months of the Rooster year can be a special time.

The Year of the Dog starts on 29 January and will be a variable one for the Rat. In some areas of his life he will enjoy considerable good fortune while in others problems and pressures could loom and he will need to be careful. However, the Rat has an alert and canny nature and is often able to foresee problems before they arise or extricate himself from difficult situations, and this year his abilities will serve him well.

As far as his work is concerned, this will be a busy year. However, there will be good opportunities to make progress. In order to get the most from the year, though, the Rat will need to remain disciplined. This is not a time when he can afford to spread his attention or energies too widely or become distracted by lesser matters.

One of the Rat's strengths is his ability to work well with others. With his personable manner, he is able to win the respect of others and this year again he will benefit by showing himself a good team member and taking chances to meet others. Not only will this help him in his duties, but if he needs support or advice on any matter, there will be many people he can consult. Also, there will be occasions when others are able to alert him to possibilities worth considering or to put in a good word for him. Over the year, the Rat's many contacts and work friends can be of great help *and* value to him.

There will also be good opportunities for the Rat to make progress over the year, and he will often find himself in a strong position for promotion or to take on other responsibilities. Those Rats who are keen to extend their experience in other ways or who are looking for work will again find some of their contacts can be helpful. By talking over their situation with others (including employment advisers), they could be given suggestions worth following up. By actively pursuing openings that interest them, many Rats will find their initiative and determination serving them well. Admittedly, it could take several attempts before they make the breakthrough they want, but their tenaciousness *will* be rewarded. The Rat's best prospects will generally be in the second half of the year, but April and the period from mid-August to November could see some good opportunities arising.

The progress the Rat makes in his work will lead to a rise in income and the Rat's earning abilities in the Dog year will be strong. Some Rats may even be able to supplement their income with additional work or by putting a skill or hobby to profitable use. For the enterprising, the Dog year holds much promise. However, the Rat does need to be alert. If he enters into any important transaction or is considering anything of a speculative nature, he does need to check the details and, when appropriate, obtain advice. A risk or oversight could cost him dear.

This need for care also extends to the Rat's personal life. In view of the busy nature of the year and sometimes considerable demands of his work, there will be times when the Rat will feel under pressure or preoccupied with his own concerns. Without care, there is a risk that strains or tensions could arise. If the Rat does sense his domestic life is beginning to suffer, he would do well to spend more time with others and share any concerns he might have. This will not only lead to a better understanding but also enable others to support and advise.

While the Rat will need to remain mindful of others, there will, however, be much to enjoy in his domestic life. It does mean a lot to him and over the year it is important that he gives time to others, is forthcoming and plays his usual full part in what goes on.

The Rat should also not allow his social life to suffer due to the other demands on his time. By keeping in contact with friends and setting time aside for recreational pursuits, he will again find his leisure activities doing him good as well as helping to keep his lifestyle in balance.

Overall, the Rat can certainly fare well over the year, particularly in his work. What he learns now will often lay the foundation for the success he will enjoy in following years. Financially, too, his prospects are promising, but despite these encouraging trends, there is an underlying need for care. This is a year for being thorough, staying alert and paying close attention to others. Particularly in his personal life, it is important that the Rat gives time to others and remains his attentive self. If he bears this in mind, however, this can be a busy and satisfying year.

The Metal Rat

This will be an important year for the Metal Rat, particularly as it will allow him to build on his skills and further his ideas. This is very much a year for positive action.

In his work the Metal Rat's prospects are especially encouraging. Often as a result of his considerable experience he will find himself being offered the chance to take on other responsibilities or will win some well-deserved promotion. There will certainly be several good opportunities for him and by making the most of these this year he can mark an important and often defining moment in his career.

Many Metal Rats will be able to further their position with their present employer, but those who feel there are better prospects elsewhere or who are keen to extend their skills in other ways should actively follow up any vacancies that interest them as well as make enquiries about possible openings. These Metal Rats will also be helped by talking to their many friends and contacts. By remaining active and persistent, almost all Metal Rats will be able to make important career advances over the year. April and the months from mid-August to early December could see some interesting developments.

However, while this is a year for progress, much will be expected of the Metal Rat. Sometimes his workload will be heavy and when taking on new responsibilities, there could be a lot to learn. At such times the Metal Rat would do well to remain focused and concentrate on his priorities. If he remains committed, his efforts over the year will not only win him much credit but also help his reputation and his future prospects.

Another important aspect of the year is the way in which it will allow the Metal Rat to develop his skills. Sometimes this will come as a result of the duties he carries out, but if he has the chance to go on any training courses, he should make the most of them. Something learned now could prove significant in time. Again, this is a year to make the most of opportunities.

In addition to developing his work skills, the Metal Rat should also consider his own personal development. If there is a pursuit he wants to take up or a skill or technique that could be helpful to him, he should follow this up. Also, if he does not tend to get much exercise during the day, he should consider making up for this in some way. Enrolling at a gym or on a fitness course could help, or doing yoga or tai chi. Whatever he does, by obtaining proper medical advice, the Metal Rat will benefit from his exercise programme.

As far as money matters are concerned, this will be a generally positive year. The progress the Metal Rat makes in his work will often bring a welcome increase in income and he could also benefit from a financial gift or find an enterprising idea bringing a useful return. However, while this may be a favourable year, the Metal Rat does still need to manage his money carefully. Also, if he is able to add to his longer-term savings he could be grateful for it in years to come. With good control over his finances, though, the Metal Rat will be pleased with how he fares.

Being born under the sign of charm, the Rat does value his relations with others and the Metal Rat is no exception. However, in the Dog year these do need care. Sometimes when work pressures are heavy or he is embarking on a period of change, the Metal Rat will be preoccupied, tense and lacking his usual patience. At such times he should take into account how he feels and tell others about any pressures or worries he may have. At demanding times good communication really will help and will be in the interests of all concerned.

Also, the Metal Rat should make sure he sets time aside to share with others. By showing that he cares, being open and contributing to family life, he will be able to make a real difference to his relations with others. This is, though, a year for care and consideration.

This also applies to the Metal Rat's social life. When he is with friends, he does need to be attentive and aware of their views and feelings. If not, misunderstandings or disagreements could arise. Fortunately the Metal Rat's social skills are excellent and by remaining aware of the trickier aspects of the Dog year he can do much to avoid committing a *faux pas* or saying something out of place. However, as with his domestic life, this is a year for treading carefully. Nevertheless the Metal Rat can look forward to many enjoyable occasions with others, with March, July and the last quarter of the year being a busy and often rewarding time for socializing.

Overall, although the Dog year will bring its pressures and there is a need for care in personal relations, it will contain excellent opportunities for the Metal Rat to progress at work as well as to make more of himself and his skills. His accomplishments now will often mark an important stage in his career and will prove significant as he looks to make more progress in following years. However, over the year, he does need to make sure that he sets aside time for those who are special to him as well as for his personal interests and activities. This is a year when it is important that he keeps his lifestyle in balance.

TIP FOR THE YEAR
Do ask for assistance and advice and be prepared to talk over your hopes and aspirations. The input and support you receive can make a considerable difference to how you fare over the year. This is very much a time for openness and for paying attention to others.

The Water Rat

This will be an interesting year for the Water Rat and while there will be pressures and some challenging moments, he can gain a great deal from it.

In his work he would, though, do well to consider this more as a year for adding to his experience than looking to make major advances. Indeed, many Water Rats will already have seen considerable changes in their work in recent years and the Dog year will give them the chance to become more established and expert in certain areas. By making the most of any opportunities to develop their skills, they will be able to prepare themselves for the successes that lie ahead.

Coping with an often heavy workload and dealing with complex matters as well as sometimes having to learn and adjust to new procedures will test the Water Rat but will also further his skills, and this again can be to his future benefit. In addition, he will be helped by his ability to work well with others, and this will also help his future prospects.

Although many Water Rats will decide to remain with their present employer over the year, for those keen to change or who are looking for work, the Dog year will bring important developments. Although it will often require a great deal of effort, by remaining persistent and emphasizing their skills, many Water Rats will obtain an interesting new opportunity. Again, what the Water Rat achieves now can often be far-reaching. April and mid-August to early December could see some important work developments.

The Water Rat would also do well to consider his own personal development over the year, either by learning more about a particular interest he already has or taking up a new one. Also, if he feels he is lacking exercise, he could consider enrolling at a gym or on a suitable fitness course. By using some of his spare time in a purposeful and enjoyable way, he will find it bringing him pleasure and sometimes considerable personal benefit.

This will also be a positive year for financial matters. In addition to enjoying an increase in income, some Water Rats could benefit from a financial gift or find a skill or idea they have earning them something extra. The Water Rat's enterprise and industry will be well rewarded over the year and with good management he can do much to improve his financial situation.

As with all Rats, however, the Water Rat will need to give special consideration to his loved ones over the year. Sometimes, as a result of the pressures of work or having such a demanding schedule, he will feel tired and lacking his usual patience or sparkle. For those Water Rats who have young children, the occasional disturbed night will not help. However, with support and understanding the more difficult moments can be considerably eased. Setting time aside to talk will also be of great help.

While there is this need for care and mindfulness, the Water Rat's domestic life will still contain happy and memorable moments. Those Water Rats who are parents will often delight in the progress of their children and some of the ideas and activities that the Water Rat is able to carry out with loved ones will also bring much pleasure. Despite its pressures, the Dog year will certainly contain some special moments.

Although the Water Rat will often have many demands on his time, it is also important that he does not allow his social life to suffer. By keeping in contact with friends and being prepared to share news with them, he will often be grateful for the support, advice and camaraderie they are able to give. Water Rats who would welcome the chance to make new friends will find that joining an interest group or becoming involved in local activities could help. The Dog year is often supportive of any positive action that the Water Rat can take. March, July, early August and the last quarter of the year will be the busiest times socially and will contain some good opportunities to meet others.

Although the Dog year will bring its pressures, it will be a significant time for the Water Rat. What he learns and accomplishes now can be instrumental in the success he can look forward to in following years.

TIP FOR THE YEAR
Do talk to others. With some of the pressures of the year, it *is* important that you talk about any concerns you may

have or decisions you need to take. That way others will be better able to assist and advise. This is a year when dialogue really can make a difference.

The Wood Rat

There is a Chinese proverb which reminds us, 'The gem cannot be polished without friction, nor man perfected without trials,' and the challenges the Wood Rat will face over the year will certainly test him. However, what he achieves will provide him with excellent experience which he will be able to build on in future years. The trials and pressures of this year will leave *many* benefits.

Over the year the Wood Rat will find a great deal being expected of him. For those Wood Rats in work there could be a heavy workload to deal with, and some will even wonder whether they have made the right choice of career. However, one of the Wood Rat's chief qualities is his tenaciousness, and by making the most of the challenges before him, he will not only discover important strengths but also certain talents he will be able to make much of in future years. Also, his commitment will be noted by others and this will help when opportunities arise. When there is the chance of promotion or a transfer to different duties which appeal to him, by putting himself forward, he can do his prospects a lot of good.

For those Wood Rats seeking work, either as the Dog year begins or during it, again developments will often take an interesting course. Although there will be disappointments in their quest, many will be successful in securing a position which, although sometimes different from what they were originally seeking, will open up important possibilities for the future. Again, what the Wood Rat achieves in the Dog year can be significant in the longer term.

Another positive feature of the year is the opportunities the Wood Rat will have to meet different colleagues. Working well with others will not only benefit him now but also help his future prospects. In addition, a more senior colleague will be particularly impressed by his efforts over the year and become almost a mentor to him. Throughout the year, the Wood Rat would do particularly well to listen closely to the advice of those who have experience behind them.

For those Wood Rats studying for qualifications this will also be an important year, especially as many will be nearing the end of their course and will have final exams to prepare for. Again, what they do now can have an important bearing on their future and it really would be worthwhile setting about their studies in a disciplined and thorough manner. The effort and commitment they put in will be well rewarded, often opening up good opportunities both later in the Dog year and in the favourably aspected Pig year that follows.

The Wood Rat can also look forward to some good fortune in money matters over the year and many will enjoy an increase in their income. Some may also be able to supplement this by some additional work. However, despite this financial upturn, the Wood Rat will need to manage his money well. With his many plans and expenses, he does need to watch his spending and make provision for his various requirements. This is very much a year for financial control. In addition, many Wood Rats will decide to travel over the year and this too needs to be planned well. The more care the Wood Rat takes and better prepared he is, the more he will be able to do while away.

As far as the Wood Rat's personal life is concerned, this will be an important year. For those Wood Rats with a partner there will be much to share, with the year containing some wonderfully happy moments. However, the Wood Rat does need to remain aware of the views and feelings of loved ones and be prepared to consult them. Good communication and attentiveness are essential, otherwise the understanding and rapport the Wood Rat so values could suffer. Wood Rats, take note.

Also, if during the year the Wood Rat has any matters concerning him, he should be open about them. Discussing his situation with a more senior relation could be particularly helpful, especially as they will often have the experience behind them to advise as well as sometimes be able to offer assistance in other ways too.

The Wood Rat will also value his social life over the year, enjoying many of the events he goes to as well as the times he meets up with friends. Again, though, he does need to remain aware of their views and feelings and should not assume that just because they are friends he automatically has their support. This is not a year to take others for granted *or* make assumptions. Wood Rats, do take note. However, while there is this need for care, the Wood Rat's social life can certainly lead to some good times and many Wood Rats will find their social circle widening as the year progresses. Those who move to a new area, either because of work or other commitments, will find that by going out and becoming involved in various activities, they will soon get to meet others, some of whom will become close friends. March, the period from mid-July to mid-August and the last quarter of the year will see the most social activity.

Although the Dog year will be a busy and often demanding one for the Wood Rat, it can have lasting significance. In his work, the skills, experience and qualifications he is able to acquire will often be instrumental in the success he will enjoy in succeeding years. Also, by being forthcoming and remaining mindful of the views of others, he will gain much from the support he receives. This is a year for care and hard work, but the long-term rewards can be considerable.

TIP FOR THE YEAR
Rise to the challenges, demands and opportunities of the year. By doing your best you will learn much and prepare yourself for the exciting prospects that lie ahead.

The Fire Rat

This year the Fire Rat will enter a new decade of his life and, whether 10 or 70, he will find this a significant time.

For the more senior Fire Rat the year holds some positive prospects, but to benefit he does need to give some thought to what he wants to do over the year. This could be furthering a particular interest, learning a new skill, visiting certain places or carrying out domestic projects which add to the comfort and style of his home. Whatever his plans, the key message of the Dog year is to act positively.

Also, as with all Rats in 2006, good communication is essential and Fire Rat really would be helped by discussing his thoughts with others and, whenever possible, encouraging those around to join him in his activities. For some Fire Rats, carrying out household projects or pursuing new interests with a partner can make the activity all the more meaningful and successful. For others, asking friends to join in their various activities will enable them to benefit from support and encouragement.

Fortunately, much that the Fire Rat proposes will work out well, but in some instances problems could arise or others may express misgivings about some of his ideas. At such times the Fire Rat will need to be careful, otherwise his attitude could compound the situation and lead to disagreements. In tricky situations, a certain flexibility and willingness to talk would be wise. Fire Rats, take note.

One of the more promising aspects of the year, however, concerns the Fire Rat's personal interests and he would do well to further these in some way, either through adding to his knowledge, setting himself a new project, sharing his skills or passing them on to others. Fire Rats who enjoy writing could find this bringing them much pleasure, especially in view of their good communication skills and often rich imagination, while those who have gardens will often delight in the time they spend there.

There will also be opportunities for the Fire Rat to travel over the year, although to get the most out of his time away, the Fire Rat does need to go well prepared, checking his itinerary, connections, paperwork and likely requirements in advance. The better organized he is, the more he will be able to do and enjoy.

As far as money matters are concerned, this will be a generally positive year, especially as some Fire Rats will enjoy the fruition of a policy or receive a financial gift or bonus. However, while this upturn will be welcome, the Fire Rat does need to manage his money well and when considering any major purchase, should take his time in deciding what best suits his requirements. Similarly, when dealing with important paperwork he needs to be thorough, and if there is anything he does not understand or agree with, he should seek advice. This may be a good year for financial matters, but care and vigilance are still necessary.

For those Fire Rats born in 1996 this will be a year of opportunity, with many having the chance to take up new interests and activities. By acting on the opportunities available, the young Fire Rat will be pleased with what he is able to learn. Also, some new interests will be a good way for him to meet others. Over the year he can look forward to making what will become long-standing friendships.

The young Fire Rat will also be well supported by those around him and if he has any difficulties or worries, whether over schoolwork or some other matter, it is important that he talks to those close to him. However, while he will often be encouraged, there could be occasions when others have reservations over some of his ideas. Should this occur, he should not let the matter get out of proportion. Although some decisions may seem unfair, they are often taken with his best interests at heart and an accommodating attitude on his part could be the wisest course.

For both the younger and more senior Fire Rat the Dog year does offer some fine prospects, particularly regarding shared personal interests and activities. Throughout the year, he does need to be mindful of others, but he will certainly benefit from talking things through and be encouraged in much of what he does.

Look to develop yourself in some way, whether by acquiring a new skill, setting yourself an interesting project to tackle or reading up on a subject that interests you. With your keen and enquiring nature, this will often bring you pleasure as well as sometimes give rise to other benefits too.

The Earth Rat

This will be a busy year for the Earth Rat and while it will contain its pressures and more challenging moments, he will emerge from it with much to his credit. As is often the way, his resourcefulness and tenacity will serve him well.

In his work there will be some key developments. Whether he is relatively new in his present position or well established, the Dog year will bring change. Sometimes, as a result of his experience, others will look to him to take on further responsibilities and he will find himself well placed to move to a more senior role or to concentrate on more specialist duties or projects. There will certainly be opportunities for the Earth Rat to progress as well as make more effective use of his knowledge and skills. Although some of his duties will be challenging, by concentrating on what needs to be done and using his skills well, he will enjoy some notable achievements. The Dog year will ask much of the Earth Rat, but it will give him the chance to show his true worth.

Another factor which will help in his progress will be his ability to relate so effectively to others. Many not only admire his knowledge and skills but also like him as a person, and their backing can lead to him being recommended for a greater role. He will also be well supported by others. If at any time he becomes worried over a certain decision or complex matter, he must not forget the many contacts and work friends he can turn to for advice.

Although many Earth Rats will remain with their present employer over the year, for those wanting a change or who would welcome a job involving less travel or fewer hours, the Dog year will contain some interesting possibilities. By remaining alert, they will find that events will sometimes move in curious ways. A comment or idea from a friend or vacancy they see could lead to an opening which, although sometimes different from what they were originally seeking, will give them an important new opportunity. Developments during the Dog year can sometimes put the Earth Rat in a dilemma about what to do, but with good support and self-belief, he will often find them working out well. Late March, April and mid-August to November could see some interesting work opportunities.

Another positive feature of the year is the way that it will allow the Earth Rat to put some of his personal interests to good use. He could even find himself passing on some of his knowledge. In addition, any creative skills he has could bring him pleasure. For the keen photographer, writer, artist or musician, the year could bring many rewarding times.

The Dog year is also generally positive for financial matters and many Earth Rats will benefit from an additional sum of money, perhaps as a gift or the fruition of a policy. However, the Earth Rat does need to manage his money well. The care and attention he can give to his financial situation can make an important difference. And if at any time he has any concerns over financial matters, paperwork or a transaction he is considering, he would do well to seek advice rather than take risks.

As with all Rats, the Earth Rat also needs to be careful in his domestic and social life. While his relations with work colleagues will often be excellent, he does need to be attentive towards his family and friends. Too much preoccupation or time spent on other activities could lead to some ill-feeling. Over the year the Earth Rat does need to be aware of this and balance out his activities and obligations. Also, often as a result of the pressures of work, there will be times when he will feel tired and tense and will lack his usual patience. At such times he would do well to let others know how he feels rather than keep his anxieties to himself. Good communication and a willingness to talk really can help over the year. Also, at busy times, he should take up any offers of assistance he may receive or ask for more help if necessary.

While the Dog year will contain its pressures and demands (particularly in the first half of the year), there will also be many occasions for the Earth Rat to enjoy. Family interests and activities, whether a local outing, a special meal or a break or holiday, can be especially pleasing.

The Earth Rat will also enjoy many of the social occasions that he goes to, although again there is a need to be aware of the views of others. Without care, there is a risk that misunderstandings could occur, sometimes over the smallest and most innocuous of matters. Fortunately, being so adept in his dealings with others, the Earth Rat can do much to avoid some of the trickier aspects and social pitfalls of the year, but he does need to remain his tactful and discreet self. March, July and the last quarter of the year will see the most social activity.

Although the Dog year will be a busy and often demanding one for the Earth Rat, it will certainly not be without its opportunities. Over the year he will be given an excellent chance to use his skills and knowledge and advance his position. He will also derive much pleasure from his personal interests, but throughout the year it is important that he balances out his various activities and ensures that he gives time and attention to those who are special to him. With care and mindfulness, however, this can be a positive and pleasing year.

TIP FOR THE YEAR
Although there will often be many demands on your time, do set some aside to spend with loved ones. The care and attention you give to those who are important to you really will make an important difference to the year and in return you will benefit so much from the love, support and assistance that those around you can give.

FAMOUS RATS

Ben Affleck, Ursula Andress, Louis Armstrong, Charles Aznavour, Lauren Bacall, James Baldwin, Shirley Bassey, Kathy Bates, Irving Berlin, Silvio Berlusconi, Kenneth Branagh, Marlon Brando, Charlotte Brontë, Jackson Browne, George H. W. Bush, Glen Campbell, David Carradine, Jimmy Carter, Aaron Copland, Chris de Burgh, Cameron Diaz, David Duchovny, T. S. Eliot, Queen Elizabeth the Queen Mother, Eminem, Colin Firth, Clark Gable, Liam Gallagher, Hugh Grant, Geri Halliwell, Daryl Hannah, Thomas Hardy, Prince Harry, Haydn, Charlton Heston, Buddy Holly, Mick Hucknall, Henrik Ibsen, Jeremy Irons, Samuel L. Jackson, Jean-Michel Jarre, Gene Kelly, Avril Lavigne, Lawrence of Arabia, Gary Lineker, Lord Andrew Lloyd Webber, Claude Monet, Nana Mouskouri, Richard Nixon, Ozzy Osbourne, Sean Penn, Terry Pratchett, Ian Rankin, Lou Rawls, Vanessa Redgrave, Burt Reynolds, Rossini, William Shakespeare, Tommy Steele, Donna Summer, James Taylor, Leo Tolstoy, Henri Toulouse-Lautrec, Spencer Tracy, the Prince of Wales, George Washington, the Duke of York, Emile Zola.

6 FEBRUARY 1913 ～ 25 JANUARY 1914   *Water Ox*

24 JANUARY 1925 ～ 12 FEBRUARY 1926   *Wood Ox*

11 FEBRUARY 1937 ～ 30 JANUARY 1938   *Fire Ox*

29 JANUARY 1949 ～ 16 FEBRUARY 1950   *Earth Ox*

15 FEBRUARY 1961 ～ 4 FEBRUARY 1962   *Metal Ox*

3 FEBRUARY 1973 ～ 22 JANUARY 1974   *Water Ox*

20 FEBRUARY 1985 ～ 8 FEBRUARY 1986   *Wood Ox*

7 FEBRUARY 1997 ～ 27 JANUARY 1998   *Fire Ox*

THE
OX

THE PERSONALITY OF THE OX

Ideals are like stars; you will not succeed in touching them
with your hands. But like the seafaring man on the desert
of waters, you choose them as your guides, and following
them you will reach your destiny.

Carl Schurz, an Ox

The Ox is born under the signs of equilibrium and
tenacity. He is a hard and conscientious worker and sets
about everything he does in a resolute, methodical and
determined manner. He has considerable leadership qualities and is often admired for his tough and uncompro-
mising nature. He knows what he wants to achieve in life
and, as far as possible, will not be deflected from his ulti-
mate objective.

The Ox takes his responsibilities and duties very seri-
ously. He is decisive and quick to take advantage of any
opportunity that comes his way. He is also sincere and
places a great deal of trust in his friends and colleagues. He
is, nevertheless, something of a loner. He is a quiet and
private individual and often keeps his thoughts to himself.
He also cherishes his independence and prefers to set about
things in his own way rather than be bound by the dictates
of others or influenced by outside pressures.

The Ox tends to have a calm and tranquil nature, but if
something angers him or he feels that someone has let him
down, he can have a fearsome temper. He can also be stubborn and obstinate and this can lead him into conflict with
others. Usually he will succeed in getting his own way, but

should things go against him the Ox is a poor loser and will take any defeat or setback extremely badly.

The Ox is often a deep thinker and rather studious. He is not particularly renowned for his sense of humour and does not take kindly to new gimmicks or anything too innovative. He is too solid and traditional for that and prefers to stick to the more conventional norm.

His home is very important to him and in some respects he treats it as a private sanctuary. His family tends to be closely knit and the Ox will make sure that each member does their fair share around the house. The Ox tends to be a hoarder, but he is always well organized and neat. He also places great importance on punctuality and there is nothing that infuriates him more than to be kept waiting, particularly if it is due to someone's inefficiency. The Ox can be a hard taskmaster!

Once settled in a job or house the Ox will quite happily remain there for many years. He does not like change and he is also not particularly keen on travel. He does, however, enjoy gardening and other outdoor pursuits and he will often spend much of his spare time out of doors. The Ox is usually an excellent gardener and whenever possible he will always make sure he has a large area of ground to maintain. He usually prefers to live in the country rather than the town.

Due to his dedicated and dependable nature, the Ox will usually do well in his chosen career, providing he is given enough freedom to act on his own initiative. He invariably does well in politics, agriculture and in careers which need specialized training. The Ox is also very gifted in the arts and many Oxen have enjoyed considerable success as musicians or composers.

The Ox is not as outgoing as some and it often takes him a long time to establish friendships and feel relaxed in another person's company. His courtships are likely to be long, but once he is settled he will remain devoted and loyal to his partner. The Ox is particularly well suited to those born under the signs of the Rat, Rabbit, Snake and Rooster. He can also establish a good relationship with the Monkey, Dog, Pig and another Ox, but he will find that he has little in common with the whimsical and sensitive Goat. He will also find it difficult to get on with the Horse, Dragon and Tiger – the Ox prefers a quiet and peaceful existence and those born under these three signs tend to be a little too lively and impulsive for his liking.

The female Ox has a kind and caring nature, and her home and family are very much her pride and joy. She always tries to do her best for her partner and can be a most conscientious and loving parent. She is an excellent organizer and also a very determined person who will often succeed in getting what she wants in life. She usually has a deep interest in the arts and is often a talented artist or musician.

The Ox is a very down-to-earth character. He is sincere, loyal and unpretentious. He can, however, be rather reserved and to some he may appear distant and aloof. He has a quiet nature, but underneath he is very strong-willed and ambitious. He has the courage of his convictions and is often prepared to stand up for what he believes to be right, regardless of the consequences. He inspires confidence and trust, and throughout his life he will rarely be short of people who are ready to support him or who admire his strong and resolute manner.

THE FIVE DIFFERENT TYPES OF OX

In addition to the 12 signs of the Chinese zodiac there are five elements and these have a strengthening or moderating influence on the sign. The effects of the five elements on the Ox are described below, together with the years in which the elements were exercising their influence. Therefore those Oxen born in 1961 are Metal Oxen, those born in 1913 and 1973 are Water Oxen, and so on.

Metal Ox: 1961

This Ox is confident and very strong-willed. He can be blunt and forthright in his views and is not afraid of speaking his mind. He sets about his objectives with a dogged determination, but he can become so involved in his various activities that he can be oblivious to the thoughts and feelings of those around him, and this can sometimes be to his detriment. He is honest and dependable and will never promise more than he can deliver. He has a good appreciation of the arts and usually has a small circle of very good and loyal friends.

Water Ox: 1913, 1973

This Ox has a sharp and penetrating mind. He is a good organizer and sets about his work in a methodical manner. He is not as narrow-minded as some of the other types of Ox and is more willing to involve others in his plans and aspirations. He usually has very high moral standards and is often attracted to careers in public service. He is a good judge of character and has such a friendly and persuasive manner that he usually experiences little difficulty in securing his objectives. He is popular and has an excellent way with children.

Wood Ox: 1925, 1985

The Wood Ox conducts himself with an air of dignity and authority and will often take a leading role in any enterprise in which he becomes involved. He is very self-confident and is direct in his dealings with others. He does, however, have a quick temper and has no hesitation in speaking his mind. He has tremendous drive and willpower and an extremely good memory. The Wood Ox is particularly loyal and devoted to the members of his family and has a most caring nature.

Fire Ox: 1937, 1997

The Fire Ox has a powerful and assertive personality and is a hard and conscientious worker. He holds strong views and has very little patience when things do not go his own way. He can also get carried away in the excitement of the moment and does not always take into account the views of those around him. He nevertheless has many leadership qualities and will often reach positions of power, eminence and wealth. He usually has a small group of loyal and close friends and is very devoted to his family.

Earth Ox: 1949

This Ox sets about everything he does in a sensible and level-headed manner. He is ambitious but also realistic in his aims and is often prepared to work long hours in order to secure his objectives. He is shrewd in financial and business matters and is a very good judge of character. He has a quiet nature and is greatly admired for his sincerity and integrity. He is also very loyal to his family and friends and his views and opinions are often sought.

PROSPECTS FOR THE OX IN 2006

The Year of the Rooster (9 February 2005 to 28 January 2006) will have been a generally constructive one for the Ox and a lot will happen in the closing months. In keeping with the nature of the Rooster year this is, though, very much a time for good planning and persistence.

At work there will be some excellent chances for the Ox to make good progress. For those Oxen wanting to further their career or secure a position, October could see some positive developments, but the remaining months are also favourably aspected and whenever the Ox sees an opportunity, he should be swift in following it up.

The Ox's domestic and social life will also become busier in the last quarter of the year. In his home life there will often be much to arrange and again the Ox's planning and involvement will be appreciated. Any additional support and advice he is able to give a close relation at this time will be of more value than he may realize. The Ox will also have many opportunities to go out and will often thoroughly enjoy himself. For the unattached, someone met at this time could quickly become special. For relations with others, the closing months of the year are well aspected.

The area requiring the greatest care concerns money. While the Ox is usually careful in dealing with his finances, this is not a time for risks.

In general, the Rooster year offers good prospects for the Ox and by making the most of the opportunities that arise, he will do well. His personal life too will be pleasing and he will value the love and support of those close to him.

The Year of the Dog starts on 29 January and will be a busy one for the Ox. However, the Ox is made of stern stuff and due to his tenacity and strength of character will not only accomplish a great deal but also further his experience. And the year will also contain some memorable and personally happy times.

As far as the Ox's work is concerned, this will be a demanding year with a sometimes heavy workload as well as new responsibilities. The Dog year will ask a lot of the Ox but it will give him an excellent chance to add to his experience and reveal new strengths that he will be able to make much of in following years.

Oxen who are keen to move on from their current work or who are seeking work may not, however, find their quest easy. The Dog year requires the Ox to work for results and it could be only after several attempts – and some disappointments – that these Oxen manage to obtain something suitable. The positions offered will sometimes be different from what they were originally seeking, but their new duties will give them the chance to extend their experience in other areas as well as widen their scope for the future. The Dog year can teach the Ox a lot, as well as be of long-term value. April, May, September and November could be the best times for career developments.

In addition to what he learns in carrying out his duties, the Ox should also make the most of any training opportunities that are offered and any chances to meet other colleagues. Any positive action he can take during the year will be helpful to his position and prospects.

As far as his finances are concerned, the Ox will need to remain careful. Although many Oxen will enjoy an increase in income, outgoings will need to be watched and whenever possible early provision should be made for larger purchases and expenses. If the Ox is considering any expensive work on his home, he should get a breakdown of costs as well as check the terms carefully. If not, an oversight could cause problems later. Similarly, when dealing with tax returns and other financial forms, the Ox needs to be his thorough and vigilant self. Although he may find certain matters irksome, to delay a response or not give the required information could lead to further correspondence and be to his detriment. The Year of the Dog *does* require thoroughness and care in money matters.

Travel, though, is more positively aspected and the Ox could have several opportunities to go away over the year. Sometimes family and friends living some distance away will invite him to stay or he may see a travel offer which appeals to him. By following these up, the Ox will enjoy seeing both old friends and new places. Even those Oxen who are not keen travellers can greatly benefit from going away and having a break from their usual routine.

As far as the Ox's domestic life is concerned, this will be an active year. Home life will often be conducted at a fast pace and again the Ox's organizational talents will be greatly valued. The Ox also recognizes the value of spending time together and despite the often considerable activity will always try to ensure that there are times to talk and special occasions for everyone to enjoy. Once again, his input will be significant. Also, with travel favourably aspected, a family holiday could be a special time.

However, while much can go well, there could also be some matters which could concern the Ox over the year, possibly the attitude and actions of a close relation or the plans that a loved one may be considering. At such times the Ox would find it helpful to talk things over quietly, explaining his viewpoint and any misgivings, but also listening to others. He will find such a discussion more productive than going off in a tirade, as Oxen sometimes do! In 2006 dialogue and good communication really can help in many areas.

Always one to choose his friends with care, the Ox will find his social life will bring him much pleasure over the year. In some cases his work or special interests will lead to invitations and as a result, his social circle will widen. Those Oxen who may be lonely or have recently had personal problems will find that joining an interest group or becoming involved in local activities can lead to making new friends as well as being a satisfying use of their time. For unattached Oxen, the Year of the Dog is splendidly aspected, with affairs of the heart often bringing much happiness and with good prospects of settling down with a partner, becoming engaged or marrying. The months from

March to May and August and September may well see some splendid personal occasions.

The Year of the Dog certainly holds many interesting prospects for the Ox. With opportunities to travel, to socialize and to enjoy some special times with loved ones, there will certainly be much to appreciate. Although he will often face pressures and demands in his work, the Ox has never been one to shrink from a challenge, and by giving his best he will not only learn a great deal but also discover new talents, some of which will be instrumental in the success he will enjoy in following years.

The Metal Ox

There is a Chinese proverb that reminds us, 'With aspirations you can go anywhere; without aspirations you can go nowhere.' The Metal Ox certainly does have aspirations and in the Dog year his resolve and determination will take him forward and allow him to accomplish a great deal.

In his work this will be a year of significant developments. Sometimes, as more senior colleagues move on or other changes in personnel take place, the Metal Ox will be well placed for promotion or will have the opportunity to become involved in other duties.

The prospects are also encouraging for those Oxen who want to change what they do or who are seeking work. By following up any openings that interest them *and* remaining persistent, many will be successful in setting their career off on an interesting new track. The months from April to early June and September and November could see some positive developments.

However, while there will be opportunities for the Metal Ox to make progress, the Dog year will also bring its challenges. When taking on new duties or moving to a new role, there will often be a great deal to learn as well as a heavy workload and challenging objectives. For one such as the Metal Ox, who prides himself on high standards, some parts of the year *will* be demanding. However, by remaining focused, using his strengths and expertise and rising to the challenges, he will not only accomplish a great deal but in the process gain invaluable experience.

The Metal Ox will also be helped by his ability to forge good working relations with others and should take advantage of any opportunities he has to meet those engaged in similar types of work. Establishing good connections will help both his current position and his future prospects.

The progress the Metal Ox makes in his work will also lead to a rise in income and financially this will be a reasonable year. However, in view of some of the costs he will face, especially connected with his family and accommodation, the Metal Ox does need to manage his finances well. If he does not already do so, he could find it helpful to keep a set of accounts. Also, when considering more expensive purchases, he would do well to review the options available. And if the Metal Ox has any financial problems or uncertainties, it would be worth seeking advice rather than dealing with what could be complex matters single-handedly. Where finance is involved, the Dog year does require care and thoroughness.

This will also be a busy year domestically. The Metal Ox will often give advice and help to those dear to him and the progress of younger relations could be the source of much pride. For some there could be a major family event or celebration to arrange and again the Metal Ox's organizational talents will prove a real asset. However, with some of the work pressures and decisions the Metal Ox will face, it *is* important that he shares any concerns and frustrations he may have. He may be willing to help others over the year, but he must also give others the opportunity to help in return.

This will also be a fairly active year socially. With his work and personal interests the Metal Ox will have many chances to go out and meet others, with some months seeing a flurry of social activity. The period from March to May and August and September could be especially busy. And while, as with most Oxen, the Metal Ox does take his time in building friendships, some of the people he meets during the year, particularly those with similar interests and outlooks, could become close friends. For those Metal Oxen who may have had personal difficulties or found their social life in the doldrums recently, the Dog year offers considerable promise, and for some unattached Metal Oxen, significant romance too.

Travel is also positively aspected over the year and will not only do the Metal Ox good and provide a welcome break from his usual routine but will also allow him to rest and enjoy himself as well as seeing some often interesting places.

Although this will be a busy and sometimes demanding year for the Metal Ox, by making the most of the opportunities that arise, he will not only make useful headway but also gain useful experience. On a personal level, the Metal Ox's domestic and social life and travel prospects will bring him particular pleasure.

TIP FOR THE YEAR

In view of the busy nature of the year it is important that you look after yourself as well as appreciate the rewards you work so hard for. Set time aside to spend with others and on recreational pursuits.

The Water Ox

This will not be the easiest of years for the Water Ox and much will be asked of him. However, despite the challenging aspects, the Water Ox should not be too despairing. The events of the year will give him the chance to broaden his experience and will provide some learning opportunities which will be of value in the longer term.

In his work there will be some good opportunities for the Water Ox to move on to other responsibilities which will give him new experience and extend his skills. While he will be pleased with the progress he makes, his workload will sometimes be considerable, however, especially in view of some of the new duties and procedures he will have to learn. But by setting about his duties in his usual efficient manner (and the Water Ox is well known for his tenacity and drive), he will not only accomplish a great deal but also do his reputation and prospects much good. Challenge does bring out the best in the Water Ox.

The Water Ox should also look positively at any training opportunities he may be offered. Again, what he does now can stand him in good stead for the future. Similarly, if there is a certain position he would one day like to move to, perhaps one which requires more specialist skills or a specific qualification, it would be worth him looking at ways in which he could obtain this. By being willing to learn, he will again help his future prospects.

The Water Ox should also make the most of any chances to build up new contacts. The more people he gets to know, the more he will benefit from their support, and some of those he meets could also alert him to possibilities worth considering. Again, while this may not be the easiest of years, what the Water Ox can do in the way of building up experience and meeting others can prove important in the longer term. For those Water Oxen seeking a position or looking to progress in their career, the months from April to mid-June and September and November could see some interesting developments.

It is also possible that some Water Oxen will be required to travel as a result of their work and although this may sometimes put additional pressure on the Water Ox, he could learn of other work practices, build up contacts elsewhere and achieve good results for his employer. Again, making the most of the chances that arise now can lead to success in the future.

The Water Ox will, however, need to be his careful self when dealing with financial matters over the year. With his responsibilities and commitments, he does need to keep a watch over his outgoings as well as make allowance for plans and purchases. Also, should he at any time have any concerns over a financial matter or transaction, it is important that he obtains advice as well as checks the details and implications involved. This is a year for care and vigilance. Water Oxen, do take note.

In addition to the possibility of travel with his work, the Water Ox should also aim to go away for a holiday over the year. Not only will he benefit from the rest but he may also get to see to some interesting new places.

This will be a generally positive year socially and as a result of his work, personal interests and travel opportunities, the Water Ox will get to meet many people, with his circle of friends and acquaintances growing as a result. For those Water Oxen who may have had recent personal difficulties, this is very much a year to draw a line under the past and to look ahead. In some cases becoming involved in new interests and recreational pursuits can be a good way to build up a more active social life. For unattached Water Oxen, the aspects are especially promising, with many meeting their future partner over the year.

The Water Ox's domestic life will also be busy. Sometimes the home will be a whirl of activity. However, with good communication and a sharing of responsibilities, there will be much for the Water Ox to appreciate. Those Water Oxen who are parents will often be delighted with their children's progress. Being the good organizer that he is, the Water Ox will play a central and active role which will certainly be valued.

Although the Dog year will be a busy and often demanding one for the Water Ox, it will bring some very good opportunities. The progress he makes in his work will give him an excellent chance to add to his experience and domestically, the year also holds good prospects, with the love and support of others meaning a great deal. The Dog year will ask a lot of the Water Ox, but it can be a rewarding one and will prepare the way for the success that awaits in following years.

Two tips! With so much going on, do use your time well. Stay organized and at busy times, concentrate on your chief priorities. Secondly, do not neglect your personal interests. These can be an excellent way for you to relax and will keep your life in balance.

The Wood Ox
This will be an eventful year for the Wood Ox in almost all areas of his life. Although the year will contain its pressures, by making the most of opportunities, the Wood Ox will do well.

With their ambitious nature, many Wood Oxen will be keen to make advances in their work. However, progress in the Dog year will not necessarily be easy or automatic. Many Wood Oxen will face disappointments along the way, yet with each application they make they will be strengthening their application and interview skills. By remaining persistent, many will be successful in the end. Results in the Dog year *will* need to be worked hard for, but they are possible.

Also, the Wood Ox should take advantage of any training he may be offered or consider taking extra courses himself. By furthering his skills he will not only be helping his current situation but also investing in his future. He is at the start of his working life and what he does will prove highly significant in time.

Those Wood Oxen seeking work will need to be active in putting themselves forward. Although progress may sometimes be difficult, they should not allow themselves to become too discouraged. Persistence *will* be rewarded and, in some cases, early disappointments could turn out to be blessings, with the Wood Ox managing to obtain a better position following a rejection. Also, whenever he is starting in a new position or taking on other duties, by showing commitment and a willingness to learn, he will be quick to make a favourable impression and mark himself out for further responsibilities. The months from April to mid-June and September and November could see some interesting developments. However, the key message for the Wood Ox throughout the year is to believe in himself and be willing to learn.

For those Wood Oxen studying for qualifications this will be an important year. With exams approaching and much material to cover, they will need to remain disciplined and organized in their approach. This is not a time to leave too much to the last moment. Fortunately, the Wood Ox's disciplined nature will often lead to the results he wants.

As far as money matters are concerned, this is a year for care and discipline. The Wood Ox will need to manage his money well and, where possible, try to make early provision for some of his plans and more expensive purchases. He also needs to be careful if entering into any agreement and, particularly if borrowing, should check the terms and commitments involved. Where money matters are concerned, this is a year for vigilance and control.

Travel will figure prominently for many Wood Oxen over the year and by saving up in advance, reading about their destination and going well prepared, they will often thoroughly enjoy themselves as well as see some impressive sights. Their travels can turn out to be one of the high points of the year.

Another positive aspect will be the way in which the Wood Ox is able to develop some of his skills and interests. And for Wood Oxen with thoughts of perhaps turning an interest into a vocation, what they learn now can come to be significant in the longer term.

The Dog year will also be an active one socially. While in true Ox style it does take the Wood Ox some time to build up good friendships, some people he gets to know during the year will become long-standing and loyal friends. Affairs of the heart are excellently aspected and there will be quite a few Wood Oxen who marry or settle down with a partner over the year, while for those who may have had a recent romance turn sour, there is every prospect that they will meet someone new, possibly even their true soul mate. The months from March to May and August to early October could be especially busy.

The Wood Ox's relationships with family members will also be important to him over the year. Although he may value his independence, he should not let this prevent him from seeking advice. By being prepared to share his ideas, he will allow others, especially more senior relations, to prove helpful and supportive. In the Dog year it *is* important he remembers that advice is there should he need it.

Overall, this will be an important year for the Wood Ox, especially in the way that he is able to further his skills. These can be very helpful to his future prospects. Socially, too, he will often have a rich and personally rewarding time.

TIP FOR THE YEAR

Make the most of any opportunities to learn. With your future holding so much promise, the achievements and lessons of the Dog year can be far-reaching.

The Fire Ox

This can be a rewarding year for the Fire Ox, although just how he fares depends largely on his attitude. The Fire Ox does tend to have set ways of going about things, but in the Dog year a certain flexibility would be wise. This is very much a time to take careful note of the prevailing situations and of the opinions of others, and if he does, the Fire Ox will find the year that much more satisfying.

He will also be helped by talking to those around him. That way he will find others not only offering more support but sometimes also coming up with useful suggestions. In 2006 discussion really *can* make a difference.

One area which the Fire Ox will spend much time on is his accommodation. Over the year many Fire Oxen will decide to alter furnishings and add new comforts. In addition many will be tempted to sort out certain storage areas and so make their home neater and more efficient. By carrying out these projects in consultation with others, the Fire Ox will be satisfied with what he is able to achieve over the year.

With the year's emphasis on the home, there will also be some Fire Oxen who decide to move to accommodation more suitable for their present needs. However, with the exertion and pressures moving can bring, these Fire Oxen should ensure that they draw on the assistance of others rather than try to deal with too much single-handedly. In some cases the assistance of younger relations can make the moving process that much smoother. Also, if at any time the Fire Ox has any concerns over any aspect of the move, it is important that he obtains professional advice. This is a year for care and vigilance. However, whether he moves or not, the Fire Ox will be pleased with what he accomplishes in the home over the year.

Travel, too, will figure prominently, with many Fire Oxen having opportunities to visit family and friends living some distance away. Also, some of the more spur-of-the-moment decisions to go on outings and trips will lead to some enjoyable occasions, often made all the more fun by their spontaneity.

The Fire Ox would do well to devote time to his personal interests over the year and by setting himself some interesting projects to do or adding to his knowledge and skills, he will find them bringing him pleasure and satisfaction. Fire Oxen with gardens will enjoy the times they spend out of doors tending their plants and crops. Creative pursuits, too, are well aspected and some Fire Oxen could enjoy success if they decide to enter their work into a competition.

As far as money matters are concerned this will, though, be a year for care. Financially related forms and any new agreements entered into *do* need to be studied carefully. If the Fire Ox has any difficult problem to deal with, especially of a more bureaucratic nature, it would be worth him contacting a helpline or someone able to give expert advice rather than tackle what could be a complex matter single-handedly. Help is there should he need it.

In addition to the various projects the Fire Ox carries out on his accommodation, this will often be a full and interesting year for domestic activities. If a grandparent, the Fire Ox will take a fond interest in the progress and activities of grandchildren and will sometimes have the chance to offer what will be helpful and far-reaching advice. There could be a significant family celebration over the year and this too will mean a great deal to the Fire Ox. Domestically, the year will certainly contain quite a few happy and meaningful times, but throughout the Fire Ox must not forget that his loved ones are keen to help should he have problems or require assistance.

This will be an interesting year socially and by meeting up with friends as well as those who share similar interests, perhaps through a local society, the Fire Ox's social life can mean a lot to him as well as be fun.

For those Fire Oxen born in 1997 the Dog year will also bring many opportunities. Whether they are extending their interests, developing their skills or undertaking activities at school, by making the most of the opportunities available to them, the young Fire Oxen can make this a constructive and pleasurable year. Much does depend on the Fire Ox's attitude and willingness to be involved, but with support and encouragement, many Fire Oxen will greatly enjoy themselves and will make good progress.

Overall, this can be a fine year for the Fire Ox, though to benefit fully he does need to liaise with others rather than be too independent in his approach. With the support of others and the many plans and ideas he is keen to carry out, this can be a pleasing, busy *and* fulfilling year.

Be forthcoming. To make the most of your ideas you *do* need to get support and assistance rather than try to do too much on your own. With the help of others, so much more can be accomplished. Also, this is a good year to make the most of travel opportunities.

The Earth Ox

This will be a year of important developments for the Earth Ox and while he will face pressures as he sets about some of his activities, his redoubtable nature will bring him many successes. Indeed, the Earth Ox has never been one to shrink from a challenge and this year will allow him to demonstrate many of his fine qualities.

In his work there will be some excellent chances for him to draw on his experience and make headway. As colleagues move on and new opportunities arise, the Earth Ox will often be well placed for promotion or to take on more specialist duties. However, while there will be some good chances to make progress over the year, his new duties could often be demanding, with new procedures and responsibilities to learn as well as high expectations being placed upon him. Being conscientious, there will be times when the Earth Ox will be anxious about some of the pressures he faces. However, he will find his efficient nature and good organizational skills great assets. Also, his ability to maintain good working relations with others will both bring him support and assist his future prospects.

While many Earth Oxen will remain with their present employer over the year and benefit from opportunities that arise there, others will feel that they would like to try something different and perhaps work nearer to where they live. For these Earth Oxen too the Dog year will contain some interesting developments. Although their quest for a new position will not always be as easy or straightforward as they hoped, many will be successful in securing a position which will allow them to use their skills in other ways and so gain both a new opportunity and a new challenge. April, May, September and November could see some particularly positive work developments.

Another important aspect of the year concerns the Earth Ox's own personal interests and he should look to develop these in some way, either by setting himself a new project, learning a new skill, finding out more about a subject that interests him or enrolling on a course. By doing something positive, he will find his interests bringing him pleasure and often other benefits too. Also, if he is sedentary for much of the day, he could find giving more attention to his well-being helpful. By following medical advice on the best way to proceed, he will often find he can make a difference to how he feels.

With travel well aspected, the Earth Ox should also make the most of any opportunities he has to go away. Whether visiting family and friends or going on holiday, he will enjoy the chance to meet others as well as see some interesting new places. If there is a particular destination he is keen to visit, he would do well to mention it to others. By talking over his ideas he could find they start to take on a momentum of their own and some of his suggestions could lead to some appreciated holidays. Travel-wise, this can be a successful year.

As far as money matters are concerned, this is, though, a year for care. With all the opportunities for travel, improvements he is considering for his home and family activities he has planned, the Earth Ox would do well to manage his money well and make early provision for forthcoming expenses. The more control he has over his finances, the more he will be able to do. Also, in view of the trickier aspects of the Dog year, if he has problems of a more bureaucratic nature or a particularly complex matter to deal with, he would do well to seek advice. Otherwise, problems can linger or even escalate. Earth Oxen, do take note.

This will be quite an active year as far as the Earth Ox's family life is concerned, with many Earth Oxen having good cause to celebrate what could be a memorable family event. The Earth Ox will also follow the progress of loved ones with much interest and several times will be asked for advice and guidance which he will be pleased to give. However, in view of the pressures of the year, if he would welcome more assistance with some of his own activities or another opinion on a matter that may be concerning him, he should not hesitate to ask. Those close to him will be glad to reciprocate his kindnesses and provide additional help and support. Also, the way in which the Earth Ox is able to encourage others to share in his plans will be appreciated and will help to make home life all the richer.

The Earth Ox will also find his work and interests will give rise to some good social opportunities over the year. For those Earth Oxen who may be lonely, have kept their social life low key or had some personal difficulty in recent years, this is very much a year to go out more and become involved in different activities. Positive action really will pay off and many will make significant new friendships. The months from March to May and from August to early October will be particularly active months socially.

Although the Dog year will demand much of the Earth Ox and he will need to be thorough and vigilant in many of his activities, it will certainly not be without its opportunities. By making the most of situations and using his talents well, he will not only accomplish a great deal but also find his actions helping to make this a fulfilling and personally rewarding time.

TIP FOR THE YEAR

Remain organized and prioritize your various activities, especially at busy times. Also, throughout the year do draw on the help of others. You may like to do a great deal on your own (a typical Ox trait!), but your plans and activities will go that much better and faster with the assistance that those around you can give.

FAMOUS OXEN

King Abdullah of Jordan, Robert Altman, Anastacia, Hans Christian Andersen, Johann Sebastian Bach, Warren Beatty, Kate Beckinsale, David Blaine, Napoleon Bonaparte, Rory Bremner, Albert Camus, Jim Carrey, Charlie Chaplin, George Clooney, Natalie Cole, Bill Cosby, Tom Courtenay, Tony Curtis, Diana, Princess of Wales, Marlene Dietrich, Walt Disney, Patrick Duffy, Harry Enfield, Jane Fonda, Gerald Ford, Edward Fox, Michael J. Fox, Peter Gabriel,

Richard Gere, Ricky Gervais, Handel, King Harald V of Norway, Adolf Hitler, Dustin Hoffman, Anthony Hopkins, Saddam Hussein, Billy Joel, King Juan Carlos of Spain, B. B. King, Mark Knopfler, Burt Lancaster, Jessica Lange, Kate Moss, Alison Moyet, Eddie Murphy, Paul Newman, Jack Nicholson, Leslie Nielsen, Gwyneth Paltrow, Oscar Peterson, Colin Powell, Paula Radcliffe, Robert Redford, Lionel Richie, Wayne Rooney, Tim Roth, Rubens, Meg Ryan, Jean Sibelius, Sissy Spacek, Bruce Springsteen, Meryl Streep, Lady Thatcher, Alan Titchmarsh, Scott F. Turow, Vincent van Gogh, Gore Vidal, Minette Walters, Zoë Wanamaker, Sigourney Weaver, the Duke of Wellington, Arsène Wenger, W. B. Yeats.

26 JANUARY 1914 ～ 13 FEBRUARY 1915   *Wood Tiger*

13 FEBRUARY 1926 ～ 1 FEBRUARY 1927   *Fire Tiger*

31 JANUARY 1938 ～ 18 FEBRUARY 1939   *Earth Tiger*

17 FEBRUARY 1950 ～ 5 FEBRUARY 1951   *Metal Tiger*

5 FEBRUARY 1962 ～ 24 JANUARY 1963   *Water Tiger*

23 JANUARY 1974 ～ 10 FEBRUARY 1975   *Wood Tiger*

9 FEBRUARY 1986 ～ 28 JANUARY 1987   *Fire Tiger*

28 JANUARY 1998 ～ 15 FEBRUARY 1999   *Earth Tiger*

THE
TIGER

THE PERSONALITY OF THE TIGER

You cannot dream yourself into a character, you must
hammer and forge one for yourself.
                              James A. Froude, a Tiger

The Tiger is born under the sign of courage. He is a charismatic figure and usually holds very firm views. He is strong-willed and determined, and sets about most of his activities with tremendous energy and enthusiasm. He is very alert and quick-witted and his mind is forever active. He is a highly original thinker and is nearly always brimming with new ideas or full of enthusiasm for some new project or scheme.

The Tiger adores challenges and loves to get involved in anything which he thinks has an exciting future or which catches his imagination. He is prepared to take risks and does not like to be bound either by convention or the dictates of others. He likes to be free to act as he chooses and at least once during his life he will throw caution to the wind and go off and do the things he wants to do.

The Tiger does, however, have a somewhat restless nature. Even though he is often prepared to throw himself wholeheartedly into a project, his initial enthusiasm can soon wane if he sees something more appealing. He can also be rather impulsive and there will be occasions in his life when he acts in a manner he later regrets. If the Tiger were to think things through or be prepared to persevere in his various activities, he would almost certainly enjoy a greater degree of success.

Fortunately the Tiger is lucky in most of his enterprises, but should things not work out as he hoped, he is liable to suffer from severe bouts of depression and it will often take him a long time to recover. His life often consists of a series of ups and downs.

The Tiger is, however, very adaptable. He has an adventurous spirit and rarely stays in the same place for long. In the early stages of his life he is likely to try his hand at several different jobs and he will also change his residence fairly frequently.

The Tiger is very honest and open in his dealings with others. He hates any sort of hypocrisy or falsehood. He is also well known for being blunt and forthright and has no hesitation in speaking his mind. He can be rebellious at times, particularly against any form of petty authority, and while this can lead him into conflict with others, he is never one to shrink from an argument or avoid standing up for what he believes is right.

The Tiger is a natural leader and can invariably rise to the top of his chosen profession. He does not, however, care for anything too bureaucratic or detailed and he does not like to obey orders. He can be stubborn and obstinate and throughout his life he likes to retain a certain amount of independence in his actions and be responsible to no one but himself. He likes to consider that all his achievements are due to his own efforts and he will not ask for support from others if he can avoid it.

Ironically, despite his self-confidence and leadership qualities, the Tiger can be indecisive and will often delay making a major decision until the very last moment. He can also be sensitive to criticism.

Although the Tiger is capable of earning large sums of money, he is rather a spendthrift and does not always put his money to its best use. He can also be most generous and will often shower lavish gifts on friends and relations.

The Tiger cares very much for his reputation and the image that he tries to project. He carries himself with an air of dignity and authority and enjoys being the centre of attention. He is very adept at attracting publicity, both for himself and for the causes he supports.

The Tiger often marries young and he will find himself best suited to those born under the signs of the Pig, Dog, Horse and Goat. He can also get on well with the Rat, Rabbit and Rooster, but will find the Ox and Snake a bit too quiet and serious for his liking, and he will be highly irritated by the Monkey's rather mischievous and inquisitive ways. He will also find it difficult to get on with another Tiger or a Dragon – both partners will want to dominate the relationship and could find it difficult to compromise on even the smallest of matters.

The Tigress is lively, witty and a marvellous hostess at parties. She takes great care over her appearance and is usually most attractive. She can be a very doting mother and while she believes in letting her children have their freedom, she makes an excellent teacher and will ensure that her children are well brought up and want for nothing. Like her male counterpart, she has numerous interests and likes to have sufficient independence and freedom to go off and do the things she wants to do. She has a most caring and generous nature.

The Tiger has many commendable qualities. He is honest, courageous and often a source of inspiration to others. Providing he can curb the wilder excesses of his restless nature, he is almost certain to lead a fulfilling and satisfying life.

THE FIVE DIFFERENT TYPES OF TIGER

In addition to the 12 signs of the Chinese zodiac there are five elements, and these have a strengthening or moderating influence on the sign. The effects of the five elements on the Tiger are described below, together with the years in which the elements were exercising their influence. Therefore those Tigers born in 1950 are Metal Tigers, those born in 1962 are Water Tigers, and so on.

Metal Tiger: 1950
The Metal Tiger has an assertive and outgoing personality. He is very ambitious and while his aims may change from time to time, he will work relentlessly until he has obtained what he wants. He can, however, be impatient for results and become highly strung if things do not work out as he would like. He is distinctive in his appearance and is admired and respected by many.

Water Tiger: 1962
This Tiger has a wide variety of interests and is always eager to experiment with new ideas or satisfy his adven-

turous nature by going off to explore distant lands. He is versatile, shrewd and has a kindly nature. He tends to remain calm in a crisis, although he can be annoyingly indecisive at times. He communicates well with others and through his many capabilities and persuasive nature usually achieves what he wants in life. He is also highly imaginative and is often a gifted orator or writer.

Wood Tiger: 1914, 1974

The Wood Tiger has a friendly and pleasant personality. He is less independent than some of the other types of Tiger and is more prepared to work with others to secure a desired objective. However, he does have a tendency to jump from one thing to another and can easily become distracted. He is usually very popular, has a large circle of friends and invariably leads a busy and enjoyable social life. He also has a good sense of humour.

Fire Tiger: 1926, 1986

The Fire Tiger sets about everything he does with great verve and enthusiasm. He loves action and is always ready to throw himself wholeheartedly into anything which catches his imagination. He has many leadership qualities and is capable of communicating his ideas and enthusiasm to others. He is very much an optimist and can be most generous. He has a likeable nature and can be a witty and persuasive speaker.

Earth Tiger: 1938, 1998

This Tiger is responsible and level-headed. He studies everything objectively and tries to be scrupulously fair in all his dealings. Unlike other Tigers, he is prepared to specialize in certain areas rather than get distracted by other matters, but he can become so involved with what he is doing that he does not always take into account the opinions of those around him. He has good business sense and is usually very successful in later life. He has a large circle of friends and pays great attention to both his appearance and his reputation.

PROSPECTS FOR THE TIGER
IN 2006

The Year of the Rooster (9 February 2005 to 28 January 2006) will have been an interesting one for the Tiger and in what remains of it he will certainly have the opportunity to use his skills and strengths well. However, to benefit, he will need to be flexible in outlook and prepared to adapt to prevailing situations. This is a time for him to work closely with colleagues and keep his independent nature in check.

For those Tigers who are looking to make progress in their career or are seeking work, November could see some interesting openings. During the remaining part of the year, the Tiger will find it is better for him to stick to the areas in which he has most experience rather than aim for anything too different.

The Tiger's domestic and social life will also see much activity in the last months of the Rooster year and in view of all that is being planned, he does need to consult others regularly and be mindful of their views. Good communication is very important in preventing disagreements from arising. October and December could be especially active months socially. There will also be some good travel opportunities for the Tiger in the closing months of the year.

Overall, the Rooster year does hold good prospects for the Tiger, but it is very much a case of making the most of the opportunities that arise. What the Tiger can achieve now will serve him well in the following 12 months.

The Year of the Dog starts on 29 January and holds encouraging prospects for the Tiger. This is a year in which his experience and efforts can lead to success, while his personal life will be active and often pleasurable.

In his work the year will bring some interesting developments, although to benefit the Tiger *will* need to work hard and be prepared to put himself forward. This is no year for him to rest on his laurels or be slow in following up opportunities. Action is the key.

Many Tigers will have done their reputation much good recently and early in the Dog year the Tiger could find himself being singled out for other duties or given opportunities to progress. Whether he is approached directly or sees an opening that interests him, he should make the most of it. By showing himself keen, he will often be able to make good headway, and with the aspects as they are, one step forward could lead to others. For the ambitious Tiger, the Dog year holds excellent potential.

Similarly, for those Tigers who may be in a rut or feeling unfulfilled in their present position, this is a time when they should seize the initiative and look to make changes. Although change will bring pressures and anxious moments, especially if the Tiger has been in the same position for some time, he will often revel in the chance to try something different and use his skills in other ways. Even if some of his initial applications fail, he should not lose heart. The Dog year rewards the dedicated and determined, and during it many Tigers will be able to set their career off on a more rewarding path. February, March and the months from July to mid-October could see important career developments, but such is the promising nature of the year that whenever an interesting opportunity appears, the Tiger should act quickly.

This also applies to those Tigers seeking work. Again, many will be successful over the year in obtaining a position which will broaden their experience and offer a good platform for further development in the future.

With the progressive aspects of the year, this is also an excellent time for the Tiger to further his skills. What he learns over the year, whether through training or in the course of his duties, will not only help him in the present but also widen his scope for the future. Those Tigers who may have been seeking work for some time will find that by exploring the possibilities of retraining or taking advantage of any courses they may be eligible for, they can greatly improve their prospects.

Travel, too, is favourably aspected and the Tiger should aim to go away at some time over the year. With his keen and adventurous nature, he could find his travels bringing him a lot of fun as well as the chance to see some often impressive sights. For those Tigers who decide to travel considerable distances, it would, though, be worth planning their itinerary carefully, reading up about their destination and checking what they may need well in advance. This way they will often get far more out of their trips.

As far as money matters are concerned, this will be a generally favourable year, with the Tiger's enterprise and hard work often leading to an increase in income. However, to benefit, the Tiger does need to manage his money well. This is a year for keeping control over his purse-strings rather than proceeding on too much of an ad hoc basis.

This will be a rewarding year as far as the Tiger's home life is concerned. He will be particularly grateful for the support of those around him and should be forthcoming about any ideas he has, as well as any hopes and concerns, as he will be able to do much more as a result of the advice and encouragement he receives. He will enjoy many of the family activities that take place too, including setting about home projects, sharing interests or simply enjoying time with his loved ones. However, as with any year, problems will sometimes emerge. When they do, the Tiger should address these before they start to sour domestic life. Fortunately such situations will be few, but when they do occur the Tiger does need to act quickly. Talking, listening and a willingness to take a more accommodating attitude will help. Overall, though, this will be a pleasing year domestically, with the Tiger appreciating the support and encouragement his loved ones are able to give.

The Tiger's social prospects are also favourably aspected. With his various interests and contacts, he will have many opportunities to go out, with April, June, September and December being particularly active months. As the year progresses, he will often find his social circle widening and for those Tigers who may have felt lonely or would welcome a more fulfilling social life, the Dog year can bring quite a transformation. For the unattached, this can be an exciting year, with many meeting someone who will quickly become special. Romantically, this can be a significant and memorable year.

In almost all areas of the Tiger's life, the aspects are promising. In his work there will be chances to make progress and further his skills, while his domestic and social life will also bring much satisfaction. However, to benefit from the favourable aspects, the Tiger will need to act upon his ideas and take his opportunities. This is a year when hard work and a willing attitude will be rewarded.

The Metal Tiger

This year will contain some good opportunities for the Metal Tiger. However, these opportunities will also bring change and there will be times over the year when the Metal Tiger will need to draw on his tenacious qualities and show his resolve. The Dog year will demand a lot of him, but it can reward him well.

In his work the aspects are especially encouraging. In view of his considerable experience the Metal Tiger will often find colleagues looking to him for advice and guidance. He may also have the chance to become involved in more specialist duties. By acting positively on any offers that come his way, he will not only be able to advance his career but also find his duties more fulfilling.

Over the year some Metal Tigers will feel they have accomplished all they can in their present role and will welcome a new challenge. For these Metal Tigers, as well as for those currently seeking work, the Dog year holds much promise. By putting themselves forward and remaining persistent, many will be successful in securing a position which can set their career off on an interesting new track. Those who are keen to change their role would be helped by discussing this with colleagues and other contacts who are in a position to give informed advice. With others thinking so highly of the Metal Tiger, words put in on his behalf can prove very helpful. Work-wise, the Dog year is one of considerable opportunity, but it is very much a case of acting positively and following up ideas and advice. For work developments February to early April and July to mid-October are favourable times.

The advances that the Metal Tiger makes in his work will also lead to an increase in his income and some Metal Tigers may be able to supplement this further through an interest or idea they have. The Metal Tiger's earning abilities will certainly be in good form over the year. To reap the benefits, though, he does need to manage his money well. Although money may flow into his account, there will be many temptations to spend it, and succumbing to too many of these could prevent the Metal Tiger from putting it to its best use. While still enjoying the fruits of his labours, he should consider making savings for the longer term, reducing any borrowings he has and setting sums aside for travel, accommodation plans and any other ideas he has. With good planning and control, he can strengthen his financial position as well as enjoy himself.

With travel prominently aspected, the Metal Tiger should also give some thought to a holiday he would like to take over the year. By discussing this with loved ones, he will find some exciting plans starting to emerge. Some Metal Tigers could also decide to go away for a break at the last moment and the spontaneity will add considerably to the enjoyment. Overall, this is a good year for travel and the Metal Tiger should make the most of it.

Domestically, this will be a busy year, with the Metal Tiger's practical nature often getting the better of him. Over the year many Metal Tigers will decide to go ahead with some major projects on their home. Whether this is redecorating, having alterations carried out or re-equipping certain rooms, it could entail considerable disruption as well as take up a lot of time. Where practical undertakings are concerned, patience will be called for! Also, with this being a year for change, there will be some Metal Tigers who decide to move. Domestically, it will certainly be a full and active year. Throughout, however, the Metal Tiger will be supported by those around him and home life, while busy, will often be enjoyable. There will also be occasions that will mean a great deal. Whether these involve pursuing joint interests, following the progress of close relations (and for some there could be a celebration connected with a younger family member), holidays or other treats, the Metal Tiger will value these special times.

The favourable aspects also extend to the Metal Tiger's social life, with many invitations and opportunities to go out. Those Metal Tigers who would welcome a more active social life will find that by going out more and meeting those who share similar interests (perhaps at a local group), they could see quite a transformation in their situation. Some excellent friendships could also be made while travelling, and for the unattached, there could be an exciting new romance. Socially and personally, this is a positive year, with late March, April, June, September and December being busy and active months.

In so many respects the Metal Tiger can do well in the Dog year. However, to reap the benefits, he will need to put himself forward. This is a year when positive action and a determined attitude will be well rewarded.

TIP FOR THE YEAR
Do consult others. Over the year it really is worth being open about ideas and plans and listening carefully to what others say. Their input, assistance and support can make an real difference to how you fare.

The Water Tiger

This is a year of opportunity for the Water Tiger and one in which he will enjoy positive developments in many areas of his life. However, to make the most of his chances, he will need to show some flexibility in attitude.

In his work there will be some excellent opportunities for him to make further advances. As colleagues move on, vacancies will become available which the Water Tiger may be well placed to put in for, or he could be offered the chance to become involved in a more specialist role. Whenever an opening arises, he will need to be quick in showing an interest and putting in an application. His eagerness and enthusiasm will be noted and will often be to his advantage.

Also, the Water Tiger should make much of his talent for coming up with ideas and if there are practical suggestions he can make or he has a solution to a problem, he should put his ideas forward. His initiative and enterprise will often be well received.

For those Water Tigers who are keen to further their career in other directions, are feeling unfulfilled or are seeking work, this is a year to take the initiative. By making enquiries and following up any vacancies that interest them, they will find their efforts can lead to some important developments. Admittedly, it may require quite a few attempts and there will be disappointments along the way, but the aspects *are* on the Water Tigers' side and with their talents and tenaciousness, many will secure a position which will suit them well. This is also a year when a certain flexibility could be helpful and these Water Tigers should aim to consider a range of possibilities rather than restrict themselves to too narrow a focus. February, March and the period from July to mid-October could be especially positive for work developments.

The Water Tiger will derive much pleasure from his personal interests over the year and should make sure he spends time on them. Not only will they help him relax and unwind but they will also give him the chance to do something different from his usual daily activities. Any Tigers who may have let their interests lapse recently, perhaps due to pressure of work or other commitments, should seek to set time aside for recreational pursuits that appeal to them. Also, any attention they can give to their well-being could be helpful, although before starting on any new fitness campaign, the Water Tiger should seek proper guidance on the best way to proceed.

The Dog year favours travel and the Water Tiger should also aim to go away over the year. A break and change of scene will do him good and by choosing his destination with care, he will often enjoy the places he visits as well as the rest and fun his travels bring.

As far as money matters are concerned, this will be a generally positive year, with many Water Tigers enjoying a noticeable rise in income. However, while this increase will be welcome, the Water Tiger would do well to manage his money carefully, including reducing any borrowings as well as saving towards any large purchases or costly plans he has in mind. By controlling his financial situation he will notice an improvement over the year as well as appreciate his purchases all the more.

This will also be a pleasing year domestically, with the Water Tiger valuing the support and assistance he receives from those close to him. In view of the many developments and sometimes pressures of his work, any extra help he receives, especially with household activities, will be particularly welcome. He will also be grateful for any advice he receives and should be prepared to discuss his activities and ideas with those around him. Over the year his loved ones really can make a difference to how he fares. The Water Tiger will also enjoy many of the domestic activities that take place, including spending time with others and on home and garden projects as well as a possible holiday. However, while a lot will go well, as with any year problems and disagreements will also arise, often as a result of tiredness. When they do, the Water Tiger will find that a willingness to talk and show understanding can do much to diffuse them. Here again his communication skills will serve him well. Overall, though, this will be a pleasing and often full year with the Water Tiger valuing his domestic life.

The Water Tiger's social life will also see much activity. With his wide interests, he will nearly always have something lined up and those Water Tigers who would welcome new friendships will find that becoming more involved in activities in their area can lead to quite a transformation in their situation. April, June, September and December could be particularly active socially.

Generally, the Water Tiger will have much in his favour over the year and by acting upon the opportunities that arise and using his experience and ideas to advantage, he will not only be able to make good progress but also help his future prospects. Also, throughout the year he will be helped by the support and advice he receives, with his relations with others again being important to him. Overall, a year of much potential and good fortune.

TIP FOR THE YEAR
You have the talents, the ideas and the experience – use them well. This is a year when initiative, hard work and a willingness to put yourself forward can bring some very positive results.

The Wood Tiger

This will be a busy year for the Wood Tiger and will see interesting developments in many areas of his life. However, he would do well to remember the Chinese proverb, 'Better to do it than to miss it.' This is a year for seizing chances, otherwise some good opportunities could be lost.

As the Dog year starts, the Wood Tiger would find it helpful to give some thought to his aims for the year. This way he will find he is able to direct his energies in a more purposeful way as well as to be alert for the right opportunities to follow up. The support he enjoys will also be helpful to him and by talking over his aims and hopes – whether domestic plans, work matters or other ideas – he really will gain a great deal of useful advice and assistance.

Over the year his home life in particular will see much activity. If a parent, he is likely to spend much time attending to the needs of young ones, encouraging them and following their progress. With the demands of children as well as all his other activities, he will often be grateful for any help offered by more senior relations and close friends. Also, he will be keen to make some improvements to his home, including adding new comforts and equipment to make life easier. Some Wood Tigers may even decide to move to somewhere that better suits their requirements. With his often ambitious domestic plans, the Wood Tiger does need to think everything through carefully as well as allow plenty of time for his ideas to be realized. However, while his home life will often be busy, there will be much to enjoy. And, as the Wood Tiger appreciates, it is important that home life is not just one round of continual activity but has its fun times as well.

The Dog year will also see much social activity, with the Wood Tiger's work and interests often bringing invitations to go out. With his ability to get on well with so many, he will often find himself in demand and forging some new friendships. For those Wood Tigers who move to new areas, are keen to build up their social life or may have had some recent personal disappointments, the Dog year offers considerable promise, with the events of the year and their various activities bringing them good opportunities to meet others and build up a new social circle. For socializing, late March, April, June, September and December are particularly favourable times.

For the unattached Wood Tiger this can be an important year, with an existing friendship suddenly becoming more significant or the chance to meet someone who will quickly become special. For affairs of the heart, this can be an exciting year.

With travel also well aspected, the Wood Tiger should take advantage of any chances he gets to go away. Travelling can lead to some very enjoyable and interesting times as well as giving him the chance to have a welcome break from his usual routine.

Although the Wood Tiger will often have many demands on his time, he should also make sure his personal interests and recreational pursuits do not suffer as a result. He does need to give himself the opportunity to unwind and any time he can set aside for activities he enjoys – perhaps involving additional exercise – will be important. Again he could find it helpful to set himself a goal to reach over the year or, if there is a skill he would like to learn, he should follow it up. Whatever he does, by pursuing his interests in a purposeful way, he will find them rewarding and satisfying.

This will also be a positive year as far as the Wood Tiger's work is concerned. With his skills, reputation and experience, there will be good opportunities for him to take on greater responsibilities, whether through promotion or moving to another employer. However, when a vacancy arises or the Wood Tiger sees a situation he feels could be to his advantage, he does need to be quick in following it up.

For those Wood Tigers who are unfulfilled in their present role or are seeking work, events can move in fortuitous ways. By talking to others, making enquiries and remaining alert for openings, these Wood Tigers will often be successful in securing a new position which could lead to exciting possibilities in the future. The Dog year is a time of opportunity, but the Wood Tiger does need to act quickly.

As far as money matters are concerned, with his accommodation plans, existing obligations and family expenses, the Wood Tiger will need to manage his situation well. Good planning and budgeting can make a real difference and enable the Wood Tiger to do more than if he were to proceed in too much of an ad hoc manner. Also, should he enter into an important agreement or have a particularly complex financial matter to deal with, he would do well to seek advice rather than try to tackle this on his own. If not, he could find problems arising or that it takes up a disproportionate amount of time. Wood Tigers, take note, and remember that support is available.

Although this will be a busy and sometimes demanding year for the Wood Tiger, by deciding upon his aims and plans and acting with the support of others, he can accomplish a great deal. This is a year of potential and progress and one that he can enjoy too.

TIP FOR THE YEAR
As the Chinese proverb suggests, it is 'Better to do it than to miss it' and this is very much a year for doing it. By making plans, acting positively whenever opportunities arise and using your talents well, you can make this a successful and productive year.

The Fire Tiger

This is a year of great possibility for the Fire Tiger, but to benefit he will need to work hard as well as make the most of the opportunities that arise. Throughout the year, however, he will be encouraged by the support of others and if at any time he is in a dilemma over a decision he has to take, has a problem or would welcome some assistance, he should not hesitate to ask. There are many who are willing to help him and, as he will find, their advice and support can make a considerable difference to how he fares.

In addition to the encouragement he receives, the Fire Tiger can look forward to a full and active personal life. He will have many chances to go out and some weeks could be a whirl of social activity with the Fire Tiger being in great demand. Affairs of the heart are splendidly aspected, with many existing romances becoming more meaningful, while for the unattached Fire Tiger there will some good opportunities to meet others, including someone who will become very special. For socializing, April, June, September and December will be active, but with the year so favourably aspected for affairs of the heart, the unattached could feel the effects of Cupid's arrow at almost any time. And for those who may realize a certain romance is not working or have experienced some recent hurt, the Dog year will provide the chance to meet others and, in some cases, build up a new social circle.

The Fire Tiger will also enjoy his personal interests over the year and should look to develop these further. If he is keen on sporting and outdoor pursuits, anything he can do to add to his skills will often increase the pleasure they bring, while for those who enjoy creative and more expressive activities, including music, again time spent furthering their talents can be very rewarding.

With the Fire Tiger's active and adventurous nature, he may well decide to travel over the year and in some cases cover considerable distances. To help make the most of his time away he would do well to read up about his destination and go well prepared. With good planning his travels can be both interesting and great fun.

For those Fire Tigers in work, the Dog year offers good prospects. However, the Fire Tiger will need to put in the effort to make headway. This includes mastering the different aspects of his work as well as building up his experience. With a willing attitude he can impress others and will often find himself being considered for greater responsibilities as the year progresses. This is a time when effort and commitment will be recognized and rewarded. Also, with the Fire Tiger being in the early stages of his career, what he learns now can stand him in good stead for later.

Those Fire Tigers who are seeking a position should actively follow up any openings that appeal to them. They could also find it helpful to talk to members of professional organizations, career advisers or any contacts they may have. By remaining persistent, many will be successful in securing a useful position. February, March and the months from July to mid-October could see some good career developments.

As far as money matters are concerned, the Fire Tiger will, however, need to be careful. With his many plans and often busy social life, his outgoings could be considerable and as far as possible he should keep a close watch on his spending as well as set funds aside for other expenses and requirements. With care and control he can manage well, but this is a year for financial discipline.

For those Fire Tigers in education this can be a significant year and while there will often be many distractions with student life, the Fire Tiger should make the most of his studying opportunities and aim to give his best. Good qualifications can open up so much and it really would be worth his while to make every effort to work well and consistently. Again, the Dog year does reward those prepared to show commitment.

In many respects this will be an important year for the Fire Tiger and whether in work or studying, what he learns now can prepare him for the success he will enjoy in following years. Personally, the year holds excellent prospects, with the Fire Tiger being encouraged by the support he receives as well as enjoying a lively social life. By making the most of this and the opportunities available to him, he will find that a lot can go in his favour this year.

TIP FOR THE YEAR

As a Tiger you value your independence, but with important decisions to take, activities to do and goals to reach this year, you will fare much better by drawing on the assistance of others. In 2006, do be forthcoming.

The Earth Tiger

This can be a rewarding year for the Earth Tiger, although to benefit from the prevailing aspects he will need to act upon his ideas and opportunities. With willingness on his part and good support from others, however, he can accomplish and enjoy a great deal.

Accommodation is likely to figure prominently, with some Earth Tigers deciding to move to accommodation more suitable to their present needs and others carrying out improvements they have had in mind for some time. Those who do move will spend a lot of time sorting out belongings as well as finding somewhere suitable to live. The process will involve considerable effort and there will be occasions when these Earth Tigers will wonder if they have made the right decision, but by allowing plenty of time and drawing on the assistance of others, in the end they will be satisfied with what they have accomplished.

In addition all Earth Tigers, whether they move or remain where they are, will decide to proceed with some major purchases for their home, and whether these are equipment, furnishings or other enhancements, they would do well to take their time and carefully consider the ranges, options and terms available. This way their purchases will often be more suitable and better value too.

Also, should any of the Earth Tiger's plans involve anything strenuous, he should seek help. Although he may be keen to get the job done, this is *not* a year to take risks with his well-being. Earth Tigers, take note.

The Earth Tiger will value his domestic life over the year, and if a grandparent, he will enjoy the opportunities he has to see his grandchildren. He will also follow the progress and activities of family members with much interest and several times over the year those close to him will seek out his views and advice. His approachability and good sense really will be valued by family members and his words of advice will be welcome.

The Earth Tiger will also get much pleasure from his personal interests over the year, especially from some of the more creative projects he tackles. In addition, if there is a subject that has been intriguing him or a skill he feels it could be useful to learn, he should find out more and perhaps enrol on a course. If he does something positive and practical, he will be pleased with the results. Sometimes taking up a new interest with a partner or a friend could also be worth considering.

This is also a favourable year for travel and the Earth Tiger should make the most of any chances he has to visit others as well as follow up any offers that appeal to him. Again, by acting positively, he will enjoy what he does, and many Earth Tigers will visit some interesting places over the year. There could also be the chance of meeting others while away, and for some, new friendships will be forged.

As far as money matters are concerned, the year could see much outlay. With his plans for his accommodation, travel opportunities and the many other things he wants to do, the Earth Tiger's spending will sometimes be considerable. However, by taking care with any transactions he enters into and seeking advice where appropriate, he will often be pleased with the results. To prevent problems it is, though, a case of proceeding steadily and carefully, particularly as too much rush could lead to mistakes and less satisfactory choices. Also, should the Earth Tiger have any questions or uncertainties over any financial matter, it is important that he gets these resolved before proceeding. This can often prevent problems from occurring later.

The Dog year is a generally favourable one for the Earth Tiger and by following up his ideas, he will be pleased with the often considerable amount he is able to do.

TIP FOR THE YEAR

Do draw on the advice and assistance of those around you. So much more can be accomplished with the help of others. Also, spend time on your interests and hobbies. These can bring you much pleasure as well as do you good.

FAMOUS TIGERS

Debbie Allen, Kofi Annan, Sir David Attenborough, Queen Beatrix of the Netherlands, Victoria Beckham, Beethoven, Tony Bennett, Tom Berenger, Chuck Berry, Jon Bon Jovi, Sir Richard Branson, Emily Brontë, Garth Brooks, Mel Brooks, Isambard Kingdom Brunel, Agatha Christie, Charlotte Church, Charles Clarke, Phil Collins, Robbie Coltrane, Sheryl Crow, Tom Cruise, Penelope Cruz, Charles de Gaulle, Leonardo DiCaprio, Emily Dickinson,

David Dimbleby, Dwight Eisenhower, Queen Elizabeth II, Enya, Roberta Flack, E. M. Forster, Frederick Forsyth, Jodie Foster, Crystal Gayle, Buddy Greco, Germaine Greer, Ed Harris, Hugh Hefner, Tim Henman, William Hurt, Ray Kroc, Stan Laurel, Jay Leno, Groucho Marx, Karl Marx, Marilyn Monroe, Demi Moore, Alanis Morissette, Jeremy Paxman, Marco Polo, Beatrix Potter, John Prescott, the Princess Royal, Renoir, Kenny Rogers, Dame Joan Sutherland, Dylan Thomas, Liv Ullman, Jon Voight, Julie Walters, H. G. Wells, Oscar Wilde, Robbie Williams, Dr Rowan Williams, Tennessee Williams, Terry Wogan, Stevie Wonder, William Wordsworth.

14 FEBRUARY 1915 ⁓ 2 FEBRUARY 1916	*Wood Rabbit*
2 FEBRUARY 1927 ⁓ 22 JANUARY 1928	*Fire Rabbit*
19 FEBRUARY 1939 ⁓ 7 FEBRUARY 1940	*Earth Rabbit*
6 FEBRUARY 1951 ⁓ 26 JANUARY 1952	*Metal Rabbit*
25 JANUARY 1963 ⁓ 12 FEBRUARY 1964	*Water Rabbit*
11 FEBRUARY 1975 ⁓ 30 JANUARY 1976	*Wood Rabbit*
29 JANUARY 1987 ⁓ 16 FEBRUARY 1988	*Fire Rabbit*
16 FEBRUARY 1999 ⁓ 4 FEBRUARY 2000	*Earth Rabbit*

THE

RABBIT

THE PERSONALITY OF THE RABBIT

The thing always happens that you really believe in; and
the belief in a thing makes it happen.

Frank Lloyd Wright, a Rabbit

The Rabbit is born under the signs of virtue and prudence. He is intelligent, well-mannered and prefers a quiet and peaceful existence. He dislikes any sort of unpleasantness and will try to steer clear of arguments and disputes. He is very much a pacifist and tends to have a calming influence on those around him. He has wide interests and usually a good appreciation of the arts and the finer things in life. He also knows how to enjoy himself and will often gravitate to the best restaurants and nightspots in town.

The Rabbit is a witty and intelligent speaker and loves being involved in a good discussion. His views and advice are often sought by others and he can be relied upon to be discreet and diplomatic. He will rarely raise his voice in anger and will even turn a blind eye to matters which displease him just to preserve the peace. He likes to remain on good terms with everyone, but he can be rather sensitive and takes any form of criticism very badly. He will also be the first to get out of the way if he sees any form of trouble brewing.

The Rabbit is a quiet and efficient worker and has an extremely good memory. He is very astute in business and financial matters, but his degree of success often depends on the conditions that prevail. He hates being in a situation which is fraught with tension or where he has to make sudden decisions. Wherever possible he will plan his various activities with the utmost care and a good deal of caution. He does not like to take risks and does not take kindly to change. Basically, he seeks a secure, calm and stable environment, and when conditions are right he is more than happy to leave things as they are.

The Rabbit is conscientious and because of his methodical and ever-watchful nature he can often do well in his chosen profession. He makes a good diplomat, lawyer, shopkeeper, administrator or priest, and he excels in any job where he can use his superb skills as a communicator. He tends to be loyal to his employers and is respected for his integrity and honesty, but if he ever finds himself in a position of great power he can become rather intransigent and authoritarian.

The Rabbit attaches great importance to his home and will often spend a lot of time and money maintaining and furnishing it and fitting it with all the latest comforts – the Rabbit is very much a creature of comfort! He is also something of a collector and there are many Rabbits who derive much pleasure from collecting antiques, stamps, coins, *objets d'art* or anything else which catches their eye or particularly interests them.

The female Rabbit has a friendly, caring and considerate nature, and will do all in her power to give her home a happy and loving atmosphere. She is also very sociable and enjoys holding parties and entertaining. She has a great ability to make the maximum use of her time and although she involves herself in numerous activities, she always manages to find time to sit back and enjoy a good read or a chat. She has a great sense of humour, is very artistic and is often a talented gardener.

The Rabbit takes considerable care over his appearance and is usually smart and well turned out. He also attaches great importance to his relations with others and matters of the heart are particularly important to him. He will rarely be short of admirers and will often have several serious romances before he settles down. The Rabbit is not the most faithful of signs, but he will find that he is especially well suited to those born under the signs of the Goat, Snake, Pig and Ox. Due to his sociable and easy-going manner he can also get on well with the Tiger, Dragon, Horse, Monkey, Dog and another Rabbit, but he will feel ill at ease with the Rat and Rooster as both these signs tend to speak their mind and be critical in their comments, and the Rabbit just loathes any form of criticism or unpleasantness.

The Rabbit is usually lucky in life and often has the happy knack of being in the right place at the right time. He is talented and quick-witted, but he does sometimes put pleasure before work and wherever possible will tend to opt for the easy life. He can at times be a little reserved and suspicious of the motives of others, but generally will lead a long and contented life and one which – as far as possible – will be free of strife and discord.

THE FIVE DIFFERENT TYPES OF RABBIT

In addition to the 12 signs of the Chinese zodiac there are five elements and these have a strengthening or moderating influence on the sign. The effects of the five elements on the Rabbit are described below, together with the years in which the elements were exercising their influence. Therefore those Rabbits born in 1951 are Metal Rabbits, those born in 1963 are Water Rabbits, and so on.

Metal Rabbit: 1951
This Rabbit is capable, ambitious and has very definite views on what he wants to achieve in life. He can occasionally appear reserved and aloof, but this is mainly because he likes to keep his thoughts to himself. He has a quick and alert mind and is particularly shrewd in business matters. He can also be very cunning in his actions. The Metal Rabbit has a good appreciation of the arts and likes to mix in the best circles. He usually has a small but very loyal group of friends.

Water Rabbit: 1963
The Water Rabbit is popular, intuitive and keenly aware of the feelings of those around him. He can, however, be rather sensitive and tends to take things too much to heart. He is very precise and thorough in everything he does and

has an exceedingly good memory. He tends to be quiet and at times rather withdrawn, but he expresses his ideas well and is highly regarded by his family, friends and colleagues.

Wood Rabbit: 1915, 1975

The Wood Rabbit is likeable, easy-going and very adaptable. He prefers to work in a group rather than on his own and likes to have the support and encouragement of others. He can, however, be rather reticent in expressing his views and it would be in his own interests to become a little more open and let others know how he feels on certain matters. He usually has many friends, enjoys an active social life and is noted for his generosity.

Fire Rabbit: 1927, 1987

The Fire Rabbit has a friendly, outgoing personality. He likes socializing and being on good terms with everyone. He is discreet and diplomatic and has a very good understanding of human nature. He is also strong-willed and provided he has the necessary backing he can go far in life. He does, not, however, suffer adversity well and can become moody and depressed when things are not working out as he would like. He has a particularly good manner with children, is very intuitive and there are some Fire Rabbits who are even noted for their psychic ability.

Earth Rabbit: 1939, 1999

The Earth Rabbit is a quiet individual, but he is neverthe-less very astute. He is realistic in his aims and is prepared to work long and hard in order to achieve his objectives. He has good business sense and is invariably lucky in financial matters. He also has a most persuasive manner and usually experiences little difficulty in getting others to fall in with his plans. He is held in high esteem by his friends and colleagues and his views are often sought and highly valued.

PROSPECTS FOR THE RABBIT
IN 2006

The Year of the Rooster (9 February 2005 to 28 January 2006) will have been a variable one for the Rabbit and not all his activities will have gone as well as he would have liked. However, as the Rooster year draws to a close, the Rabbit can look forward to an improvement in his fortunes.

In what remains of the Rooster year the Rabbit should look positively at any opportunities that arise. In his work, if he can extend his role or add to his skills, he will find this will help his prospects. Also, working well with colleagues and showing himself an effective team member will help his reputation and with the aspects so encouraging in the Dog year, what the Rabbit can do at this time can be *very* constructive in the longer term.

The Rabbit will, though, need to be his usual careful self when dealing with money matters and with the closing months of the year being a more expensive time, he could find it helpful to make early provision for some of his larger outgoings. Also, if he has any problems, especially of a bureaucratic nature, he would do well to get additional advice or contact a helpline.

With his sociable nature the Rabbit sets much store by his relations with others and his social life is set to become busier as the year draws to a close. There will be plenty of chances for him to go out, with invitations to various social events and opportunities to meet up with others. He will also value his home life and play a full part in many of the activities that take place. Also, by being forthcoming over any concerns he may have, he will find that others will be supportive and can offer good advice.

Both domestically and socially the closing months of the Rooster year can be a pleasing time and with the friendship and support of those around him, the Rabbit may sense that his fortunes are on the turn and look forward to the approach of the Dog year with a greater optimism and a determination to make the most of the year ahead.

The Year of the Dog starts on 29 January and will be a constructive one for the Rabbit. Over the year he will be able to build on his recent activities and make good headway, while his personal life is also favourably aspected.

In his work the Rabbit's prospects are especially encouraging. In view of his recent experience, he will often find himself in an excellent position to make important headway. For many Rabbits this will be with their current employer, which will allow them to benefit from their in-house knowledge and the good reputation they have built up. When these Rabbits see an opening or are offered greater responsibilities, they should seize the chance. This is very much a year for growth and for moving their career forward.

For those Rabbits who feel there are better opportunities elsewhere or that it would help their career to move to another employer, again the Dog year holds excellent prospects. By making enquiries and following up any openings that become available, these Rabbits will find their initiative and determination will often lead to them securing a position which can represent an important step forward as well as further their experience.

Similarly, for those Rabbits seeking work, either as the Dog year starts or during it, this is a time to follow up vacancies that interest them as well as draw on the help that is available. This can range from advice offered by employment agencies and professional organizations to retraining and refresher courses. Anything positive that these Rabbits can do to help their prospects *can* make a difference and many will secure what will be an interesting position. March, May, June and September could see important developments work-wise, but with the aspects so encouraging throughout the year, whenever an opportunity arises, the Rabbit should act quickly.

The progress that the Rabbit makes in his work will also lead to an increase in his income and some Rabbits could also benefit from some further financial good fortune, including a bonus, a gift or being able to supplement their income through a skill they have. The Rabbit's financial prospects are certainly encouraging and this will enable many Rabbits to go ahead with plans they have for their home, as well as recreational pursuits and travel. The Rabbit will certainly enjoy the rewards of his labours over the year. He could also find it helpful to give some thought to his future and if he is able to start or add to a savings scheme or pension policy, in years to come he could be grateful for what he has been able to put aside.

The Rabbit will also derive much pleasure from his interests over the year, especially those which have a social element or allow him to draw on his more creative talents. By setting time aside for activities he enjoys, the Rabbit will not only find them rewarding but also a good way to relax and do something different from his usual daily activities. In addition, if he is able to learn any new techniques and skills that could help him to get more from his interests or can set himself an interesting project to do, he will find it giving his interest added purpose and meaning.

This will also be an important year as far as the Rabbit's relations with others are concerned. Others do feel at ease in his company and over the year he will find himself in demand, with many invitations and chances to go out as well as opportunities to meet others. For those Rabbits who would welcome more company and are keen to build up their social life, the year is pleasingly aspected. By making the most of their chances and getting involved in various activities, they will find their social life improving and becoming more fulfilling as the year progresses.

For the unattached Rabbit the Dog year can also bring the chance to meet someone who can quickly become special. So encouraging are the aspects that many Rabbits will settle down with a partner over the year or become engaged or married. For personal relationships this can be a favourable *and* significant year. For meeting others and socializing, March, June to August and November will be busy and important months.

The Rabbit will also value his domestic life over the year and there may be good cause for a celebration. This could be an addition to the family, a wedding, graduation, career success or some other key event, but whatever happens, it will often be the source of great joy and may mean more to the Rabbit than others realize.

The Rabbit will also appreciate the support he is given by his loved ones, and by being open with his ideas and any concerns he will not only find himself benefiting from their ideas and advice but will also maintain the good rapport he enjoys with those around him. As far as his home life is concerned, this may be a busy and eventful year but it can be a rewarding one too.

Also, with this being a year for positive developments, some Rabbits will decide to move to new accommodation. Although this will involve considerable effort on their part, by setting about their plans in good time and using their organizational skills well, they will be pleased with how the move works out and the new opportunities it offers.

The Year of the Dog certainly holds encouraging prospects for the Rabbit, especially in terms of his career. His personal interests too can give him much satisfaction, while his social and domestic life will both see much activity and some pleasing times. Overall, much can go in the Rabbit's favour in 2006, but to benefit he should be willing to move his situation forward. For those who act, the rewards, pleasures and achievements of the year can be significant indeed.

The Metal Rabbit

This will be a year of considerable opportunity for the Metal Rabbit. In his work the aspects are promising and the year will bring some excellent chances to make progress. However, this *does* mean change and if the Metal Rabbit is to benefit, he must accept this. It will involve moments of uncertainty, pressure and, for some, a wrench from the familiar, but from this will come growth and opportunity. This is very much a year for the Metal Rabbit to look forward and to advance his career.

Metal Rabbits who are seeking work or keen to move their career in another direction could find it useful to talk to those who are able to advise them – and here some of their contacts could be helpful – as well as put themselves forward whenever they see a suitable opportunity. In many cases, their determination and resolve will lead to them securing a good position. March, May, June and September could see some positive career developments.

For those Metal Rabbits who are content in their career choice and well-established in their present position, this is also a year of considerable opportunity. With their experience, skills and ability to relate well to others, these Metal Rabbits will find themselves excellently placed to make progress. As more senior colleagues retire or move to other positions, they will be strong candidates for promotion or more specialist duties. This is a year when they can really benefit from their knowledge and skills.

The Metal Rabbit will also get much pleasure from his personal interests over the year and should look to build on them, perhaps by enrolling on a course or learning new techniques. Those who, due to work and other commitments, have let their interests lapse should aim to rectify this over the year. Setting time set aside for activities they enjoy really can benefit them.

The Metal Rabbit should also give consideration to his well-being over the year and if he does not get much daily exercise or is reliant on convenience foods, he should look at ways of correcting this. By seeking medical guidance and acting on the advice given he will often feel much better. Again, positive action will be rewarded.

The year is also well aspected for money matters, with many Metal Rabbits enjoying an increase in income as well as possibly a gift, an unexpected payment or a bonus. However, while the aspects may be encouraging, the Metal Rabbit should manage his money well rather than be tempted to spend anything extra all too readily. By reducing his borrowings and setting sums aside for the longer term as well as making provision for specific requirements, he will find his financial position improving and will be able to do that much more as a result. This is a year when planning can make an appreciable difference.

With his approachable nature and wide interests, the Metal Rabbit gets on well with most people and he will find himself much in demand over the year. With his work, his interests and his circle of friends, he will have many chances to go out and socialize. Changes in his work and personal activities (including new interests) can also lead to him meeting others and extending his social circle. March, June to early September and November could be active and interesting months socially. Those Metal Rabbits who may have let their social life lapse and would welcome some new friendships will find that by making the most of chances to go out and becoming more involved in interests that allow them to meet others, their social life can become more active and meaningful over the year.

This will also be a busy year as far as the Metal Rabbit's domestic life is concerned. With his ability to relate so effectively to others and his good judgement, he will find his views and advice will often be sought. Also, with younger relations often having to cope with a great deal (possibly including babies and young children), any practical help and support the Metal Rabbit can offer will be appreciated.

The Metal Rabbit will also value the interests and activities that he carries out with his loved ones over the year, including tackling projects that will enhance the home and garden. By setting time aside for joint activities and interests, he will find his home life very rewarding.

In so many ways this can be a positive and pleasing year for the Metal Rabbit, bringing him the chance to progress in his work as well as to further his talents. However, while so much can go well, it is important that he keeps his lifestyle in balance and sets time aside for spending with others, recreational pursuits, socializing and developing his interests. This is a year of much potential, but the Metal Rabbit does need to maintain a balance in all his activities. Overall, though, a positive year.

TIP FOR THE YEAR
This is a year for positive action and if you have certain ambitions you are keen to reach, plans you want to realize and ideas you are keen to try out, *now* is the time to act upon them. Follow up any opportunities, make enquiries

and talk to those who may be able to help you. By doing something definite you can set a lot in motion.

The Water Rabbit

This is a year of considerable opportunity for the Water Rabbit and by pursuing his aims and making the most of the situations that arise, he can advance his position as well as enjoy himself.

In his work the Water Rabbit will have much in his favour and with his fine reputation and the considerable experience he has built up, he will be well placed to benefit from any openings that arise. These may be in his existing place of work or with another employer, but over the year many Water Rabbits will reap the rewards of their recent efforts. The months from March to mid-April and June and September could see some interesting promotion possibilities or other career developments.

For those Water Rabbits who feel unfulfilled in their present position or are seeking work, again this is a year for positive change. By making enquiries, taking advantage of any retraining opportunities and following up any openings that interest them, many will find their persistence and self-belief leading to an important new opportunity. Many will secure a position quite different from their previous duties and it will be an interesting challenge as well as open up other possibilities for later.

The progress the Water Rabbit makes in his work will lead to a welcome and often noticeable increase in income. As a result many Water Rabbits will be tempted to go ahead with certain ideas they have had for some time, especially regarding their accommodation. Where home purchases and décor are concerned, the Water Rabbit's fine taste will be appreciated and often admired by others. In addition, if he is able to use any increase in income to reduce any borrowings he has or make early provision for some of his more expensive outgoings he will find this helpful. With good management, his financial situation can certainly improve over the year.

Although the Water Rabbit will have many demands on his time, he should also make sure he sets some aside for more recreational pursuits. With his often busy lifestyle, he does need time to himself. He should also consider going away for a break over the year. A holiday will do him a lot of good.

As far as the Water Rabbit's domestic life is concerned this will be a busy year. With his own activities and those of his family members, there will often be a lot to do, think about and organize, and the Water Rabbit's ability to keep tabs on everything really will be an asset. However, at busy times, he does need to make sure that everyone does their fair share of household tasks and, if necessary, to ask for additional help.

Several times over the year the Water Rabbit will himself help both younger and more senior relations with decisions that need taking as well as assist them with their various activities. Again, his ability to relate so well to others will be particularly appreciated. However if, at any time, he has any concerns or reservations about a family matter, he should let his feelings be known. As he will find, openness on his part will be far better than saying nothing and letting any awkward matter linger in the background.

However, while his domestic life will often be busy, it will mean a great deal to him. The year will contain some very pleasurable times, with interests and home projects, family get-togethers and a possible holiday all helping to make his home life a valuable aspect of his life during the year.

His social life, too, will be fairly busy. Over the year he will have many opportunities to go out and his social circle is set to increase. For those Water Rabbits whose personal life may have been disappointing in recent years, this will be a much more favourable time, with the chance to forge some new friendships and, for some who are unattached, find romance. The Dog year can often mark an important upturn in the Water Rabbit's fortunes. March, the period from June to August and November are particularly favourable times for meeting others.

Overall, this is a year of opportunity for the Water Rabbit, but to benefit he does need to make the most of his ideas and talents. With positive action and the support of others, however, he is set to make good progress.

TIP FOR THE YEAR

This is a year for progress, but to benefit you do need to have faith in yourself and your abilities and make the most of your opportunities. With determination and self-belief, you can make this a great and important year.

The Wood Rabbit

The Dog year holds considerable opportunity for the Wood Rabbit and will see some significant developments.

In recent years the Wood Rabbit will have accomplished a great deal in his work but there will still be many Wood Rabbits who will feel they could be making more of their skills and potential. For these Wood Rabbits, the Dog year will offer the chance they have been seeking.

Wood Rabbits who are discontent with their current situation or seeking work should actively look for new positions and follow up those that interest them, emphasizing to prospective employers their previous experience and what they could bring to the position. In some cases they *will* need be more assertive in order to be noticed, but with persistence, initiative and confidence in what they can offer, many will be given what will be an excellent platform to build on. And if the Wood Rabbit decides to pursue a type of work which is different from what he has been doing, any studying he can do, retraining courses he can go on and information he can get will help his prospects. This is a year which rewards hard work and initiative.

For those Wood Rabbits who are satisfied with their career, this is also a year which offers considerable scope. With their reputation and experience, they will often have the chance to become involved in more specialist work or will find themselves excellently placed for promotion.

The Wood Rabbit will also be helped by his ability to work well with others and in some cases more senior colleagues could be particularly helpful in giving advice and encouragement. The Wood Rabbit should also make the most of any chances he has to meet colleagues and build up contacts.

The progress the Wood Rabbit makes in his work will lead to an increase in his income, but while this will be welcome, he still needs to manage his finances well. With the plans he has for his accommodation (with some Wood Rabbits moving during the year), family expenses and commitments, he does have considerable outgoings and would do well to budget for these as well as keep a close watch on his overall situation. However, with good control and his usual good financial sense, he will be able to carry out many of his plans.

The Wood Rabbit will also derive much pleasure from his recreational pursuits over the year. Not only will some of these have an enjoyable social element, but in some cases they will give him the chance to take additional exercise. Also, if he feels it would be useful to learn or perfect a skill connected to one of his interests, he should follow it up. Any way in which he can further his talents this year can have considerable benefit.

Wood Rabbits who do not tend to get much exercise and/or rely on convenience foods could also find it helpful to get advice on how best they can correct this. By making a few modifications, they really can make a difference to how they feel. Those who may have neglected their well-being lately will find any changes they can make can be another positive aspect of the year.

As far as the Wood Rabbit's home life is concerned, this will be a busy and often rewarding year. Those who are parents or who become parents in 2006 will often be kept busy with the demands of babies and young children and some parts of the year *will* be tiring. Work commitments and other demands will add to the pressure. However, by staying well organized (and the Wood Rabbit *is* methodical) and drawing on the support of his loved ones, the

Wood Rabbit will not only manage well but often enjoy his domestic life, including spending time with loved ones, making improvements to the home (or for those who move, setting up a new one) and, if a parent, watching over and encouraging his children. Domestically, this may be a hectic year but it can be a special one too.

Many Wood Rabbits will be particularly grateful for the assistance given by more senior relations over the year and if at any time they have problems or concerns, they would do well to talk these over. With the experience that more senior relations have, their knowledge, advice and understanding can often be of great help.

In view of the pressures and activity of the year, many Wood Rabbits will decide to keep their social life low-key this year, but this will often make the times that they do go out that much more special. Any Wood Rabbit who would welcome more companionship will often find that changes in his work or interests will lead to his meeting others, some of whom will, in time, become important and close friends. The months of March, June to August and November could bring some fine social occasions.

The Dog year may be a busy one for the Wood Rabbit, but it will certainly give him the chance to make important headway. What he accomplishes now will often be significant in terms of the success he will enjoy in following years. In addition, the encouragement and goodwill of others will help him throughout the year.

TIP FOR THE YEAR
With important decisions to take and good chances in the offing, do talk to others and listen to their advice. The

support and co-operation of those around you can make a big difference to how you fare over the year.

The Fire Rabbit

There is a Chinese proverb which reminds us 'Diligence leads to riches' and in the Dog year, the Fire Rabbit's diligence and determination can lead to so much.

For those Fire Rabbits in work there will be some excellent chances to move on to greater responsibilities. One step forward can quickly lead to others and for the keen and determined, this really is an auspicious year.

These Fire Rabbits should also make the most of any training opportunities available to them. Learning about the various aspects of their work and adding to their skills will not only be helpful to their present situation but can also open up other possibilities for later. In addition, some will find that some training they do and new responsibilities they take on will give a good indication of where their strengths lie and in this way the Dog year can prove highly significant in their future career development.

This also applies to those Fire Rabbits seeking work. Although they may feel disillusioned with their situation, especially when applications do not go their way, by remaining determined, many will be given the chance they have been striving so hard for. And, as they will find, once they secure a position, it will give them a good platform to build on and will widen their experience. March, May, June, September and early October could see some positive career developments.

For those Fire Rabbits in education and studying for further qualifications this will also be an important year. By working well and making most of the facilities and opportunities available, these Fire Rabbits will find that what they learn and the qualifications they gain can lead to some good openings later on. Again, as most Rabbits will discover, what is accomplished in the Dog year can have considerable long-term significance.

This is also a splendid year as far as the Fire Rabbit's personal interests are concerned and he should look to develop these, either by setting himself a particular project to carry out or furthering his skills in some other way. Those Fire Rabbits whose interests are more creative, especially those who like music, art, writing or drama, will find by experimenting that their talents can develop in an encouraging manner. This is a year when positive action will pay off.

As far as money matters are concerned, the Fire Rabbit's careful and resourceful nature will serve him well over the year. As he will want to do a lot on often limited means, he will need to plan carefully as well as keeping a close watch on his overall spending. Although there will be times when he may be concerned about his situation, he could find that he is able to improve his position by doing some extra work or helping another. Willingness and enterprise can make a difference and while the Fire Rabbit will need to be careful with his money over the year, he will generally cope well.

The Dog year is splendidly aspected as far as his social life is concerned and he will often meet up with friends and greatly enjoy himself. He will also find his work, interests or, if studying, student friends will lead to some fun occasions. Those Fire Rabbits who move over the year, whether for work or education, will soon find themselves making a new circle of friends too. Socially, this is a fine year and for some Fire Rabbits there is the chance of significant romance. The months of March, June to August and November could see much social activity as well as good chances to meet others.

In addition, those who decide to travel or take a holiday over the year will find this will also lead to some enjoyable times and, for many, could prove to be one of the high points of the year.

Although the Fire Rabbit will value a greater independence as he sets about his various activities, he will still be grateful for the support and advice of family members. As he faces certain decisions, he would do well to talk to those close to him and listen to their views. The support, advice and reassurance they can offer *can* make a difference. And if at any time the Fire Rabbit has a problem, by being open about it he will again appreciate the understanding shown by others and the help he is given.

In so many ways this will be a significant year for the Fire Rabbit, particularly as it will allow him to further his position and prepare himself for the advances that await in following years. Personally, the Dog year holds good prospects, with an often busy and pleasing social life and enjoyable interests and recreational pursuits. The Fire Rabbit certainly has much in his favour over the year and it rests with him to make the most of his many fine qualities and the opportunities available.

TIP FOR THE YEAR
Regard this as a time for personal development. What you accomplish now will, in time, prove significant. Remember, 'Diligence leads to riches' – and your efforts now can ultimately lead on to much more.

The Earth Rabbit
This will be a satisfying year for the Earth Rabbit and by spending time on interests and activities he enjoys, he will gain a great deal of pleasure from it.

With his keen and enquiring nature the Earth Rabbit may well want to advance his personal interests in some way, perhaps by reading, learning, experimenting with new ideas and techniques or enrolling on a course. If there is a particular skill he feels could be useful, such as extending his computer knowledge or finding out more about a certain subject, this would be an excellent year to follow it up. It is very much a time for acting on ideas.

Those Earth Rabbits with gardens will also find that whether growing their own crops, experimenting with new stock or adding some features, they will again take great satisfaction in what they do. Overall, their gardening talents will serve them well over the year.

The Earth Rabbit will also value the support he is given and will find that encouraging family and friends to share in his various activities will add to the pleasure they bring. If he does enrol on a course, encouraging his partner or a close friend to join him can help to make the subject more meaningful, and sometimes more fun too.

In addition to his interests, the Earth Rabbit will also give some attention to his home over the year, carrying through some of the alterations and improvements he has often considered. In some cases he will decide to alter the décor and arrangement of certain rooms as well as buy new equipment that will help make certain tasks easier. He will be helped by setting about his ideas with those close to him and will be delighted as he sees his ideas take shape. Also, where décor and any new home furnishings are concerned, his fine taste will be evident and much admired.

The Earth Rabbit will also enjoy many of the family activities that take place and will be able to support those dear to him. Several times over the year younger relations will seek out his views on certain matters and will set much store by what he says. Once more, his approachable nature and ability to understand and empathize will be much appreciated by his loved ones.

There will also be some good chances for the Earth Rabbit to travel over the year. In addition to invitations to visit family and friends who may be living some distance away, he could be tempted by certain travel offers. By following up his ideas, he will enjoy some interesting times away. This is a year for seizing opportunities.

There could also be some good fortune in money matters, with many Earth Rabbits receiving a gift or bonus or enjoying the fruition of a policy. As a result, many will be tempted to travel or go ahead with ideas they have for their home. However, while the aspects are positive, the Earth Rabbit needs to be his usual careful self when entering into new agreements. This includes checking the terms and implications as well as keeping paperwork and guarantees safely. Also, care needs to be taken when completing financial forms. Contacting a helpline or adviser could help. Financial aspects are generally positive, however, and the Dog year will bring an element of luck too, so if the Earth Rabbit sees a competition that interests him or a contest which allows him to use his specialist knowledge or skills, he would do well to enter it. The Dog year could have some surprises in store!

In so much of what he does, the Earth Rabbit will be encouraged and supported by those around him. And by acting upon his ideas and carrying through his plans, he will find the year will bring him a great deal of satisfaction.

TIP FOR THE YEAR
Do be prepared to talk over any ideas you may have. Just mentioning them could set some important wheels in motion. Also, look to develop your interests in some way.

FAMOUS RABBITS

Bertie Ahern, Margaret Atwood, Drew Barrymore, David Beckham, Harry Belafonte, Ingrid Bergman, St Bernadette, Gordon Brown, James Caan, Nicolas Cage, Lewis Carroll, Fidel Castro, John Cleese, Confucius, Marie Curie, Johnny Depp, Albert Einstein, George Eliot, W. C. Fields, James Fox, Sir David Frost, James Galway, Cary Grant, Edvard Grieg, Oliver Hardy, Seamus Heaney, Tommy Hilfiger, John Howard, Bob Hope, Whitney Houston, Helen Hunt, John Hurt, Anjelica Huston, Chrissie Hynde, Enrique Inglesias, Clive James, Henry James, David Jason, Angelina

Jolie, Michael Jordan, Michael Keaton, John Keats, Judith Krantz, Lisa Kudrow, Danny La Rue, Cheryl Ladd, Patrick Lichfield, Gina Lollobrigida, George Michael, Colin Montgomerie, Sir Roger Moore, Mike Myers, Brigitte Nielsen, Graham Norton, Jamie Oliver, George Orwell, Edith Piaf, Sidney Poitier, Romano Prodi, Ken Russell, Mort Sahl, Elisabeth Schwarzkopf, Neil Sedaka, Jane Seymour, Maria Sharapova, Neil Simon, Frank Sinatra, Sting, Joss Stone, Quentin Tarantino, J. R. R. Tolkien, Arturo Toscanini, Tina Turner, Luther Vandross, Queen Victoria, Muddy Waters, Orson Welles, Walt Whitman, Robin Williams, Kate Winslet, Tiger Woods.

16 FEBRUARY 1904 ⌣ 3 FEBRUARY 1905   *Wood Dragon*

3 FEBRUARY 1916 ⌣ 22 JANUARY 1917   *Fire Dragon*

23 JANUARY 1928 ⌣ 9 FEBRUARY 1929   *Earth Dragon*

8 FEBRUARY 1940 ⌣ 26 JANUARY 1941   *Metal Dragon*

27 JANUARY 1952 ⌣ 13 FEBRUARY 1953   *Water Dragon*

13 FEBRUARY 1964 ⌣ 1 FEBRUARY 1965   *Wood Dragon*

31 JANUARY 1976 ⌣ 17 FEBRUARY 1977   *Fire Dragon*

17 FEBRUARY 1988 ⌣ 5 FEBRUARY 1989   *Earth Dragon*

5 FEBRUARY 2000 ⌣ 23 JANUARY 2001   *Metal Dragon*

THE
DRAGON

THE PERSONALITY OF
THE DRAGON

To accomplish great things, we must not only act, but also
dream, not only plan, but also believe.

Anatole France, a Dragon

The Dragon is born under the sign of luck. He is a proud
and lively character and has a tremendous amount of
self-confidence. He is also highly intelligent and very
quick to take advantage of any opportunities. He is ambitious and determined and will do well in practically
anything he attempts. He is also something of a perfectionist and will always try to maintain the high standards
he sets himself.

The Dragon does not suffer fools gladly and will be
quick to criticize anyone or anything that displeases him.
He can be blunt and forthright in his views and is certainly
not renowned for being either tactful or diplomatic. He
does, however, often take people at their word and can
occasionally be rather gullible. If he ever feels that his trust
has been abused or his dignity wounded, he can sometimes
become very bitter and it will take him a long time to
forgive and forget.

The Dragon is usually very outgoing and is particularly
adept at attracting attention and publicity. He enjoys being
in the limelight and is often at his best when he is
confronted by a challenging situation. In some respects he
is a showman and he rarely lacks an audience. His views

are highly valued and he invariably has something interesting – and sometimes controversial – to say.

He has considerable energy and is often prepared to
work long and unsocial hours in order to achieve what he
wants. He can, however, be rather impulsive and does not
always consider the consequences of his actions. He also
has a tendency to live for the moment and there is nothing
that riles him more than to be kept waiting. The Dragon
hates delay and can get extremely impatient and irritable
over even the smallest of hold-ups.

The Dragon has an enormous faith in his abilities, but
he does run the risk of becoming over-confident and unless
he is careful he can sometimes make grave errors of judgement. While this may prove disastrous at the time, he does
have the tenacity and ability to bounce back and pick up
the pieces again.

The Dragon has such an assertive personality, so much
willpower and such a desire to succeed that he will often
reach the top of his chosen profession. He has considerable
leadership qualities and will do well in positions where he
can put his own ideas and policies into practice. He is
usually successful in politics, show business, as the
manager of his own department or business, and in any job
which brings him into contact with the media.

The Dragon relies a tremendous amount on his own
judgement and can be scornful of other people's advice. He
likes to feel self-sufficient and there are many Dragons
who cherish their independence to such a degree that they
prefer to remain single throughout their lives. However,
the Dragon will often have numerous admirers and many
will be attracted by his flamboyant personality and striking

looks. If he does marry, he will usually marry young, and will find himself particularly well suited to those born under the signs of the Snake, Rat, Monkey and Rooster. He will also find that the Rabbit, Pig, Horse and Goat make ideal companions and will readily join in with many of his escapades. Two Dragons will also get on well together, as they understand each other, but the Dragon may not find things so easy with the Ox and Dog, as both will be critical of his impulsive and somewhat extrovert manner. He will also find it difficult to form an alliance with the Tiger, for the Tiger, like the Dragon, tends to speak his mind, is very strong-willed and likes to take the lead.

The female Dragon knows what she wants in life and sets about everything she does in a determined and positive manner. No job is too small for her and she is often prepared to work extremely hard until she has secured her objective. She is immensely practical and somewhat liberated. She hates being bound by routine and petty restrictions and likes to have sufficient freedom to be able to go off and do what she wants to do. She will keep her house tidy, but is not one for spending hours on housework – there are far too many other things that she prefers to do. Like her male counterpart, she has a tendency to speak her mind.

The Dragon usually has many interests and enjoys sport and other outdoor activities. He also likes to travel and often prefers to visit places that are off the beaten track rather than head for popular tourist attractions. He has a very adventurous streak in him and providing his financial circumstances permit – and the Dragon is usually sensible with his money – he will travel considerable distances during his lifetime.

The Dragon is a very flamboyant character and while he can be demanding of others and in his early years rather precocious, he will have many friends and will nearly always be the centre of attention. He has charisma and so much confidence that he can often become a source of inspiration to others. In China he is the leader of the carnival and he is also blessed with an inordinate share of luck.

THE FIVE DIFFERENT TYPES OF DRAGON

In addition to the 12 signs of the Chinese zodiac there are five elements and these have a strengthening or moderating influence on the sign. The effects of the five elements on the Dragon are described below, together with the years in which the elements were exercising their influence. Therefore those Dragons born in 1940 and 2000 are Metal Dragons, those born in 1952 are Water Dragons, and so on.

Metal Dragon: 1940, 2000

This Dragon is very strong-willed and has a particularly forceful personality. He is energetic, ambitious and tries to be scrupulous in his dealings with others. He can also be blunt and to the point and usually has no hesitation in speaking his mind. If people disagree with him or are not prepared to co-operate, he is more than happy to go his own way. The Metal Dragon usually has very high moral values and is held in great esteem by his friends and colleagues.

Water Dragon: 1952

This Dragon is friendly, easy-going and intelligent. He is quick-witted and rarely lets an opportunity slip by. However, he is not as impatient as some of the other types of Dragon and is prepared to wait for results rather than expect everything to happen at once. He has an understanding nature and is prepared to share his ideas and co-operate with others. His main failing is a tendency to jump from one thing to another rather than concentrate on the job in hand. He has a good sense of humour and is an effective speaker.

Wood Dragon: 1904, 1964

The Wood Dragon is practical, imaginative and inquisitive. He loves delving into all manner of subjects and can quite often come up with some highly original ideas. He is a thinker and a doer and he has the drive and commitment to put many of his ideas into practice. He is more diplomatic than some of the other types of Dragon and has a good sense of humour. He is very astute in business matters and can also be most generous.

Fire Dragon: 1916, 1976

This Dragon is ambitious, articulate and has a tremendous desire to succeed. He is a hard and conscientious worker and is often admired for his integrity and forthright nature. He is very strong-willed and has considerable leadership qualities. He can, however, rely a bit too much on his own judgement and fail to take into account the views and feelings of others. He can also be rather aloof and it would certainly be in his own interests to let others join in more with his various activities. The Fire Dragon usually enjoys music, literature and the arts.

Earth Dragon: 1928, 1988

The Earth Dragon tends to be quieter and more reflective than some of the other types of Dragon. He has a wide variety of interests and is keenly aware of what is going on around him. He also has clear objectives and usually has no problems in obtaining support and backing for any of his ventures. He is very astute in financial matters and is often able to accumulate considerable wealth. He is a good organizer, although he can at times be rather bureaucratic and fussy. He mixes well with others and has a large circle of friends.

PROSPECTS FOR THE DRAGON IN 2006

The Year of the Rooster (9 February 2005 to 28 January 2006) holds encouraging prospects for the Dragon and in the closing months he can accomplish a great deal. Also, in many of his activities, he will enjoy good support and this will have a positive bearing on his progress.

In his work the Dragon will have many opportunities to use his skills and for those who are looking to make headway or seeking work this can be an encouraging time, with November seeing some interesting developments.

With the closing months of the year being a generally expensive time, the Dragon would, though, do well to keep watch on his spending and where possible make early provision for his increased outlay. Control and good management can make a difference.

The Dragon's domestic life is pleasingly aspected at this time and he will again enjoy planning and sharing activities with those around him. However, with so much happening, if he is contemplating any major household projects, he should allow plenty of time for them as well as be wary of starting too many all at once. His intentions may be good, but at times it would be wise to keep his sometimes over-zealous nature in check.

The Dragon's social life will also become busier as the Rooster year draws to a close, with many opportunities to go out and meet up with friends. And with his sociable and outgoing nature, the Dragon will often thoroughly enjoy himself. Overall, the closing months of the year will be a busy but rewarding time for him.

The Year of the Dog starts on 29 January and will be a variable one for the Dragon. However, while he will need to proceed with care, this can still be a constructive year, with what he accomplishes during it often having an important bearing on following years.

In his work the Dragon should make the most of the opportunities he has to add to his experience and skills. If he is relatively new to his position, he will find taking advantage of any training courses that are available and learning more about the various aspects of his work not only beneficial for his current duties but also for his future prospects. All Dragons, whether new or well established in their work, should make the most of any chances they have to extend their experience.

Many Dragons will decide to remain with their present employer over the year, but for those eager to move elsewhere or seeking work, the Dog year will present some interesting openings. In some cases these could arise in fortuitous ways, with friends and colleagues advising the Dragon of a particular vacancy or type of position it would be worth considering. By acting positively on any openings that appeal to them *and remaining persistent,* many Dragons will be successful in securing a new position which will not only broaden their experience but can also lead to other possibilities in the future. April, June and the period from late September to November could see some positive career developments.

The Dragon will need be careful, however, when dealing with money matters. This is not a year to take risks and if he is entering into a new commitment, he does need to check the small print as well as address any questions and uncertainties before proceeding. Also, throughout the year, he should keep a close watch on his financial position. If he has any large expenses looming, he would do well to allow for these in advance. The more he can plan ahead, the better.

There will be several chances for the Dragon to travel quite extensively over the year, either on holiday or through his work. When travelling some distance, he could find it helpful to read up about his destination beforehand and check up on his likely requirements while away. The better prepared he is, the more comfortable and enjoyable his trips will be. As with so many areas of his life this year, the extra care he takes *can* make a difference.

With his often busy lifestyle, the Dragon should also give some thought to his general well-being over the year, including diet, exercise and rest. To drive himself too hard could leave him tired and prone to minor ailments. He does need to keep his lifestyle in balance and if at any time he feels low or lacking his usual sparkle, he would do well to seek advice. This is not a year to neglect his well-being.

With the Dragon's outgoing nature and wide interests, he will often have a busy social life. He could also find himself meeting others through his travels or through existing friends, and there will certainly be chances for him to extend his social circle during the year. Those Dragons who would like more companionship, perhaps having just moved to a new area, will find that by involving themselves in local activities and pursuing their interests they will soon get to meet others. Socially, this is a promising year, with February, May, August and December seeing a lot of activity.

The Dog year does, though, contain its trickier aspects and one area which requires care is the Dragon's home life. Sometimes, due to his busy lifestyle, pressure and tiredness can bring irritability. Failure to communicate properly or give adequate attention to domestic matters can also lead to disagreements. In the Dog year the Dragon *does* need to be aware of this and set aside time to spend with family members. Talking about his ideas and involving his loved ones will also help. Positive input into family life can make an important difference. With travel favourably aspected, the Dragon should also give some thought to a family holiday over the year. With a well-chosen destination, this could often surpass expectations.

Although the Dog year will contain its trickier aspects, it will certainly not be without its more pleasurable times. And with the following Pig year holding so much promise, what the Dragon does now can pave the way for the success he is soon to enjoy.

The Metal Dragon

The Metal Dragon can accomplish a great deal this year, but a lot hinges on his willingness to liaise and co-operate with others. If he adopts too independent an attitude – and the Metal Dragon does have an independent streak to his nature – then the year will not nearly be as satisfying. This is a time when consulting others and getting support and advice can make a substantial difference.

As the Dog year starts the Metal Dragon would find it helpful to discuss with his loved ones his ideas for the year ahead. By being prepared to do so, he will find that others will not only be able to help but may also make useful suggestions. A willingness to consult others can be of great value over the year.

As far as any plans he has for his home, whether buying new equipment, adding comforts or making alterations, the Metal Dragon will again find that discussion and taking the time to consider various possibilities will lead to better decisions than proceeding in too much haste. While he may be eager to get his plans underway, by waiting for sales and favourable buying opportunities he could make considerable savings.

Some Metal Dragons will decide to move in 2006 and again this is not something that should be rushed. By talking to estate agents and others about their requirements and taking the time to view different places, these Metal Dragons will find their efforts *and patience* will lead to somewhere that will suit them well.

Whether the Metal Dragon moves or not, the year will see much practical activity, and despite the pressures, he will often find the considerable effort he puts into his plans well worth his while. Apart from all the practical activity, there will also be many domestic occasions that the Metal Dragon will particularly value including shared interests, garden projects, visiting local places of interest and other domestic and family activities.

The Dog year will certainly be a full and active one, though while much will go well, as with any year, differences of opinion will sometimes raise their head. When they do, the Metal Dragon should talk these through and try to resolve them as quickly as he can. If this means accepting a compromise or apologizing if at fault, better this than allowing what can be relatively small matters to escalate. Fortunately, by being aware of the trickier aspects of the year and remaining mindful of the views of others, the Metal Dragon will find many problems can be averted or amicably resolved. In the main, his relations with others will go well and will mean much to him over this often busy year.

The Metal Dragon will also get much contentment from his social life. In addition to regularly meeting up with friends, he will enjoy going to a variety of special occasions and local events and for those Metal Dragons who are involved in a club or society, there could be the chance to play a greater role or to pass on their knowledge to others. On a social level, this can be a busy year. Some Metal Dragons may also decide to contribute more to the community, perhaps through charity work. Whatever they do, by following through their ideas, they can make their social life all the more enriching.

As far as money matters are concerned this is, though, a year for care. If the Metal Dragon enters into any major agreement, particularly if moving or involved in any other large expense in connection with his accommodation, he does need to check the terms and obligations and seek advice if he has any questions or uncertainties. In addition he could find it helpful to look at his overall financial situation. In some cases he could find he has funds languishing in low-yielding accounts when he could be getting better returns elsewhere. Similarly, certain outgoings may no longer be necessary or could be reduced and so leave him more money for other activities and plans. By reviewing his situation and, when necessary, obtaining advice, the Metal Dragon can often gain a great deal from the modifications he is able to make. This is a year when good management can do much to help his financial situation.

Generally, this will be a busy and important year for the Metal Dragon, but throughout he does need to be wary of acting too hastily or independently. In particular, this is not a year to rush what could be important decisions. By being willing to discuss ideas and plans with others and listen closely to advice given, the Metal Dragon will accomplish much more. The involvement of others can make an appreciable difference too. With care and good support, though, it can be a busy and often rewarding time.

TIP FOR THE YEAR
Avoid rush. The more thought, time and consideration you can give to your activities, the better. Do draw on the readiness of others to support and advise. Also, take advantage of any travel opportunities. A break from your usual routine will do you a lot of good.

The Water Dragon

This will be a generally satisfying year for the Water Dragon, although he will need to act in close co-operation with others. Too independent an attitude could spell trouble.

At work many Water Dragons will decide to remain in their present position and, with their knowledge and expertise, they will often be satisfied in the way that they are able to use their skills. Colleagues will often look to them for guidance and some will be given the chance to become involved in training and a more supervisory role.

However, for those particularly keen to advance their career, there will be some very good opportunities. When they arise, these Water Dragons *will* need to act quickly. As they will find, they will fare best in positions which are related to what they have been doing. This is a year to make the most of existing skills and expertise.

Whether he remains in his current position or moves, the Water Dragon would also do well to take advantage of any training that may be available. In some cases learning additional skills will pave the way to future opportunities, particularly in the following and more auspicious Pig year.

Similarly, those Water Dragons seeking work could also find it helpful to enquire about any training or refresher courses they may be eligible for. By doing something positive, they can often strengthen their prospects as well as discover suitable opportunities. With persistence, many of these Water Dragons will be able to secure a position with good potential for further development. April, June and late September to November could see interesting and positive career developments, but generally this is a year to act swiftly on opportunities as they occur.

Also, whether the Water Dragon remains in his existing position or not, he does need to act in close co-operation with colleagues. This way he will not only benefit from the support good relations will bring but if problems occur or pressures mount, he will also be grateful for the help that others can give. And if he does put in for another position, he will find his chances that much better with the backing of his colleagues behind him.

The year will also bring several travel opportunities and the Water Dragon should make the most of them. Whether travelling in connection with his work, for a holiday or visiting those living some distance away, he could not only get to see some interesting sights but, in many cases, will particularly enjoy visiting somewhere he has long wanted to see. A family holiday could work out well and by choosing his destination carefully, the Water Dragon could find it turning out to be one of the best he has had for some time. For travel, this really is a year to make the most of opportunities.

Another favourably aspected area is the Water Dragon's personal interests and despite the many demands on his time, he should look to further these in some way, either by starting a new project, learning more about a certain skill or getting to meet other enthusiasts. By doing something positive, the Water Dragon will find his interests a source of much pleasure and sometimes bringing other benefits (including social) too.

The Water Dragon could also find it helpful to give consideration to his well-being over the year. If he is sedentary for large parts of the day or relies a lot on convenience foods, he could find taking more exercise or switching to a more balanced diet could lead to an improvement in how he feels. Before proceeding he should seek medical advice, but any attention he can give to his well-being can make a difference.

As far as money matters are concerned, this is a year for care and vigilance. If taking on a new commitment or conducting an important transaction, the Water Dragon does need to take the time to check the implications and small print and, if appropriate, seek professional advice. Without care, problems could loom. The Water Dragon would also find it helpful to make early provision for some of the plans he has over the year, whether a large purchase, expenses connected with a family member (including a possible wedding) or travel. This is a year for care, good control and planning ahead.

The Water Dragon also needs to pay close attention to family matters over the year. Although usually thoughtful and enjoying a good rapport with loved ones, with pressures of work, possible preoccupation with other matters and a busy lifestyle, he may find disagreements arising. Tiredness, too, could lead to some irritability or impatience. To help deal with this, the Water Dragon will find that a general willingness to discuss matters can make a difference. Also, he should encourage everyone to share in household tasks. With good communication and co-operation, not only will family life be that much better but more will get done too.

However, while there is this need for mindfulness, the year will also contain some exciting domestic events, with many Water Dragons celebrating a wedding in the family, the birth of a grandchild or some other good news. To help his realtions with those special to him a meaningful gesture or token of affection could also be especially appreciated – perhaps a surprise present or treat, such as a special meal. This gesture may come to mean a great deal. Water Dragons, do bear this in mind and show others that you care.

The Water Dragon's social life will be fairly active over the year and with his work, interests and circle of friends, he will have many chances to go out. Those Water Dragons who are keen to build up their social life will find that by taking up invitations, going to social events and becoming involved in more local activities, they can experience quite a transformation in their situation. February, late April, May, August and December could be active months.

Although the Water Dragon will need to be his careful and thorough self this year, it can still be a positive and pleasing time. With good travel and social opportunities, his own interests and the activities shared with loved ones, there will be much for him to enjoy. In his work, too, by building on his skills, he will often find a greater fulfilment. However, in all areas, the Water Dragon does need to communicate well with others as well as watch his sometimes independent-minded nature. With support and goodwill so much more can be achieved.

TIP FOR THE YEAR
Look to develop your knowledge and skills. Going on training courses, reading or setting yourself a new challenge will not only be personally satisfying but will also help your prospects. And with the aspects being so encouraging in 2007, what is accomplished this year could be especially significant in the near future.

The Wood Dragon

This will be a busy and often demanding year for the Wood Dragon, but during it he will discover new strengths and gain experience as well as pave the way for some significant successes in following years. This may not be the easiest of years for him, but it can be an important one.

In his work the Wood Dragon would do well to regard this as a time to build on his present position rather than look to make major changes. By taking advantage of any chances he has to further his skills, whether deputizing for colleagues, becoming involved in new responsibilities, putting forward ideas (something he is good at) or taking up training opportunities, he will gain invaluable experience.

Also, he could discover certain strengths which he will decide to make more of in the future. By developing his skills and showing commitment, he will be able to do his prospects a lot of good.

For those Wood Dragons who are seeking work or feeling dissatisfied with their current situation, the Dog year can bring important developments. Although their quest for a new position will not be easy and there will be disappointments when certain applications do not work out, events can move in curious ways. In some cases a position they did not expect to get may be offered to them or they may find a suitable vacancy almost by chance. By making the most of any openings, these Wood Dragons will not only further their experience but also establish a platform from which to progress. April, June and late September to mid-November will see some particularly positive career developments.

With the pressures of the Wood Dragon's work and other commitments, it is important that his interests and more recreational pursuits do not suffer over the year. Activities which allow them to get additional exercise can be especially beneficial. Some Wood Dragons may well decide to walk more, swim, cycle or do some other form of exercise which appeals. And with the Wood Dragon's imagination and often good visual sense, photography, painting or some other expressive interest could also bring pleasure. Whatever he does, it *is* important that the Wood Dragon does not neglect himself in the Dog year and miss out on the often considerable benefits that his interests and recreational pursuits can bring.

With travel favourably aspected, the Wood Dragon would also do well to go away for a break at some time over the year. A trip arranged at short notice could work out especially well. This is a year for the Wood Dragon to make the most of his ideas and opportunities that arise.

As far as money matters are concerned, the Wood Dragon will enjoy a modest rise in his income over the year, and, with good planning and budgeting, we will be generally pleased with how he manages and all that he is able to do. The Wood Dragon will also need to be thorough when dealing with financial forms and other paperwork and will need to keep receipts, guarantees and policies safe, as in time he could need to refer back to them.

As far as his domestic life is concerned, this is also a year for care. Although the year will bring some very happy family times, there could also be tension and disagreements. Sometimes these will not be helped by outside pressures or busy lifestyles. Whenever any differences of opinion do arise, the Wood Dragon would do well to talk these over and set more time aside to spend with those close to him. As he will find, good communication and input into family life can be of great help over the year. Fortunately, with his thoughtful nature and ability to relate so well to others, he will often be able to avert more awkward situations or deal amicably with them, but this is something he *will* need to watch.

However, despite the trickier aspects of the Dog year, there will be much in the Wood Dragon's domestic life that will bring him real pleasure, including family interests and activities, a possible holiday or trips out, as well as projects that enhance the home and possibly garden in some way. In addition, the Wood Dragon will often be pleased by the progress made by younger relations.

The Wood Dragon's social life will also be active over the year, with some important new friendships being forged. Those Wood Dragons who may have let their social life lapse recently due to other demands on their time will find that by going out more, joining interest groups and treating themselves to events that appeal, they can bring a sparkle back into their lives that may have been lacking for some while. February, May, August and December will be the best and busiest months for socializing.

Although the Dog year will require the Wood Dragon to proceed carefully, it can be an important time. The experience gained and skills acquired now can be particularly helpful in following years. By spending time with loved ones and making sure his lifestyle has balance, the Wood Dragon will be satisfied with much that he does and how the year develops.

TIP FOR THE YEAR

Do spend time with others. You will gain much from the support and advice you receive. Also, your ability to relate so effectively to others will prove a valuable asset. Use it well.

The Fire Dragon

This year marks a new decade in the Fire Dragon's life and he may well be keen to make more of himself. With his drive and tenacity, he certainly has the attributes to take him far and what he does in the Dog year will often be significant in terms of his future progress.

As far as his work is concerned, this will be both an important and valuable year. Those Fire Dragons who decide to remain with their current employer will often find themselves excellently placed to take on greater responsibilities. As so many will find, the experience they can gain now can be an important stage in their career development.

For those Fire Dragons who would like to move on, again the events of the year can be significant. By actively following up any openings that appeal to them, many will be successful in securing a position which will represent an interesting step up from what they have been doing. Although their new responsibilities may initially be daunting, these Fire Dragons will often feel invigorated by the challenge and, in the process, find strengths that they are keen to develop. As so many will discover, the Dog year can give their career an exciting boost.

This also applies to those Fire Dragons seeking work. Again, by actively following up any advice given and openings that interest them, they will find their prospects can suddenly become much brighter.

Over the year, in addition to the experience the Fire Dragon will gain through carrying out his duties, he should aim to make the most of any training that is available to him. By improving his skills, he will not only help his present position but may also learn of other possibilities worth considering in the future. The Dog year can have far-reaching significance.

Another of the Fire Dragon's strengths is his ability to relate well to others and he should make the most of his chances to get to know his colleagues. By building up contacts, he can improve his present situation as well as sometimes bring a pleasing social element to his work.

The months of April, June and from mid-September to November could see some interesting career developments.

This will be a reasonable year as far as financial matters are concerned. In addition to an increase in income, some Fire Dragons can look forward to receiving a bonus or a financial gift. However, to benefit, the Fire Dragon will need to manage his money well rather than spend it too impulsively. If he can set funds aside for his commitments and plans as well as reduce any loans and interest payments he may have, he will find he can make a real difference to his position. Financially, this can be an improved year, but it still requires good management.

Travel is favourably aspected and the Fire Dragon would do well to consider taking a special holiday over the year, perhaps to mark his thirtieth birthday. By discussing his ideas with his loved ones, he could find some exciting possibilities emerging. In addition, some Fire Dragons could travel through their work or receive invitations to visit those living some distance away. There will certainly be opportunities for some extensive travelling during the year and with his adventurous and outgoing nature, the Fire Dragon will often enjoy it enormously.

As far as domestic matters are concerned, however, this is a year for care and the Fire Dragon would find it of immense value to set aside some quality time for spending with his loved ones. In some cases pursuing interests and tackling projects together, including those that enhance the home, will lead to some pleasurable occasions. This is very much a year when the Fire Dragon's contribution to home life can make a difference.

For those Fire Dragons who are parents or who become parents over the year there will be much joy as they follow the progress of their babies and young children, but new pressures and times of tiredness too. In view of this, the Fire Dragon would do well to take up any offers of assistance he receives as well as be willing to talk over any concerns he may have. Although he may like to do a great deal by himself, sharing pressures and any worries can be very helpful.

Also, to keep his lifestyle in balance, the Fire Dragon would do well to set a regular time aside for recreational activities, including those that allow him to get some additional exercise. This can help to keep him in good form as well as be an often enjoyable way to relax and unwind. In this full and busy year, the Fire Dragon does need to give some time to himself. Fire Dragons, do take note.

Overall, this will be a significant year for the Fire Dragon. By looking to build on his experience, getting to know others connected with his work and making the most of the opportunities that arise, he can prepare the way for future success. However, in view of the active nature of the year, he does need to make sure he gives time to those who are important to him and ensures that his lifestyle has balance. In this way the Dog year will not only be important but often pleasurable too.

TIP FOR THE YEAR
Although you may like to deal with a lot of things by yourself, do draw on the support, advice and help that others can give. This can make a real difference to how you fare. Also, allow time for recreational pursuits and interests. These will

not only do you good but also help you to relax and unwind and may have a pleasing social element too.

The Earth Dragon

This will be a mixed year for the Earth Dragon with some successes and times of great happiness but a few disappointments too. But, as is often the way, there will be important lessons to be learned from these setbacks and the Earth Dragon will emerge from the Dog year considerably wiser as a result.

One of the most important factors in how he fares over the year will be the amount of effort he is prepared to put into his activities. When he is motivated and does his best then he is capable of achieving some impressive results, but if he becomes complacent or does not put in the effort, then things can start to go awry. And the Dog year, which demands effort and commitment, can be a hard taskmaster.

For those Earth Dragons studying for qualifications, this really is a year when they will need remain disciplined and focused upon the work they have to do. For many this will be their main chance of getting certain qualifications and it *is* worth making the necessary commitment. To help keep themselves motivated, these Earth Dragons could find it helpful to think of the possibilities that will open up if they do well, and with their future looking so promising, particularly in the favourably aspected Pig year that follows, what is achieved this year can be especially significant.

Earth Dragons in education could also find it helpful to talk to tutors and career advisers about the next stage in their development, particularly whether to go on to further education or take up certain careers. By talking over their options, they can come to some important decisions. However, to benefit, the Earth Dragon *will* need to be prepared to talk openly to those who can help.

Similarly, if at any time he is having difficulty with any aspect of his studying, he should ask for help rather than be held back or remain worried over a certain topic. Sometimes just one additional explanation is all that is needed, but he *does* need to ask.

For those Earth Dragons in work or seeking work, this is a year for putting themselves forward whenever they see a suitable opportunity. By showing commitment and a willingness to learn, these Earth Dragons will quickly impress. Again, this is a year when effort can make a big difference. However, should the Earth Dragon decide not to apply himself or just do enough to get by, then his work is not only likely to become uninspiring but he will also undermine his chances of moving to something more interesting. The Earth Dragon may be on the first rungs of the career ladder, but the effort he makes now can make a difference to his future prospects.

Also, if the Earth Dragon finds himself in a position he does not like or feel suited for, he should look to change it, otherwise there is a danger that he could remain in a rut for a little while. Earth Dragons, do take note. This is a year when positive action and effort can make so much difference to what happens both now and in the future. April, June and the period from mid-September to early December could see some interesting opportunities.

The Dog year is favourably aspected for travel and the Earth Dragon should make the most of any ideas that he has. Also, the more he can save and plan ahead for any holidays and other trips, the better his time away will be. In addition to visiting some often impressive areas, he will find his travels can often have a great social element and lead to some fun times. In this respect this can be a positive and exciting year.

The Earth Dragon's social life will also be lively. Those Earth Dragons who move over the year, perhaps for work or education, will soon get to meet others in similar positions to their own and will make what will become special and long-lasting friendships. The year can also bring romance and while sometimes the path of love may not always run smoothly, some Earth Dragons will get to meet someone who will play a significant part in their lives. For meeting others and socializing, February, May and the last quarter of the year are particularly favourable.

The Earth Dragon's domestic life will, though, need careful handling over the year. Sometimes he would welcome more independence and he could find differences of opinion arising with older relations too. Rather than allow any matter to escalate, the Earth Dragon would do well to discuss any problems and see if a compromise or agreement can be reached. He should not forget that those around him do care deeply for him and will often be very willing to help and support him, but for this to happen the Earth Dragon does need to be receptive. However, despite the sometimes tricky aspects, there will be much for him to appreciate in his home life, including some of the activities he helps with and the interests he shares with others.

Although the Earth Dragon leads an often full and lively lifestyle, he would also do well to give some consideration to his well-being over the year. To skimp on healthy food or sufficient sleep could leave him prone to minor ailments. If taking part in sporting or more strenuous activities, he should also follow recommended procedures rather than take risks or be foolhardy. Earth Dragons, do take note.

As far as money matters are concerned, the Earth Dragon will often manage well, despite his sometimes limited means. With his resourceful nature, he could find ways to supplement his finances by helping others or doing some casual work. With care and good planning, he will cope well.

In so many respects the Dog year can be a significant one for the Earth Dragon and by putting in the effort, whether in his studying or his work, he can do much to pave the way for his future progress, especially in the auspicious Pig year that follows. On a personal level, the year will often bring a lot of fun as well as the chance to make some important new friends. Also, the Earth Dragon should remember that help, support and advice are available and he only has to ask.

TIP FOR THE YEAR
Believe in yourself and be prepared to make the effort. This is a year to rise to the occasion and show what you are capable of. Much can happen as a result.

FAMOUS DRAGONS

Clive Anderson, Maya Angelou, Jeffrey Archer, Joan Armatrading, Dan Ackroyd, Joan Baez, Roseanne Barr, Count Basie, Maeve Binchy, Dan Brown, Sandra Bullock, Julie Christie, James Coburn, Courteney Cox, Bing Crosby, Russell Crowe, Roald Dahl, Salvador Dali, Charles Darwin, Neil Diamond, Bo Diddley, Matt Dillon, Christian Dior, Placido Domingo, Fats Domino, Kirk Douglas, Faye Dunaway, Bruce Forsyth, Sigmund Freud, Graham Greene, Che Guevara, David Hasselhoff, James Herriot, Paul Hogan, Joan of Arc, Tom Jones, Immanuel Kant, Martin Luther King, John Lennon, Abraham Lincoln, Dame Ellen MacArthur, Elle MacPherson, Queen Margrethe II of Denmark, Andrew Motion, Hosni Mubarak, Florence Nightingale, Nick Nolte, Sharon Osbourne, Al Pacino, Gregory Peck, Pelé, Edgar Allan Poe, Vladimir Putin, Keanu Reeves, Sir Cliff Richard, Ronaldo, Ariel Sharon, George Bernard Shaw, Martin Sheen, Alicia Silverstone, Ringo Starr, Princess Stephanie of Monaco, Dave Stewart, Karlheinz Stockhausen, Shirley Temple, Maria von Trapp, Andy Warhol, Johnny Weissmüller, Raquel Welch, The Earl of Wessex, Mae West.

4 FEBRUARY 1905 ～ 24 JANUARY 1906   *Wood Snake*

23 JANUARY 1917 ～ 10 FEBRUARY 1918   *Fire Snake*

10 FEBRUARY 1929 ～ 29 JANUARY 1930   *Earth Snake*

27 JANUARY 1941 ～ 14 FEBRUARY 1942   *Metal Snake*

14 FEBRUARY 1953 ～ 2 FEBRUARY 1954   *Water Snake*

2 FEBRUARY 1965 ～ 20 JANUARY 1966   *Wood Snake*

18 FEBRUARY 1977 ～ 6 FEBRUARY 1978   *Fire Snake*

6 FEBRUARY 1989 ～ 26 JANUARY 1990   *Earth Snake*

24 JANUARY 2001 ～ 11 FEBRUARY 2002   *Metal Snake*

THE
SNAKE

THE PERSONALITY OF THE SNAKE

Just trust yourself, then you will know how to live.
Johann Wolfgang von Goethe, a Snake

The Snake is born under the sign of wisdom. He is highly intelligent and his mind is forever active. He is always planning and always looking for ways in which he can use his considerable skills. He is a deep thinker and likes to meditate and reflect.

Many times during his life he will shed one of his famous Snake skins and take up new interests or start a completely different job. The Snake enjoys a challenge and he rarely makes mistakes. He is a skilful organizer, has considerable business acumen and is usually lucky in money matters. Most Snakes are financially secure in their later years, provided they do not gamble – the Snake has the distinction of being the worst gambler in the whole of the Chinese zodiac!

The Snake generally has a calm and placid nature and prefers the quieter things in life. He does not like to be in a frenzied atmosphere and hates being hurried into making a quick decision. He also does not like interference in his affairs and tends to rely on his own judgement rather than listen to advice.

At times the Snake can appear solitary. He is quiet, reserved and sometimes has difficulty in communicating with others. He has little time for idle gossip and will certainly not suffer fools gladly. He does, however, have a good sense of humour and this is particularly appreciated in times of crisis.

The Snake is certainly not afraid of hard work and is thorough in all that he does. He is very determined and can occasionally be ruthless in order to achieve his aims. His confidence, willpower and quick thinking usually ensure his success, but should he fail it will often take a long time for him to recover. He cannot bear failure and is a very bad loser.

The Snake can also be evasive and does not willingly let people into his confidence. This secrecy and distrust can sometimes work against him and it is a trait which all Snakes should try to overcome.

Another characteristic of the Snake is his tendency to rest after any sudden or prolonged bout of activity. He burns up so much nervous energy that he can, if he is not careful, be susceptible to high blood pressure and nervous disorders.

It has sometimes been said that the Snake is a late starter in life and this is mainly because it often takes him a while to find a job in which he is genuinely happy. However, he will usually do well in any position which involves research and writing and where he is given sufficient freedom to develop his own ideas and plans. He makes a good teacher, politician, personnel manager and social adviser.

The Snake chooses his friends carefully and while he keeps a tight control over his finances, he can be particularly generous to those he likes. He will think nothing of buying expensive gifts or treating his friends or loved ones to the best theatre seats in town. In return he demands loyalty. The Snake is very possessive and he can become extremely jealous and hurt if he finds his trust has been abused.

The Snake is also renowned for his good looks and is never short of admirers. The female Snake in particular is most alluring. She has style, grace and excellent (and usually expensive) taste in clothes. A keen socializer, she is likely to have a wide range of friends and a happy knack of impressing those who matter. She has numerous interests and her opinions are often highly valued. She is generally a calm-natured person and while she involves herself in many activities, she likes to retain a certain amount of privacy in her undertakings.

Affairs of the heart are very important to the Snake and he will often have many romances before he finally settles down. He will find that he is particularly well suited to those born under the signs of the Ox, Dragon, Rabbit and Rooster. Provided he is allowed sufficient freedom to pursue his own interests, he can also build up a very satisfactory relationship with the Rat, Horse, Goat, Monkey and Dog, but he should try to steer clear of another Snake as they could very easily become jealous of each other. The Snake will also have difficulty in getting on with the honest and down-to-earth Pig, and will find the Tiger far too much of a disruptive influence on his quiet and peace-loving ways.

The Snake certainly appreciates the finer things in life. He enjoys good food and often takes a keen interest in the arts. He also enjoys reading and is invariably drawn to subjects such as philosophy, political thought, religion or the occult. He is fascinated by the unknown and his enquiring mind is always looking for answers. Some of the world's most original thinkers have been Snakes, and although he may not readily admit it, the Snake is often psychic and relies a lot on intuition.

The Snake is certainly not the most energetic member of the Chinese zodiac. He prefers to proceed at his own pace and to do what he wants. He is very much his own master and throughout his life he will try his hand at many things. He is something of a dabbler, but at some time – usually when he least expects it – his hard work and efforts will be recognized and he will invariably meet with the success and the financial security which he so desires.

THE FIVE DIFFERENT TYPES OF SNAKE

In addition to the 12 signs of the Chinese zodiac there are five elements, and these have a strengthening or moderating influence on the sign. The effects of the five elements on the Snake are described below, together with the years in which the elements were exercising their influence. Therefore those Snakes born in 1941 and 2001 are Metal Snakes, those born in 1953 are Water Snakes, and so on.

Metal Snake: 1941, 2001
This Snake is quiet, confident and fiercely independent. He often prefers to work on his own and will only let a privileged few into his confidence. He is quick to spot opportunities and will set about achieving his objectives with an awesome determination. He is astute in financial matters and will often invest his money well. He also has a liking for the finer things in life and a good appreciation of the

arts, literature, music and good food. He usually has a small group of extremely good friends and can be generous to his loved ones.

Water Snake: 1953

This Snake has a wide variety of interests. He enjoys studying all manner of subjects and is capable of undertaking quite detailed research and becoming a specialist in his chosen area. He is highly intelligent, has a good memory and is particularly astute when dealing with business and financial matters. He tends to be quietly spoken and a little reserved, but he does have sufficient strength of character to make his views known and attain his ambitions. He is very loyal to his family and friends.

Wood Snake: 1905, 1965

The Wood Snake has a friendly temperament and a good understanding of human nature. He is able to communicate well and often has many friends and admirers. He is witty, intelligent and ambitious. He has numerous interests and prefers to live in a quiet, stable environment where he can work without too much interference. He enjoys the arts and usually derives much pleasure from collecting paintings and antiques. His advice is often highly valued, particularly on social and domestic matters.

Fire Snake: 1917, 1977

The Fire Snake tends to be more forceful, outgoing and energetic than some of the other types of Snake. He is ambitious, confident and never slow in voicing his opinions – and he can be very abrasive to those he does not like. He does, however, have many leadership qualities and can win the respect and support of many with his firm and resolute manner. He usually has a good sense of humour, a wide circle of friends and a very active social life. He is also a keen traveller.

Earth Snake 1929, 1989

The Earth Snake is charming, amusing and has a very amiable manner. He is conscientious and reliable in his work and approaches everything he does in a level-headed and sensible way. He can, however, tend to err on the cautious side and never likes to be hassled into making a decision. He is adept in dealing with financial matters and is a shrewd investor. He has many friends and is very supportive towards the members of his family.

PROSPECTS FOR THE SNAKE IN 2006

The Year of the Rooster (9 February 2005 to 28 January 2006) will have been an important one for the Snake. However, to get the best from the remaining months, he would do well to decide on his priorities and concentrate on them. To spread his energies too widely will reduce his effectiveness as well as increasing the pressures on him.

In his work the Snake will find his best results will come from concentrating on areas in which he is able to make the most effective use of his experience. By using his skills well, he can help his prospects in the forthcoming Dog year. For those Snakes who are seeking work or considering moving from their present position, October could see some interesting opportunities.

In the closing months of the Rooster year the Snake would also be helped by being more forthcoming. Often he likes to keep his thoughts to himself, but if he is willing to talk over his ideas and hopes, he will be given some often excellent support and advice. Those Snakes who tend to keep themselves to themselves should also make the effort to get out more as the year draws to a close, as this can help to make the last quarter of the year a pleasing and personally rewarding time.

Generally, the Rooster year is a constructive one for the Snake and making the most of his talents at this time can be of great help to him in the next Chinese year.

The Year of the Dog begins on 29 January and holds considerable potential for the Snake. By seizing his opportunities, he can look forward to making excellent progress. However, to benefit from the prevailing aspects, the Snake *does* need to put himself forward and remain active. For those Snakes who are reticent or reserved, this really is a year when they should have faith in themselves and let their true strengths come to the fore. Fortune, in the Dog year, will favour the bold.

The Snake's work prospects are especially promising and whenever he has the chance to become involved in greater responsibilities or seek promotion, he should put himself forward. Also, if there are certain types of work he would like to become more involved in or certain positions he would like to move to, he should make enquiries. This really is a year for seizing the initiative.

The Snake should also aim to make the most of his experience and talents as well as put forward any ideas he may have. Action on his part can lead to positive developments.

The year will also bring excellent chances for the Snake to extend his skills. Sometimes, by taking on a new role, he will not only further his experience but also open the way to other possibilities in the near future. Those Snakes who feel in a rut or disenchanted with their present position will find that they too can set their career on a brighter path. The months from February to April and September and November could see some interesting developments, but throughout the year the Snake should act upon his ideas and opportunities.

Another interesting feature of the Dog year is that it rewards long-term effort and for those who have been working in a particular area or on a project for a long time, it can often bring recognition and success. Accordingly, for those Snakes who are involved in creative areas, this is very much a year to promote their work. The Dog year will reward dedication as well as originality.

In view of their success at work, many Snakes will see a noticeable rise in their income over the year. Some will also be able to supplement this through additional work or putting an enterprising idea to good use. However, the Snake's hard work will often be well rewarded. To enjoy the benefits, though, the Snake should manage his money well. Some Snakes could find that a savings plan started during the Dog year could build up into a useful sum in years to come. Overall, with good planning and control, the Snake's financial position can be much improved during the year.

The Snake would also do well to give some consideration to his well-being over the year. He does drive himself hard and parts of the year will be demanding. In view of this, and all the mental and physical energy the Snake burns up, it is important that he gives himself the opportunity to relax. Some Snakes could find tai chi or yoga helpful, or even just allowing themselves time to meditate or reflect quietly. Whatever he does, it is important that the Snake allows himself to enjoy a respite from all the activity. Also, if at any time he feels below par, it would be worth him seeking medical advice. To keep himself in good form, he does need to look after himself.

Travel is favourably aspected and the Snake could find a holiday or short break another excellent way to have a rest and a break from his routine. If he chooses his destination with care, his time away could work out especially well.

The Snake will also value his domestic life over the year. Those close to him will be particularly supportive and whenever he is facing important decisions he will be grateful for their advice and encouragement. In addition to his own successes, other family members could enjoy pleasing news and several times during the year there could be good reason for a celebration or to go out for a special family treat.

The Snake will also be pleased with some of the projects he tackles with loved ones over the year and even when he is busy, by ensuring time is still spent with those who are special to him, he will find his home life rewarding.

With all the activities of the year the Snake may be tempted to cut back on his social life, however it is important that this does not suffer, as it does provide him with an excellent chance to unwind and enjoy himself. So, in this full and active year, the Snake really would do well to ensure he keeps in regular contact with his friends and takes up any invitations he may receive. For the unattached or those Snakes who would welcome more companionship, a fortuitous meeting can lead to a significant friendship and, for some, romance. For socializing, February, May, July and September are particularly favourable months.

The Dog year can be a highly successful one for the Snake and his hard work, talents and enterprise will often be well rewarded. To benefit fully, the Snake will need to remain active and put himself forward, but for the bold and determined, the Dog year can be one of the best. And by ensuring his lifestyle has balance, including spending time with loved ones and on recreational pursuits, the Snake can make this a personally rewarding year too.

The Metal Snake

This will be a year of opportunity for the Metal Snake and as it begins, he would do well to give some thought to what he would like to achieve over the next 12 months. If he talks through his ideas with those around him, he will find many hopes being realized during the course of the year.

Some Metal Snakes will retire over the year and will now have the chance to explore some of the ideas they have had in mind for some time. These Metal Snakes will be excited by the prospects and possibilities before them.

This will be a particularly satisfying year as far as the Metal Snake's personal interests are concerned and he would do well to further these in some way. This could be by setting himself a fulfilling project, learning a new technique or skill or trying out a completely different interest. Joining other enthusiasts at a local society or even perhaps corresponding with them over the internet can also add to his knowledge and enjoyment. The Metal Snake also has a creative side to his nature and should aim to make the most of this talent this year.

The Metal Snake will also value the support he is given by those around him and will find that sharing his ideas and plans will help many to be realized. Also, with the year so favouring travel, if there are any places he would like to visit, he should mention them. Sometimes he will find his ideas taking root and being advanced far more quickly than he anticipated. In particular a break taken at short notice could turn out to be great fun. This *is* a year for seizing chances.

The Metal Snake will also enjoy some of the domestic occasions that take place over the year and whether these involve entertaining friends or relations (and the Metal Snake does make an attentive host) or sharing interests and projects with others, they will often mean a great deal to him. In addition, several times during the year those close to him will ask him for advice or help, and again his willingness to assist will be appreciated. As far as the Metal

Snake's home life is concerned, this can be a rich and meaningful year.

He will also value meeting up with friends as well as other social activities. Those Metal Snakes who would welcome more companionship will find that becoming involved in local activities and joining courses or societies can lead to a more fulfilling social life. February, late April, May, July and September could be pleasing months for socializing.

Although the Metal Snake usually keeps himself active, he would also do well to give some thought to his well-being over the year. He could find switching to a more balanced diet will give him more energy and some suitable exercise could help his fitness levels. And if over the year he does have any medical concerns, it would be worth seeking advice. By taking good care of himself he will find he is able to accomplish that much more.

Some Metal Snakes could also be attracted to more thoughtful and reflective disciplines over the year and could find meditation or relaxation techniques bringing pleasure and often much benefit too.

This will be a positive year for financial matters, with many Metal Snakes receiving a bonus, payment or gift. However, as with most of their activities in 2006, good planning and careful thought will help. In particular, when making major purchases, it would be worth the Metal Snake taking the time to compare the options available.

The one word of warning that does need to be sounded concerns important paperwork. If certain policies are due for renewal or forms need attention, the Metal Snake should deal with these promptly. If not, oversights could be to his detriment. Metal Snakes, do take note.

Overall, this can be a rewarding year for the Metal Snake, but to benefit he does need to act upon his ideas.

TIP FOR THE YEAR
Share your plans and ideas with others. With the support and involvement of those around you, so much more can be achieved and enjoyed.

The Water Snake

This will be a significant year for the Water Snake and one which will often mark the successful culmination of many years of effort as well as bring change *and* fresh opportunity. And the Water Snake, quiet, confident and determined, will relish the prospects before him.

In his work this will be an especially important year. With the experience and skills he has behind him, he will find he is well placed for some of the openings that arise or that he is able to create. Many Water Snakes can look forward to making substantial progress within their current organization. However, those who feel there may be better prospects elsewhere or who are seeking work should be active in making enquiries. This is a year for key developments, with the Water Snake's efforts often being well rewarded.

Accordingly, the Water Snake should aim to make the most of his strengths. With Water as his element, he is often a skilful communicator and if his work involves any form of presentation or communication he could enjoy considerable success. He should also put his ideas forward, as he could find some being taken further. The months from February to April and September and November could see interesting work developments, but such are the aspects that whenever the Water Snake sees an opportunity or has an idea he believes has potential, *he should act.*

He will also get much satisfaction from his personal interests over the year and for the more creative Water Snakes, these can be especially rewarding. Any Water Snake who may not have a particular interest at the moment should aim to take one up.

It is also important that the Water Snake gives consideration to his well-being. If he does not get much regular exercise, he should seek advice on the best way to correct this. Sometimes additional walking or activities such as cycling, swimming, tai chi or yoga can help. Also, switching to a more balanced diet could make a difference to how he feels. With this being such an active year, any attention the Water Snake can give to his own well-being can make a noticeable difference.

With travel favourably aspected, the Water Snake should also make the most of any travel opportunities that come his way. By following up his ideas and invitations, he can look forward to some enjoyable times away and his travels will often having a pleasing social element too.

This will also be a promising year for the Water Snake's financial prospects, with the progress he makes at work leading to a rise in income. This will tempt many Water Snakes into proceeding with ideas they have had for a while. However, whenever considering any major outlay, the Water Snake would do well to check the implications. The more care he takes, the better he will fare. This is a year when his cautious nature will serve him well.

This will be an active year in the Water Snake's home life and both younger and more senior relations will be grateful for what he does, with his ability to empathize being especially valued. However, if at any time the Water Snake has any concerns over family activities or plans, it is important that he raises these rather than keeps them to himself. Others will appreciate his frankness as well as take note of what he says. Similarly, if there is any matter worrying him, he really will find it advantageous to be forthcoming.

Over the year there will be some family events that will be particularly special to the Water Snake, possibly a graduation, marriage or the birth of a grandchild.

With all the activities of the year, however, the Water Snake should make sure that his social life does not get side-tracked. Meeting up with friends and treating himself to trips out will be a good way for him to unwind. And if he can meet those with similar interests, perhaps through a society, he will enjoy many pleasant occasions as well as a widening of his social circle. February, late April, May, July and September could be the most favourable months socially.

Overall, this is a year of much promise for the Water Snake and by using his talents and experience well he can make important headway. For those who are prepared to put in the effort, it can be a successful and pleasing time.

TIP FOR THE YEAR
Be active. Be bold. This is very much a year to show your worth.

The Wood Snake

This is a year of opportunity for the Wood Snake and by making the most of his ideas and opportunities, he can look forward to making considerable headway.

In recent years the Wood Snake will have seen many changes and in the Dog year he will be able to build on the positive and make up for any disappointments he may have had. This is very much a year for moving forward.

At work the Dog year will bring important developments. Although many Wood Snakes will have seen considerable changes in recent years, this period of change is far from over. Often as a result of his experience and the fine reputation he has built up, the Wood Snake will have the chance to take on greater responsibilities. This will also give him the chance to broaden his experience and open the way to further possibilities later. Progress made in the Dog year can have far-reaching implications.

The Wood Snake's ability to get on with his colleagues will also serve him well. He will not only find the support he enjoys helpful for his present position but also for his future prospects. More senior colleagues could be particularly encouraging and the Wood Snake would do well to listen to any advice they give. With the backing of others, he is very much in the ascendancy.

Although many Wood Snakes will be able to make excellent progress with their current organization over the year, for those who may feel they have achieved all they can where they are and would welcome new challenges or who are seeking work, again the Dog year will bring some good possibilities. To benefit, though, these Wood Snakes would do well to give serious thought to the sort of position they would now like. If they are able to talk to those currently involved in this type of work or are eligible for training or retraining, they will find initiative and effort can open up new doors. The months from February to April and September and November could see some important developments.

The Wood Snake also possesses a fertile mind and should aim to make the most of his ideas over the year. If he takes them further, some interesting wheels can be set in motion. As Thomas Edison once wrote, 'The value of an idea lies in the using of it.'

The Wood Snake should also spend time on his personal interests. Not only will they bring him pleasure but they can also be another outlet for his many talents.

Travel too is favourably aspected and the Wood Snake should also aim to go away at some time during the year. A break from his usual routine can do him a lot of good. And if he gives careful thought to what he wants to do, he can make his trips all the more enjoyable.

As with others of his sign, the Wood Snake should also give some consideration to his well-being and if he is sedentary for much of the day or relies a lot on convenience foods, it would be worth him getting guidance on how best to correct this. Wood Snakes, do take note.

Financially, the Dog year will bring an improvement in the Wood Snake's situation, with an increase in his income as well as possibly something extra from another source. However, to benefit, the Wood Snake should manage his money well. If he is able to set funds aside for future requirements, including possibly adding to his savings, he could find this helpful. By dealing with his money with care, he will find his financial situation much improved by the year's end.

He will also be grateful for the support he is given by those close to him and his home life will mean much to him over the year. With key developments in his work and some important decisions to be taken, he will value the chance to talk over his options with his loved ones and will often benefit from the advice and encouragement they give. In return, the Wood Snake himself will do much to assist family members over the year and whether this is helping children facing pressures and decisions of their own or assisting his partner or senior relations, his advice and support will again count for a great deal.

The Wood Snake will also be pleased with how some of his plans develop over the year. Whether these are alterations and enhancements to his home, projects and interests that can be pursued with others or trips and treats, they will be appreciated and often work out well. And by spending time with loved ones, he will find his domestic life both rich and rewarding.

The Wood Snake will also appreciate meeting up with friends, although his social life may not be as active as in some years. However, when there are chances to meet colleagues on a social basis or others with similar interests, he will find himself making some very good friends. For unattached Wood Snakes, someone they are introduced to or meet by chance could quickly become important. The Dog year can have some surprises in store for the Wood Snake and a powerful new friendship or love could well be one of these. February, May, July and September are particularly favourable for socializing.

The Dog year certainly holds some encouraging prospects for the Wood Snake and by making the most of his talents, ideas and chances, he will make important headway. Overall, a rewarding and very positive year.

TIP FOR THE YEAR
Despite the many demands on your time, aim to further your interests and add to your knowledge and skills. If you have let your interests slip recently, consider taking up a new one. It could be significant in the future as well as help to give your lifestyle greater balance.

The Fire Snake

This will be an important year for the Fire Snake and will bring some special times in his personal life as well as allow him to make significant progress in his work. During the Dog year the aspects are very much on his side and this, combined with his own determined nature, can make this a year of far-reaching developments and success.

At work the Dog year holds great potential and by looking to build on his experience, the Fire Snake will find some interesting possibilities opening up. However, he must not be too narrow in what he is prepared to consider. As he will find, there are several different paths open to him, any of which can help him to further his career. For some Fire Snakes there will be excellent promotion opportunities in their present place of work, although quite a few could be attracted by vacancies elsewhere. By acting on those they feel have greatest potential, many Fire Snakes will be successful in gaining a new position which will represent an important stage in their career development. In addition, some of the responsibilities they take on over the year can help to bring out certain strengths and aptitudes and which can be built on in following years.

The aspects are also promising for those Fire Snakes seeking work and by actively following up openings, many will find their persistence being rewarded with a position which will give their career new impetus. What is achieved in the Dog year can have important long-term value.

The aspects are also encouraging as far as the Fire Snake's financial prospects are concerned and in addition to an increase in income many could enjoy some financial good fortune, including a bonus, gift or sum from another source. For the enterprising, freelance work could help them to supplement their finances. Overall, the Fire Snake's earning abilities will be on good form, particularly in the second half of the year. To benefit from this upturn, though, he does need to manage his money well rather than proceed on too much of an ad hoc basis. By budgeting rather than spending too freely, he will often be able to do more as a result. He could also find it helpful to regularly review his outgoings and commitments. In some cases he could find some of these could be modified. By taking control of his finances, he will certainly fare that much better.

With travel favourably aspected, the Fire Snake would also do well to set funds aside for a holiday or break over the year. Again, by saving for this early on, he will find he is able to do more as a result. Also, any holiday he takes will not only give him the chance to enjoy a rest and break from his usual routine but will also allow him to visit some often impressive areas.

In view of his active lifestyle it is also important that the Fire Snake does not neglect his well-being. In particular it could be worth him making sure that he eats a balanced and healthy mix of foods. Not only will this often give him more energy but it will also leave him feeling fitter in himself. With all his activities and commitments, it *is* important that he takes good care of himself.

With the progressive nature of the year the Fire Snake would also do well to spend time on his interests and look to further these in some way, perhaps by setting himself a project or challenge to tackle.

The Dog year will also be an important one for family activities and for those Fire Snakes who are parents or become parents in 2006, the needs and demands of babies and young children will bring many moments of delight and happiness but some pressure and tiredness too. Accordingly, Fire Snakes who are parents really would do well to draw on any help offered. This can make a lot of difference.

All Fire Snakes will particularly value the support of those close to them over the year and while sometimes life will be hectic and there will be moments of tiredness, by setting time aside to talk and share interests, the Fire Snake will find the Dog year containing many meaningful times. As with any year, when disagreements do arise, a willingness to talk these through and show understanding can make a big difference. Overall, though, the Fire Snake's home life, while often busy, can be immensely rewarding.

With this being a year of important developments some Fire Snakes could also decide to move during the year. For those who do, the more they can prepare for this in advance, the easier the actual move will turn out to be.

The Fire Snake's social life is well aspected this year and he will get to meet many new people either through his work, his interests or his travelling. For those Fire Snakes who may have had some personal difficulties or be feeling that their social life has reached a low ebb, the Dog year can see a marked transformation, with new friendships and chances to go out adding a new sparkle and joy to their life. And for the unattached, an important romance can result. February, May, July and the period from September to mid-October will be especially active months for socializing.

Overall, the Year of the Dog holds exciting prospects for the Fire Snake and by seizing his opportunities and using his strengths, he can make important strides.

TIP FOR THE YEAR
Extend your skills and experience. This can pay dividends both in this and following years.

The Earth Snake

This is a year of considerable opportunity for the Earth Snake and by making the most of it, he can do his prospects much good. However, to benefit, he will need to put himself forward and make the effort, otherwise important chances will be lost.

For those Earth Snakes in education there will often be a lot to learn as well as examinations to prepare for. By working steadily and consistently, the Earth Snake can look forward to making good progress, with his results often having an important bearing on future years. The effort that he puts into his work can make a significant difference to how he fares.

The Earth Snake should also take advantage of the facilities available to him and will find joining clubs or groups both helpful and fun. Those interested in music, sport or drama in particular will enjoy building on their talents. Again, though, to benefit, it is a case of making the most of the opportunities available.

Throughout the year, those around the Earth Snake will be willing to give support and guidance and if he has any problems with his work or studies, he should ask for help rather than keep any concerns to himself. He would also be helped by talking to tutors or career advisers about his future. By being willing to seek guidance, he could often be alerted to possibilities he may not have realized existed. This is a year to be forthcoming and to take advantage of the help that is available.

Those Earth Snakes seeking work can also be helped by the many services and opportunities available. These could include apprenticeship schemes and day release and vocational courses as well as advice offered by companies or professional organizations. By making enquiries and seeking guidance, the Earth Snake will find himself helping to get his career off to a good start. Even if, for some, opportunities may be sparse or the positions offered routine, getting a foot on the employment ladder will help. In the Dog year, it is a case of being willing to make the most of the chances that arise. The months from February to April could see some interesting openings and there could also be important developments in the last quarter of the year.

The Earth Snake will derive much pleasure from his personal interests over the year and in addition to getting to know other enthusiasts, he could enjoy setting himself an interesting project or challenge. By experimenting as well as adding to his knowledge and skills, he will find what he does all the more satisfying. For those Earth Snakes who have thoughts of making more of a particular interest, perhaps on a vocational basis, what is learned now can prove significant later.

Another favourably aspected area is travel and there will be some good chances for the Earth Snake to go away and have a lot of fun.

As far as money matters are concerned, the Earth Snake will be pleased with all he is able to do on often limited means. However, it would be to his advantage to watch his general level of spending and if he is considering any large and expensive purchase, he should seek the advice of others before going ahead. This is a year for care and good planning.

Many of the Earth Snakes in education will be able to supplement their means by helping others or by taking on a small job over the year and their efforts can be well rewarded. The one word of warning that does need be sounded is that the Earth Snake should be very careful if he is tempted by 'get rich quick' schemes or to put his money into anything he has not properly investigated. Without care and advice, he could be misled. Earth Snakes, do take careful note.

Another area that the Earth Snake needs to be wary of during the year is finding himself in situations he is uncomfortable with. If he has misgivings or concerns over any situation, he should stick to his principles. He will feel much better for having done so.

The Earth Snake may value his independence, but he should not let this prevent him from playing a part in domestic activities or being open with those around him. By doing so, he will not only be able to improve the rapport he has with others but will also enjoy family life all that more. Again, much depends on his willingness to be involved.

The Earth Snake's social life is favourably aspected and he will have many opportunities to go out and meet up with friends. He will also have plenty of chances to meet others by pursuing his interests and becoming involved in other activities. Over the year, some long-lasting friendships will be formed. February, May and the period from July to September will be active socially.

Overall, this is a year of considerable potential for the Earth Snake, but to benefit he does need to apply himself and make the most of situations. Determination and effort will be rewarded, however, and the Earth Snake will be helped and supported by those around him.

TIP FOR THE YEAR

Aim to develop your interests and skills. These will not only be personally satisfying but will often allow you to discover talents and strengths which you can take further in the future. This is a year to use your opportunities.

FAMOUS SNAKES

Muhammad Ali, Tim Allen, Ann-Margret, Lord Baden-Powell, Kim Basinger, Björk, Tony Blair, Michael Bloomberg, Heinrich Böll, Michael Bolton, Brahms, Pierce Brosnan, Casanova, Chubby Checker, Dick Cheney, Jackie Collins, Tom Conti, Jim Davidson, Bob Dylan, Elgar, Sir Alex Ferguson, Sir Alexander Fleming, Henry Fonda, Mahatma Gandhi, Greta Garbo, Art Garfunkel, J. Paul Getty, Dizzy Gillespie, W. E. Gladstone, Johann Wolfgang von Goethe, Princess Grace of Monaco, Stephen Hawking, Audrey Hepburn, Jack Higgins, Michael Howard, Howard Hughes, Tom Hulce, Elizabeth Hurley, James Joyce, Stacy Keach, Ronan Keating, Howard Keel, J. F. Kennedy, Carole King, Cyndi Lauper, Courtney Love, Dame Vera Lynn, Mao Tse-tung, Henri Matisse, Cecil B. de Mille, Robert Mitchum, Nasser, Alfred Nobel, Mike Oldfield, Aristotle Onassis, Jacqueline Onassis, Pablo Picasso, Mary Pickford, Brad Pitt, Daniel Radcliffe, Franklin D. Roosevelt, Mickey Rourke, J. K. Rowling, Jean-Paul Sartre, Franz Schubert, Charlie Sheen, Brooke Shields, Paul Simon, Delia Smith, Paul Theroux, Madame Tussaud, Shania Twain, Dionne Warwick, Charlie Watts, Ruby Wax, Oprah Winfrey, Victoria Wood, Virginia Woolf.

25 JANUARY 1906 ∼ 12 FEBRUARY 1907   *Fire Horse*

11 FEBRUARY 1918 ∼ 31 JANUARY 1919   *Earth Horse*

30 JANUARY 1930 ∼ 16 FEBRUARY 1931   *Metal Horse*

15 FEBRUARY 1942 ∼ 4 FEBRUARY 1943   *Water Horse*

3 FEBRUARY 1954 ∼ 23 JANUARY 1955   *Wood Horse*

21 JANUARY 1966 ∼ 8 FEBRUARY 1967   *Fire Horse*

7 FEBRUARY 1978 ∼ 27 JANUARY 1979   *Earth Horse*

27 JANUARY 1990 ∼ 14 FEBRUARY 1991   *Metal Horse*

12 FEBRUARY 2002 ∼ 31 JANUARY 2003   *Water Horse*

THE

HORSE

THE PERSONALITY OF THE HORSE

These three things – work, will, success – fill human existence. Will opens the door to success, both brilliant and happy. Work passes these doors, and at the end of the journey success comes in to crown one's efforts.

Louis Pasteur, a Horse

The Horse is born under the signs of elegance and ardour. He has a most engaging and charming manner and is usually very popular. He loves meeting people and likes attending parties and other large social gatherings.

The Horse is a lively character and enjoys being the centre of attention. He has considerable leadership qualities and is much admired for his honest and straightforward manner. He is an eloquent and persuasive speaker and has a great love of discussion and debate. He also has a particularly agile mind and can assimilate facts remarkably quickly.

He does, however, have a fiery temper and although his outbursts are usually short-lived, he can often say things which he will later regret. He is also not particularly good at keeping secrets.

The Horse has many interests and involves himself in a wide variety of activities. He can, however, get involved in so much that he can often waste his energies on projects which he never has time to complete. He also has a tendency to change his interests rather frequently and will often get caught up with the latest craze or 'in thing' until something better or more exciting turns up.

The Horse also likes to have a certain amount of freedom and independence. He hates being bound by petty rules and regulations and as far as possible likes to feel that he is answerable to no one but himself. But despite this spirit of freedom, he still likes to have the support and encouragement of others in his various enterprises.

Due to his many talents and likeable nature, the Horse will often go far in life. He enjoys challenges and is a methodical and tireless worker. However, should things go against him and he fail in any of his enterprises, it will take a long time for him to recover and pick up the pieces again. Success to the Horse means everything. To fail is a disaster and a humiliation.

The Horse likes to have variety in his life and he will try his hand at many different things before he settles down to one particular job. Even then, he will probably remain alert to see whether there are any better opportunities for him to take up. He has a restless nature and can easily get bored. He does, however, excel in any position which allows him sufficient freedom to act on his own initiative or which brings him into contact with a lot of people.

Although the Horse is not particularly bothered about accumulating great wealth, he handles his finances with care and will rarely experience any serious financial problems.

The Horse also enjoys travel and loves visiting new and faraway places. At some stage during his life he will be tempted to live abroad for a short period of time and due to his adaptable nature he will find that he will fit in well wherever he goes.

The Horse pays a great deal of attention to his appearance and usually likes to wear smart, colourful and rather distinctive clothes. He is very attractive to others and will often have many romances before he settles down. He is loyal and protective to his partner, but despite his family commitments he still likes to retain a certain measure of independence and have the freedom to carry on with his own interests and hobbies. He will find that he is especially well suited to those born under the signs of the Tiger, Goat, Rooster and Dog. He can also get on well with the Rabbit, Dragon, Snake, Pig and another Horse, but he will find the Ox too serious and intolerant for his liking. The Horse will also have difficulty in getting on with the Monkey and the Rat – the Monkey is very inquisitive and the Rat seeks security, and both will resent the Horse's rather independent ways.

The female Horse is usually most attractive and has a friendly, outgoing personality. She is highly intelligent, has many interests and is alert to everything that is going on around her. She particularly enjoys outdoor pursuits and often likes to take part in sport and keep-fit activities. She also enjoys travel, literature and the arts, and is a very good conversationalist.

Although the Horse can be stubborn and rather self-centred, he does have a considerate nature and is often willing to help others. He has a good sense of humour and will usually make a favourable impression wherever he goes. Provided he can curb his slightly restless nature and keep tight control over his temper, he will go through life making friends, taking part in a multitude of different activities and generally achieving many of his objectives. His life will rarely be dull.

THE FIVE DIFFERENT TYPES
OF HORSE

In addition to the 12 signs of the Chinese zodiac there are five elements, and these have a strengthening or moderating influence on the sign. The effects of the five elements on the Horse are described below, together with the years in which the elements were exercising their influence. Therefore those Horses born in 1930 and 1990 are Metal Horses, those born in 1942 and 2002 are Water Horses, and so on.

Metal Horse: 1930, 1990
This Horse is bold, confident and forthright. He is ambitious and a great innovator. He loves challenges and takes great delight in sorting out complicated problems. He likes to have a certain amount of independence and resents any outside interference in his affairs. He has charm and a certain charisma, but he can also be very stubborn and rather impulsive. He usually has many friends and enjoys an active social life.

Water Horse: 1942, 2002
The Water Horse has a friendly nature and a good sense of humour and is able to talk intelligently on a wide range of topics. He is astute in business matters and quick to take advantage of any opportunities that arise. He does,

however, have a tendency to get easily distracted and can change his interests – and indeed his mind – rather frequently, and this can often work to his detriment. He is nevertheless very talented and can often go far in life. He pays a great deal of attention to his appearance and is usually smart and well turned out. He loves to travel and also enjoys sport and other outdoor activities.

Wood Horse: 1954

The Wood Horse has a most agreeable and amiable nature. He communicates well with others and is able to talk intelligently on many different subjects. He is a hard and conscientious worker and is held in high esteem by his friends and colleagues. His opinions are often sought and, given his imaginative nature, he can often come up with some very original and practical ideas. He is usually widely read and likes to lead a busy social life. He can also be most generous and often holds high moral views.

Fire Horse: 1906, 1966

The element of Fire combined with the temperament of the Horse creates one of the most powerful forces in the Chinese zodiac. The Fire Horse is destined to lead an exciting and eventful life and to make his mark in his chosen profession. He has a forceful personality and his intelligence and resolute manner bring him the support and admiration of many. He loves action and excitement and his life will rarely be quiet. He can, however, be rather blunt and forthright in his views and does not take kindly to interference in his own affairs or to obeying orders. He is a flamboyant character, has a good sense of humour and will lead a very active social life.

Earth Horse: 1918, 1978

This Horse is considerate and caring. He is more cautious than some of the other types of Horse, but he is wise, perceptive and extremely capable. Although he can be rather indecisive at times, he has considerable business acumen and is very astute in financial matters. He has a quiet, friendly nature and is well thought of by his family and friends.

PROSPECTS FOR THE HORSE IN 2006

The Year of the Rooster (9 February 2005 to 28 January 2006) will have been a busy and often demanding one for the Horse and the closing months will see a lot of activity. The Horse will sometimes despair of all he has to do, but he can take satisfaction in the knowledge that what he does now can have a positive bearing on the more encouraging Dog year that follows.

In his work this is an especially important time and by setting about his duties in his usual determined way, the Horse will not only find his work becoming more satis-fying but will also enhance his prospects for the year ahead. For those Horses seeking work or hoping to make headway, a position they can secure in the closing months can often be one they can build on in the forthcoming year. November could see some interesting developments.

The Horse will, though, need to be careful in money matters and if entering into a new agreement or making a major purchase, he should check the details carefully. Important financial matters should not be rushed.

With his outgoing and sociable nature the Horse sets much store by his relations with others and both his domestic and social life will bring him considerable pleasure, with late November and December being especially active months socially. Domestically, the Horse will often be busy arranging various activities and once again his input into family life will be much appreciated. Also, some advice he gives to a close relation near the year's end could prove important and helpful.

The Rooster year is invariably a busy one for the Horse, but with his active and keen nature, he will certainly accomplish a great deal in the closing months and can look forward to reaping some fine rewards in the next Chinese year.

The Year of the Dog begins on 29 January and is one of considerable opportunity for the Horse, although to benefit he will need to watch his self-willed and independent nature. Joint enterprise and effort will be rewarded, but if the Horse adopts a go-it-alone attitude or allows his restless and impulsive nature to get the better of him, then some good opportunities could be lost.

The Horse's work prospects are, however, especially promising. Many Horses will build on their experience and make considerable headway. Also, by being active and willing to contribute, the Horse will find his initiative often being recognized. As so many Horses have found, making that little bit of extra effort *can* make so much difference.

The Horse will also benefit from the support of others and by working well as part of a team (and watching his independent nature), he will not only be able to accomplish that much more but will also help his prospects. He should also make the most of any chances to get to know other colleagues. If he is able to become better known, he will find it helpful both in the present and near future.

For those Horses who are satisfied in their present area of work the Dog year will often bring excellent chances to progress, including promotion opportunities, while for those seeking work or keen to change the nature of what they do, there will be some exciting prospects. These Horses can be greatly helped by the advice of close colleagues as well as guidance offered by professional organizations. The input of others can make a considerable difference to how the Horse fares over the year. March, May, July and September could see some positive developments, but in general this is a year when effort and talent will be recognized and well rewarded.

The favourable aspects also extend to financial matters. Many Horses will see an increase in income and some may be able to supplement this by overtime or additional work. However, while the aspects may be positive, the Horse does need to handle his finances well, including making allowances for some of the substantial outgoings he has and the plans he wants to carry through. Also, when dealing with important transactions and paperwork, he needs to be thorough. Should he face any problems, he would do well to seek advice rather than deal with some-times complex matters single-handedly.

Accommodation matters will also figure prominently over the year, with quite a few Horses deciding to move. For those who do, the process could take up considerable time and effort. However, while there will be moments of despair and these Horses may wonder if what they are embarking on is really worthwhile, events will sometimes move in fortuitous ways. In some cases a lot can happen all at once after months of inactivity. By the year's end, those who have moved will often be delighted with the amenities their new location offers. In this respect, the Dog year can be significant and eventful.

This is also a favourable year as far as the Horse's relations with others are concerned. For unattached Horses who would welcome new friendships and perhaps romance, the Dog year can bring quite a transformation and the chance to meet someone who will quickly become special. And such are the aspects that many Horses will settle down with a partner, and become engaged or married over the year. Again, the events of the year can move in exciting ways. For meeting others and socializing, April, June, August and September are particularly favourable.

The Horse will also value his domestic life over the year, especially the support given by his loved ones. With some of the opportunities that the year will bring, it is important that he talks through his thoughts and options with those close to him. Not only will this help to clarify certain situations in his own mind, but others could also raise matters that need to be addressed. This is a year when consultation can be beneficial in many ways.

In addition to the encouragement the Horse will receive for his own activities, he will also enjoy the interests and household projects he shares with family members. And with the prospects of some Horses moving and the ambitious household projects that many have lined up, this is very much a year for planning and doing things together.

In addition to all the practical activity, the Dog year will contain some memorable family highlights, possibly including a special holiday or break or a house-warming party. There will certainly be events in 2006 that the Horse will both value and long remember.

Overall, the aspects are very much on the Horse's side during the year, but to benefit he does need to act in conjunction with others and restrain his sometimes overly independent nature. With support, co-operation and the goodwill of others, however, he can achieve and enjoy a great deal during the Dog year.

The Metal Horse

This is a pleasing and productive year for the Metal Horse and by setting about his activities in his usual determined way, he will do well. However, the Dog year *does* call for effort and if the Metal Horse becomes lax or complacent in some of his activities, it can provide some sharp reminders. This is very much a year for commitment and hard work.

For those Metal Horses who are studying, great progress can be made. As they move on to more advanced work, many will find themselves being drawn towards certain subject areas and this will help indicate possible areas to concentrate on in the future. In the meantime, by working consistently and giving their best, many Metal Horses will be encouraged by their progress.

The Metal Horse should also make the most of any special talents he has and whether these are in sport or music (and many Metal Horses are talented musically), drama or some other area, he will find that furthering his skills will add to the pleasure his activities bring.

In addition the Metal Horse would also do well to considering broadening his range of interests and if there is another skill or activity that appeals to him, he should find out more. In some cases this could lead to an absorbing new hobby or discovering another talent.

Throughout the year the Metal Horse should draw on the help available to him and if there is something he would like to do or is concerned about, by talking to tutors, advisers and family members, he will find the assistance and encouragement he is given can make a difference. To benefit, though, the Metal Horse does need to be forthcoming rather than keep his thoughts to himself.

The Metal Horse will welcome the support and companionship of his close friends over the year and as he becomes involved in other activities, his social circle is set to grow. He will often find himself in demand, with opportunities to meet up with friends and attend parties and other social occasions. April, June, August, September and December will be busy and enjoyable months socially.

Those Metal Horses who decide to enter the world of work rather than remain in education over the year will find that by being flexible in what they are prepared to consider and remaining persistent, they can often secure a job which can give them a useful platform on which to build. Although their initial duties may be routine, by showing commitment and putting in that extra effort, they will soon find themselves being singled out for increased responsibilities or able to move to something more satisfying. This is a year when effort and application can make an important difference.

Also, some Metal Horses will choose to take an apprenticeship or pursue other studies in addition to their work. Although this will often demand a lot of them, by making the most of their opportunities, they will find that what they learn now will have long-term value.

The Metal Horse will need to be careful, however, in financial matters. With his many plans, full social life and travel opportunities, he does need to watch his spending and avoid succumbing to too many impulse purchases. Control over his purse-strings would be wise and if he is able to save towards any larger expenses, he will find this to his advantage. This is a year for good financial discipline.

Those Metal Horses in education will often have the chance to help their financial position by taking on a seasonal job or working for a few hours each week. This is a year when initiative and enterprise will be well rewarded.

There will also be some good travel opportunities for the Metal Horse over the year, either as part of his education or for pleasure, and he should make the most of them. With his adventurous Horse nature, he will often greatly enjoy himself.

For those Metal Horses born in 1930 this can also be a rewarding year, although again it is a case of making the most of their ideas and opportunities. Whether these involve pursuing personal interests or following up invitations to visit family and friends living some distance away, the Metal Horse will find the year containing some pleasurable occasions. Also, like the younger Metal Horses, these Metal Horses will be grateful for the support given by those around them and should they need advice or assistance, they should be forthcoming.

Overall, the Dog year is an encouraging one for the Metal Horse and by setting about his activities and putting in the effort, he will be pleased with what he is able to accomplish. Some of his achievements over the year can be of great value in the future.

TIP FOR THE YEAR
Make the most of your opportunities. Anything that you can do to further yourself, your talents and your interests will not only be personally satisfying but can also open up other possibilities for later on.

The Water Horse

This will be a significant year for the Water Horse with key developments in several areas of his life.

In his work there will be some important decisions to take. Some Water Horses, due to their seniority and experience, will have the chance to become involved in more specialist duties and to concentrate on areas they enjoy and do best. In many cases what they achieve will mark the culmination of years of hard work.

However, while there be excellent opportunities to advance, some Water Horses will decide to retire or reduce their working hours. These Water Horses will now have more opportunity and time to carry out ideas they have long considered. In many ways, the events of the Dog year can be far-reaching. March, May, July and September could see important developments and key decisions.

Also, in view of the implications of some of the decisions that need to be taken, the Water Horse will be particularly grateful for the support he receives from those around him. If there are any matters particularly concerning him, including his financial situation, it is important that he seeks proper advice. By doing so, he will find some of his questions can be quickly and satisfactorily addressed.

In addition to the important developments in the Water Horse's working life, another area which is likely to feature prominently is accommodation. During the Dog year quite a few Water Horses will decide to move to accommodation that better suits their requirements and to areas that have long attracted them. For these Water Horses a lot of time will be devoted to the moving process, including the considerable sorting out that needs to be done (and the earlier this is started, the better), and there will be occasions when these Water Horses will despair, but once they have settled into their new home, they will be pleased with what they have achieved. Again this is a year for realizing important plans.

All Water Horses, whether they move or not, will be grateful for the support given by loved ones over the year and if they need help with some strenuous tasks and activities, they should ask. As they will find, those dear to them can do much to assist.

In addition to the more practical activities of the year, the Water Horse can look forward to some pleasing family news, with a possible wedding or the birth of a grandchild or great-grandchild to celebrate as well as, for some, a house-warming gathering. The Water Horse's domestic life will certainly mean much to him and some events could make him especially proud.

The Dog year also favours travel and the Water Horse should take advantage of any invitations he receives as well as follow up any offers that appeal to him. This is a year to act on opportunities and ideas and, if there is a place the Water Horse has wanted to visit for some time, this would be an excellent year in which to do so.

The Water Horse will also get much pleasure from his social life and those Water Horses involved in a local group or society could find themselves playing an increased role. In addition, by joining others with similar interests, whether at a society or by going to particular events, they will not only enjoy what they do but also be able to make some good friends and contacts. Those who do move or would welcome more companionship will find joining a local activity group could be especially rewarding and lead to new friendships. In addition, any holidays the Water Horse takes could bring some splendid social opportunities. With his sincere and outgoing manner, he can look forward to good relations with many over the year, with late March, April, June, August and September being especially favourable months. Also, for any Water Horses who may have had recent personal problems, this is a year to move on and for some who are unattached, romance and possible marriage can beckon. This can be a special *and* auspicious year.

In addition to the positive social aspects, this is a time when the Water Horse should consider his own personal development. By giving himself something new and purposeful to do (especially if recently retired), he can add another enjoyable aspect to the year. Those Water Horses who tend to be sedentary could find a suitable keep-fit course or tai chi or yoga beneficial. However, before starting any fitness course, the Water Horse should seek proper medical guidance.

In most areas of his life the aspects are on his side, but during the year the Water Horse will need to be careful when dealing with financial paperwork and forms. A mistake, oversight or delay could be to his disadvantage and, when appropriate, he would do well to get sound advice rather than take risks or make assumptions. Similarly, in any major transaction, he needs to check all the details and implications carefully and seek professional guidance when necessary. Water Horses, do take note.

Overall, this is a significant and favourable year for the Water Horse and one which can bring many positive developments. These may include changes in his work, opportunities to move, to travel, to enjoy positive relations with many and to devote more time to personal interests. Whatever he chooses to do, by making the most of his ideas and opportunities, the Water Horse will find this a year which offers considerable scope and potential.

TIP FOR THE YEAR
Do not hesitate to ask for advice or an opinion on any decision you may be considering. Also consider developing your interests or taking up something new. This can give you a fresh and interesting challenge.

The Wood Horse

The Dog year will mark an upturn in the Wood Horse's fortunes, bringing opportunities to advance in his work as well as to further some of his ideas. However, the key for the Wood Horse in 2006 is to curb his independent Horse tendencies. In the Dog year he will fare much better, by building up support and involving others in his activities.

In the Wood Horse's work there will be some excellent opportunities for him to further his position. In view of his experience and special skills he may find himself ideally placed to put in for well-deserved promotion. By acting upon any openings that arise, he will often find that he can move to a more fulfilling role. Even if one application does not go his way, other opportunities will follow.

For those Wood Horses who may have been in the same position for some while or are seeking work, this is also a year for change. Again, by putting themselves forward and making enquiries, many will be successful in setting their career off on a more fulfilling path. For all Wood Horses, 2006 is very much a year for growth and for making the most of the often special opportunities that will come their way. March, May, July and September could see some positive career developments.

Throughout the year the Wood Horse will also be helped by the good working relations he has with his colleagues and if at any time he is in a dilemma, has a problem or needs assistance, he should be forthcoming. His colleagues, contacts and friends think highly of him and will often be able to offer help and support that will exceed what he was expecting. Those Wood Horses who do change their work over the year will find that getting to know their new colleagues, building up contacts and taking full advantage of any training opportunities will be especially helpful. This is a year for making the most of their abilities and the often excellent chances presented to them.

The Wood Horse's progress at work will lead to an increase in income and many Wood Horses could benefit from an additional sum over the year, perhaps a bonus or gift or the fruition of a policy. However, while this will be welcome, the Wood Horse does need to manage his money well rather than be tempted to spend anything extra all too readily. If he is able to reduce any borrowings or add to his longer-term savings, he could find this making a difference to his overall situation. However, with careful financial control, the Wood Horse can fare well over the year.

Domestically, the year will see much activity and during it the Wood Horse will do much to help and support family members, including those much younger and older than himself. The support and care he shows, as well as the good advice he gives, will often be more valued than he may realize. He can also look forward to celebrating some good pieces of family news and the year will contain some enjoyable and appreciated moments.

With travel favourably aspected, he should also aim to go away with loved ones at some time during the year. A change of scene will do everyone good.

The Dog year favours practical activity and during it the Wood Horse will often decide to go ahead with plans he has for his home, including adding new comforts as well as changing the layout and style of certain rooms. By discussing ideas and taking the time to compare the many different possibilities and options available (as well as the costs involved), he will often delight in what is accomplished over the year.

Also, with this being a year for change, some Wood Horses will decide to move. Although this could entail considerable upheaval and take up a lot of time, it will often mark the start of an important new chapter in their lives. In this respect, too, the events of the Dog year can be both positive and far-reaching.

The Wood Horse will appreciate his social life during the year and will particularly value the friendship of those he knows well. If at any time he is anxious over a decision or has any other concerns, talking things over with close friends will certainly help. He will also enjoy the various social events he attends over the year and these will give him the chance to add to his circle of acquaintances. Those Wood Horses who move or would welcome additional friends will find that by making the most of chances to go out, their social life can enjoy quite a transformation. For the unattached the year could mark the start of a significant romance. Late March, April, June, August and September could be especially active months socially.

The Dog year certainly holds encouraging prospects for the Wood Horse and by making the most of the chances that arise and using his talents well, he can look forward to making important progress and enjoying good results. And the more he consults others and draws on their help and support, the better he will fare.

TIP FOR THE YEAR
This is a year of considerable opportunity, but to benefit you do need to take positive and enthusiastic action. Self-

development can be significant and whether you are improving an existing skill, acquiring a new one or widening your interests in some other way, what you learn now can be very much to your future benefit.

The Fire Horse

This year marks the Fire Horse's fortieth year and as he enters a new decade of his life, important changes are on the way.

Although the Fire Horse will have accomplished a great deal in recent years, there will be quite a few Fire Horses who feel they are not yet realizing their full potential. However, good fortune will be *firmly* on the Fire Horse's side this year.

In his work this is a year both for change and important advances. For some Fire Horses promotion will beckon, particularly as more senior colleagues move on or new initiatives, changes and restructuring lead to other opportunities. With his experience and in-house knowledge, the Fire Horse will often be in an excellent position to benefit. However, whenever an opportunity does appear, he does need to be swift in putting himself forward. The Dog year is no time to delay, prevaricate or let chances slip by.

Those Fire Horses who are seeking work or feeling unfulfilled in their present role should also actively make enquiries and follow up any openings that interest them. Talking to those in a position to offer advice can also be helpful. Effort will be rewarded in the Dog year and many Fire Horses will secure a position which can give their career new impetus. March, May, July and September could see some good work opportunities, but overall this is a year when persistence can pay off.

The Fire Horse will also find that he can help his prospects by any training he can undertake, with new skills often opening up new possibilities. In addition his colleagues and the many good contacts he has can be helpful. Once again, the Fire Horse will have much on his side during the Dog year, but he does need to act.

The progress the Fire Horse makes in his work will lead to an increase in his income and some Fire Horses may also benefit from an extra payment or gift over the year. However, while any financial upturn will be welcome, the Fire Horse does need to manage his money well and set funds aside for some of his more substantial outgoings. Also, he would do well to consider adding to his savings or a pension policy. Overall, with control and good planning, the Fire Horse will fare well in financial matters.

With travel favourably aspected, he should also consider taking a holiday over the year and perhaps choose somewhere special to visit to mark his fortieth birthday. In addition there could be the opportunity to go away at relatively short notice, perhaps for an unexpected or spur-of-the-moment break and the spontaneity can help to make it all the more fun.

This will also be an active time domestically and with this being a year for change, some Fire Horses could decide to move to somewhere that better suits their requirements. Whether the Fire Horse moves or not, the year will see much practical activity and throughout he does need to liaise closely with others and preserve some time to spend with his loved ones.

There could be good cause for a family celebration over the year too, and in addition to the possible marking of his own birthday, the academic success and progress of a younger relation could mean much to the Fire Horse. The Dog year will certainly give rise to some memorable moments.

Although the Fire Horse will have much to do over the year, it is also important that he does not neglect his own interests or social life. Both can give him the chance to relax and unwind. For those Fire Horses who may have had some recent personal misfortune, the Dog year is very much a time to draw a line under the past to become involved in new activities. For the unattached Fire Horse the year can also bring the gift of a wonderful new romance. On a personal level, this can be a special and important time, with late March, April, June, August and September being particularly favourable months.

In so many ways this can be a significant year for the Fire Horse. By making the most of his chances to further himself, he will often enjoy good fortune and see positive results. This is very much a year to seize the initiative and *look to advance.*

TIP FOR THE YEAR

Two tips! First, involve others in all you do. The advice, support and encouragement you will be given can make a great difference to your level of success. This is not a year for acting alone or for being too independent. Second, strive for a balanced lifestyle and do ensure you give time to those who are important to you. Your loved ones are a truly valuable and special part of your life and you need to show that you care.

The Earth Horse

This will be an eventful year for the Earth Horse and one of considerable good fortune. In his personal life he can look forward to several significant developments, possibly including an addition to the family or some other good cause to celebrate. And he himself will often be buoyed up by the love and support of those around him.

With this being a year of important developments there will be quite a few Earth Horses who decide to move to somewhere which better suits their requirements, often somewhere which offers them additional space as well as a more convenient location. While there will be much to do to get their home as they want it, with the help and support of others, an amazing amount can be achieved. Indeed, by the year's end many Earth Horses will look back with some incredulity at the transformation that has taken place.

In addition to the often considerable activity concerning his accommodation, the Earth Horse can look forward to some important times with his loved ones over the year. If he is a parent or becomes a parent during 2006, he will take a fond interest in his young family, often forging a close bond with them. Even though there will be times when he will be tired, by giving time to others, he can make this a meaningful year on a personal level.

The favourable aspects also extend to those Earth Horses who are unattached or who may have had some recent ill fortune in their personal life. The Dog year is very much a time to move forward. For those Earth Horses who are alone, sometimes a chance introduction or meeting can quickly lead to romance, often in such a way that it will seem as if fate is playing a special part.

The Earth Horse's social life will also be important to him over the year. Not only will he value some of his close friendships – particularly as they will give him the opportunity to share his thoughts with those he trusts – but he will often have the chance to go to various social events. Some of those he meets through his work and interests will have a natural affinity with him and some new friendships and important contacts will be made. A key feature of the Dog year is that it is a time for being with others.

The prospects are also encouraging as far as the Earth Horse's work is concerned. With his ambitious nature and desire to make the most of himself, when promotion opportunities arise, the Earth Horse will often put himself forward and, with persistence, can obtain an excellent new position which will represent an important stage in his career development.

Those Earth Horses who are seeking work or feeling in a rut will also find that by actively pursuing openings that interest them, they can be successful in securing a position which they can build on in the future. March, May, July and September can see some good career developments.

However, while so much can go well for the Earth Horse in the Dog year, there are areas which do call for special care. Finance is one and although many Earth Horses will enjoy an increase in income, this will be an expensive year. There will often be a lot of pressure on their resources and they do need to manage their situation well. Over the year it certainly would be prudent for the Earth Horse to keep close track of his spending. Also, when entering into any new commitment or borrowing, it is important that he checks the terms and implications and obtains advice if he has any uncertainties. This is not a year for taking risks or making assumptions.

The Earth Horse also needs to be careful when completing important forms as well as keeping documents, receipts and guarantees safe. Mistakes or mislaid items could cause problems and result in protracted correspondence. Earth Horses, do take note.

Another area which the Earth Horse should not ignore is his own well-being and if he becomes involved in any strenuous or hazardous activities, he does need to follow safety guidelines rather than take risks. Earth Horses who are sedentary for much of the day could help themselves by ensuring that they take regular exercise. With so much going on in his life this year, the Earth Horse does need to take good care of himself.

In many respects, this will be a special year for the Earth Horse, with significant developments in his personal life and good chances to advance in his work. By using his personal qualities and skills well and seizing his opportunities, he can make this a rewarding and successful time.

TIP FOR THE YEAR
Spend time with others and be prepared to talk over your hopes and plans. Joint effort can lead to more being accomplished as well as help the year to be that much more special.

FAMOUS HORSES

Neil Armstrong, Rowan Atkinson, José Manuel Barroso, Samuel Beckett, Ingmar Bergman, Leonard Bernstein, Karen Black, Cherie Blair, Helena Bonham Carter, James Cameron, Jackie Chan, Ray Charles, Chopin, Sir Sean Connery, Billy Connolly, Catherine Cookson, Elvis Costello, Kevin Costner, Cindy Crawford, Michael Crichton, James Dean, Clint Eastwood, Thomas Alva Edison, Britt Ekland, Harrison Ford, Aretha Franklin, Bob Geldof, Samuel Goldwyn, Billy Graham, Gene Hackman, Rolf Harris, Rita Hayworth, Jimi Hendrix, John Edgar Hoover, Janet Jackson, Calvin Klein, Lenin, Annie Lennox, Sir Paul McCartney, Nelson Mandela, Princess Margaret, Michael Moore, Ben Murphy, Sir Isaac Newton, Louis Pasteur, Harold Pinter, Puccini, Lou Reed, Rembrandt, Ruth Rendell, Jean Renoir, Condoleezza Rice, Theodore Roosevelt, Helena Rubenstein, David Schwimmer, Lord Snowdon, Alexander Solzhenitsyn, Rachel Stevens, Barbra Streisand, Kiefer Sutherland, Patrick Swayze, John Travolta, Kathleen Turner, Vivaldi, Robert Wagner, Denzel Washington, Billy Wilder, Andy Williams, the Duke of Windsor, Boris Yeltsin, Will Young.

13 FEBRUARY 1907 ⁓ 1 FEBRUARY 1908	*Fire Goat*
1 FEBRUARY 1919 ⁓ 19 FEBRUARY 1920	*Earth Goat*
17 FEBRUARY 1931 ⁓ 5 FEBRUARY 1932	*Metal Goat*
5 FEBRUARY 1943 ⁓ 24 JANUARY 1944	*Water Goat*
24 JANUARY 1955 ⁓ 11 FEBRUARY 1956	*Wood Goat*
9 FEBRUARY 1967 ⁓ 29 JANUARY 1968	*Fire Goat*
28 JANUARY 1979 ⁓ 15 FEBRUARY 1980	*Earth Goat*
15 FEBRUARY 1991 ⁓ 3 FEBRUARY 1992	*Metal Goat*
1 FEBRUARY 2003 ⁓ 21 JANUARY 2004	*Water Goat*

THE
GOAT

THE PERSONALITY OF THE GOAT

Always do right; this will gratify some people and astonish the rest.

Mark Twain, a Goat

The Goat is born under the sign of art. He is imaginative, creative and has a good appreciation of the finer things in life. He has an easy-going nature and prefers to live in a relaxed and pressure-free environment. He hates any sort of discord or unpleasantness and does not like to be bound by a strict routine or rigid timetable. He is not one to be hurried against his will, but despite his seemingly relaxed approach to life, he is something of a perfectionist and when he starts work on a project he is certain to give his best.

The Goat usually prefers to work in a team rather than on his own. He likes to have the support and encouragement of others and if left to deal with matters on his own he can get very worried and tend to view things rather pessimistically. Wherever possible he will leave major decision-making to others while he concentrates on his own pursuits. If, however, he feels particularly strongly about a certain matter or has to defend his position in any way, he will act with great fortitude and precision.

The Goat has a very persuasive nature and often uses his considerable charm to get his own way. He can, however, be rather hesitant about letting his true feelings be known and if he were prepared to be more forthright he would do much better as a result.

The Goat tends to have a quiet, somewhat reserved nature but when he is in company he likes he can often become the centre of attention. He can be highly amusing, a marvellous host at parties and a superb entertainer. Whenever the spotlight falls on him, his adrenaline starts to flow and he can be assured of giving a sparkling performance, particularly if he is allowed to use his creative skills in any way.

Of all the signs in the Chinese zodiac, the Goat is probably the most gifted artistically. Whether it is in the theatre, literature, music or art, he is certain to make a lasting impression. He is a born creator and is rarely happier than when occupied in some artistic pursuit. But even in this the Goat does well to work with others rather than on his own. He needs inspiration and a guiding influence, but when he has found his true *métier*, he can often receive widespread acclaim and recognition.

In addition to his liking for the arts, the Goat is usually quite religious and often has a deep interest in nature, animals and the countryside. He is also fairly athletic and there are many Goats who have excelled in some form of sporting activity or who have a great interest in sport.

Although the Goat is not particularly materialistic or concerned about finance, he will find that he will usually be lucky in financial matters and will rarely be short of the necessary funds to tide himself over. He is, however, rather indulgent and tends to spend his money as soon as he receives it rather than make provision for the future.

The Goat usually leaves home when he is young but he will always maintain strong links with his parents and the other members of his family. He is also rather nostalgic and is well known for keeping mementoes of his childhood and souvenirs of places that he has visited. His home will not be particularly tidy, but he knows where everything is and it will also be scrupulously clean.

Affairs of the heart are particularly important to the Goat and he will often have many romances before he finally settles down. Although he is fairly adaptable, he prefers to live in a secure and stable environment and he will find that he is best suited to those born under the signs of the Tiger, Horse, Monkey, Pig and Rabbit. He can also establish a good relationship with the Dragon, Snake, Rooster and another Goat, but he may find the Ox and Dog a little too serious for his liking. Neither will he care particularly for the Rat's rather thrifty ways.

The female Goat devotes all her time and energy to the needs of her family. She has excellent taste in home furnishings and often uses her considerable artistic skills to make clothes for herself and her children. She takes great care over her appearance and can be most attractive to others. Although she is not the most organized of people, her engaging manner and delightful sense of humour create a favourable impression wherever she goes. She is also a good cook and usually derives much pleasure from gardening and outdoor pursuits.

The Goat can win friends easily and people generally feel relaxed in his company. He has a kind and understanding nature and although he can occasionally be stubborn, he can, with the right support and encouragement, live a happy and very satisfying life. And the more he can use his creative skills, the happier he will be.

THE FIVE DIFFERENT TYPES OF GOAT

In addition to the 12 signs of the Chinese zodiac there are five elements and these have a strengthening or moderating influence on the sign. The effects of the five elements on the Goat are described below, together with the years in which the elements were exercising their influence. Therefore those Goats born in 1931 and 1991 are Metal Goats, those born in 1943 and 2003 are Water Goats, and so on.

Metal Goat: 1931, 1991

This Goat is thorough and conscientious in all that he does and is capable of doing very well in his chosen profession. Despite his confident manner, he can be a great worrier and he would find it helpful to discuss his concerns with others rather than keep them to himself. He is loyal to his family and employers and will have a small group of particularly close friends. He has good taste and is usually highly skilled in some aspect of the arts. He is often a collector of antiques and his home will be very tastefully furnished.

Water Goat: 1943, 2003

The Water Goat is very popular and makes friends with remarkable ease. He is good at spotting opportunities but does not always have the necessary confidence to follow them through. He likes to have security both in his home life and at work and does not take kindly to change. He is articulate, has a good sense of humour and is usually very good with children.

Wood Goat: 1955

This Goat is generous, kind-hearted and always eager to please. He usually has a large circle of friends and involves himself in a wide variety of activities. He has a very trusting nature but he can sometimes give in to the demands of others a little too easily and it would be in his own interests if he were to stand his ground more often. He is usually lucky in financial matters and, like the Water Goat, is very good with children.

Fire Goat: 1907, 1967

This Goat usually knows what he wants in life and often uses his considerable charm and persuasive personality to achieve his aims. He can sometimes let his imagination run away with him and has a tendency to ignore matters which are not to his liking. He is rather extravagant in his spending and would do well to exercise a little more care when dealing with financial matters. He has a lively personality, many friends, and loves attending parties and social occasions.

Earth Goat: 1919, 1979

This Goat has a considerate and caring nature. He is particularly loyal to his family and friends and invariably creates a favourable impression wherever he goes. He is reliable and conscientious in his work but sometimes finds it difficult to save and never likes to deprive himself of any little luxury. He has numerous interests and is often very well read. He usually derives much pleasure from following the activities of the various members of his family.

PROSPECTS FOR THE GOAT IN 2006

The Year of the Rooster (9 February 2005 to 28 January 2006) will have been a reasonable one for the Goat, although with its emphasis on order and practicality, he will have needed to watch his capricious nature. The Rooster year is no time for wavering and indecision and as it draws to a close, the Goat should be careful not to let favourable opportunities slip by.

In his work there could be some especially good chances to further his experience. September and early October could be particularly favourable times.

The closing months of the Rooster year will also bring some excellent social opportunities and the Goat can look forward to some enjoyable times as well as to adding to his social circle. Social opportunities arising from his work or interests can lead to some important new friendships too.

The Goat will also value his home life, although the last quarter of the year could be a busy time. As far as possible the Goat should plan ahead as well as consult closely with others, otherwise certain weeks could become a frenzy of activity. Again, good organization will help.

With the closing months being a more expensive time, the Goat could also find it helpful to make early provision for his increased spending as well as any other looming expenses. Once more, planning ahead will be beneficial.

Generally, the closing months of the Rooster year will be a positive time for the Goat, but he will need to remain well-organized and act upon any opportunities that arise. On a personal level, he will value the support he receives as well as the good rapport he has with so many.

The Year of the Dog starts on 29 January and will be a mixed one for the Goat. During some parts of the year he could face some challenging situations. However, despite the variable aspects, the Dog year can teach the Goat a great deal as well as prepare him for some of the successes he will enjoy in following years. Throughout the year, however, he should try not to take certain situations too personally. Sometimes events happen that are outside his control and he should accept this rather than feel they are personal slights. If he can bear this in mind – and adopt a thicker skin – then he will find it will help. And tricky though some parts of the year may be, it will certainly not be without its positive aspects.

In the Goat's work this is a year for care and thoroughness and for concentrating on the areas he knows best. By remaining disciplined, he will not only accomplish a great deal but will also add to his experience and enhance his future prospects. And while he will face some problems and pressures, these will be good learning opportunities and will allow him to extend his skills. Some parts of the year *will* be demanding, but the Goat can emerge from them stronger, wiser and often with greater scope for the future.

Throughout the year the Goat should aim to work closely with others. Not only will this help when dealing with some of the pressures and problems that will arise, but he will also value the support and advice that those around him can give, especially more senior colleagues. If he is concerned or troubled by any problem or recent development, he would certainly find it helpful to talk matters over rather than keep his worries to himself.

Also, should any difference of opinion or tricky situation arise with a colleague, the Goat should try to resolve this as quickly and amicably as he can and certainly not allow it to overshadow what he does or spoil his good standing. Some incidents over the year may well be testing, but this is very much a time for knuckling down and concentrating on what needs to be done rather than being distracted by unproductive or unhelpful matters. Goats, do take note.

Those Goats who are particularly anxious to move on from their present position or are seeking work will fare best by looking for openings which draw on their experience rather than trying for something too different from what they have been doing. With competition for some positions being particularly keen, these Goats will find it helpful to thoroughly prepare for any interview. The more informed they are, the better their chances. They will also need to remain focused and persevering, but what they achieve now can prove very important in the longer term. April, June, October and November could see the best work opportunities.

An area which certainly requires care, however, is finance. During the Dog year, the Goat will need to keep a close watch on his spending and overall situation. If he does not already do so, keeping a set of accounts could help him to keep track of his position. This is a year for a careful and disciplined approach, and should the Goat take on any costly commitment, he does need to check the terms and implications thoroughly. This is a time for vigilance.

More positively aspected are the Goat's personal interests and despite the considerable demands on his time, it is important that he continues to develop these. The many Goats who enjoy creative pursuits will find them especially fulfilling and will often be encouraged by the feedback they receive and could find their work enjoying a certain recognition and success in the Dog year. The Goat will also find his interests a marvellous way to relax and sometimes to meet others as well. They really can do him a lot of good over the year.

The Goat will also value his domestic life and the willingness of others to help will mean a great deal to him. It is important, however, that the Goat is forthcoming with his concerns, and if he is tired or tense, he should let others know, so that they are aware and can possibly do more to help. Though a tricky year, this is also very much one for good communication and for spending time with loved ones.

The Goat also sets much store by his social life, but while the year will contain some happy and often lively occasions, the Goat does need to be his attentive self as well as watch his words, otherwise a careless comment or lack of attention could mar an occasion or even friendship.

However, provided the Goat remains aware of this, he can do much to prevent awkward or embarrassing situations from arising. Any Goats who would welcome a more fulfilling social life could find that joining an interest group, or perhaps giving time to a charitable cause will add a new dimension to their life. May, July, September and December will be the busiest and most rewarding months socially.

Overall, this is a year for treading carefully. While some of situations that arise will demand a lot of the Goat, they often *will* have hidden benefits, particularly as they will add to his experience, reveal new strengths and prepare the way for the success that awaits in the more favourable Pig year.

The Metal Goat

The Year of the Dog will be a demanding one for the Metal Goat, but while he will face pressures, by giving his best he will emerge from it with more self-confidence and much to his credit.

As far as his education is concerned, this will be an important year, especially as he will now move on to more advanced work and prepare for what could be significant exams. There will be times when he will feel under pressure but by working consistently and rising to the challenges, he can accomplish a great deal. Also, by tackling more demanding work, he will not only learn more, but often discover new strengths.

He will also be well supported by those around him and if at any time he feels concerned about any aspect of his education, he should be forthcoming rather than keep his worries to himself. By being open, he can find many problems being eased and sometimes removed altogether.

Over the year the Metal Goat may need to make decisions which will have a bearing on his future. These could include deciding which subjects to select for further study. When making these choices, it is important that the Metal Goat makes his preferences known rather than remains reliant on others to decide for him. This is a year when he must make his views heard.

There will be excellent chances for the Metal Goat to develop some of his other skills and interests over the year, particularly in sporting and recreational areas. In addition, some of the activities he gets involved with will lead to him meeting others and making some new friendships. Any Metal Goat who may feel lonely will find his interests a good way to meet those with whom he can get on well.

However, while the Metal Goat's social life is promising, a certain care is still needed. In some situations the Metal Goat could get carried away and be tempted to say or do things against his better judgement and these could lead to problems. The Dog year is not one for being foolhardy, taking risks or being indiscreet. Metal Goats, do take note. May, July to September and December will be the best and busiest months socially.

The Metal Goat will also need to be careful in money matters. Over the year he will often find himself tempted by certain things and while some of his purchases will bring him considerable pleasure, it would be wise to spend time considering his choices and avoiding more impulsive buys. Should he have any uncertainties, he would do well to seek the advice of others. This can be of considerable value.

As far as the Metal Goat's home life is concerned there will certainly be many occasions that he will enjoy. However, while a lot can go well, differences of opinion will sometimes arise and the Metal Goat may feel certain decisions are unfair. Although this may lead to frustration, he should not allow what can be relatively small issues to escalate or get out of proportion. Metal Goats, do take note. However, while there will be some awkward moments, as in any year, for the most part the Metal Goat will appreciate his home life.

For those Metal Goats born in 1931, again the Dog year will contain its tricky aspects. Sometimes plans may not be as easy or quick to put into practice as the Metal Goat would like. However, throughout the year he would do well to remember the saying 'A worry shared is a worry halved' and whenever something is worrying him, he would do well to talk it over with others.

One area which will need particular care is finance and if the Metal Goat is required to complete forms concerning benefits, tax or pensions, he does need to deal with these promptly and thoroughly. Should problems arise, he should seek advice.

However, while there is this need for care, the Dog year will not be without its happier times with family and friends and the Metal Goat's personal interests will often be the source of much pleasure too.

Although this year will demand a lot of both younger and more senior Metal Goats, it can be a significant and instructive one. For the younger Metal Goats in particular, what they learn now will prepare them for the progress they will make in following years.

TIP FOR THE YEAR
Be forthcoming. There are many who are able to help you and will be pleased to do so if asked. In addition, look to further your interests and special talents. What you learn now can be helpful in the future.

The Water Goat

The Water Goat is blessed with a highly perceptive nature and is often able to sense how others are feeling or how situations are developing. As the Dog year progresses, he would do well to pay attention to his instincts.

In his home life the Water Goat will need to be open and regularly talk over his plans and thoughts, and should encourage his loved ones to do the same. The better the communication – and the Water Goat *is* a good communicator – the better his family life will be. Failure to talk could leave problems lingering on in the background and allow unnecessary tensions to arise as well as prevent certain activities from going as well as they otherwise might. Openness in the Dog year is essential.

Also, with the Water Goat's ability to sense how others are feeling, if he thinks someone close to him is tense or worried, some gentle and understanding words may be appreciated more than he may realize.

With his practical and creative nature, he will also have some ideas that he will be keen to put into practice, including some home alterations that could make life more comfortable. Water Goats with gardens will enjoy experimenting with new stock and plants too. Whatever his plans, by talking them over with his loved ones and encouraging them to join in, the Water Goat will often be pleased with the results that follow.

In addition, spending time with loved ones and friends could lead to some enjoyable occasions and over the year the Water Goat should again be forward in suggesting ideas and activities. His input can lead to some particularly pleasant and rewarding times.

The Water Goat will also be pleased with how he is able to develop his own personal interests during the year. Those Water Goats who enjoy more creative pursuits will once again find their talents can bring them much joy.

With his outgoing nature the Water Goat also sets much store by his social life and while this will often go well, a certain care is necessary. Sometimes the Water Goat may feel that some he knows are not their normal selves and his ability to sense this and offer friendship and a listening ear will mean a great deal. However, in more delicate situations, the Water Goat *does* need to tread carefully and let friends open up and talk in their own time. A further reason for care is that sometimes the Water Goat may hear rumours or pick up only parts of a story. If concerned by something he hears or senses, he would do well to check the facts.

However, while there is this need for watchfulness, the Water Goat's social life can lead to many pleasant occasions. Those Water Goats who may be feeling lonely will find, with the Dog year's interest in humanitarian concerns, that giving time to a charitable cause or becoming more involved in the community can be rewarding. If interested, it really would be worth these Water Goats taking the initiative and finding out more. They will be glad they did so.

Another area which requires care, however, is finance and paperwork. When dealing with forms connected with finance, tax, pension or some form of benefit, the Water Goat should make sure he acts both properly and promptly. Although he may find such paperwork tiresome, to delay or not give it sufficient attention could be to his detriment. Should there be any parts he does not understand or decisions he does not agree with, it would be worth him seeking advice, either through a helpline or professional adviser. Bureaucratic matters do need to be handled with the utmost care in the Dog year.

Also, if the Water Goat makes any large purchase or enters into an agreement, possibly for work or for a task he wants carried out, he needs to check the terms and implications and make sure that everything is clear beforehand. This is not a year to be lax in such matters.

As far as work is concerned, many Water Goats will decide to remain where they are over the year. However, for those who would welcome a change or who are seeking work, events can move in curious ways and often lead to them securing a position which very much suits their talents. Those whose work involves an element of creativity or brings them into contact with others will find their skills leading to some particularly heartening results.

Although the year does contain its more awkward aspects, by being careful and taking note of his feelings and instincts, the Water Goat can do much to avoid or minimize some of the problems. More positively, by using his ideas and talents well and setting about his activities with the support and involvement of others, he can take great pleasure and satisfaction in what he achieves.

Be forthcoming and involve others in your plans. So much more can be accomplished with encouragement and support. Also spend time on activities you enjoy.

The Wood Goat

The Wood Goat is well-meaning and has a warm, friendly and sincere nature. Many do think well of him. However, despite his good intentions and the support he enjoys, this could be a mixed year for him. Progress will be difficult and there will be pressures and problems to cope with. But while the aspects may be variable, the Wood Goat can still emerge from the year with much to his credit.

As far as his work is concerned, the Wood Goat would do well to concentrate on the areas he knows best. With a sometimes increased workload or complex matters to deal with, this will allow him to use his expertise and, in the process, often earn much credit. Indeed, problems and challenges often give rise to opportunity and by working well now, the Wood Goat can find his efforts particularly well rewarded in the following Pig year.

Throughout the Dog year, however, the Wood Goat would do well to work closely with colleagues and show himself a good team member rather than be too independent. While relations with his colleagues will mostly go well, with the aspects as they are, the Wood Goat will still need to be careful. The year could see cases of petty jealousy, rumours or even a clash of personalities. While the Wood Goat may feel anxious about this, he should not get embroiled in unhelpful distractions that divert him from his work. In some cases, it would be better to address any troubling situation openly rather than let problems linger in the background. For a few Wood Goats, the Dog year will contain some uncomfortable moments, but by dealing with them as effectively as they can, they will often become stronger and more resilient as a result.

Many Wood Goats will decide to remain in their present position over the year. However, if there is a chance for the Wood Goat to take on further responsibilities, he should make the most of it. What he achieves now can be an important stepping-stone to greater advances in following years.

For those Wood Goats who are particularly anxious to change their work or are seeking work, again the Dog year can bring important developments. Although these Goats will often find themselves facing considerable competition, by making a special effort with their application form, preparing well for interviews and seeking out those who could offer advice, they will often find their initiative rewarded. April, June and the months from late September to November could see the best work opportunities.

Another important aspect of the year concerns the Wood Goat's own development and in addition to taking advantage of any courses and other training opportunities he may be offered through his work, he could find it helpful to consider studying certain subjects by himself. These can be work-related or recreational, but by improving his knowledge and skills, the Wood Goat will feel he is moving forward. And if he does not tend to get much exercise during the day, joining a keep-fit class or gym or following a fitness course could be both fun and beneficial.

With the variable aspects of the year the Wood Goat will, though, need to be careful when dealing with money matters. In particular he should make sure that essential policies are kept up to date and paperwork and documents are kept safely. He should also make allowance for his commitments and forthcoming expenses. This is very much a year for vigilance and good financial control. Should he have uncertainties or problems, he would do well to seek advice.

The Wood Goat's home life always means a great deal to him and this year will be no exception. During the year the Wood Goat will do much to help and encourage others and those both younger and more senior to him will often have excellent reason to value his advice and support. In addition, some Wood Goats could see a family member move due to education, work or marriage, and here the Wood Goat's encouragement will be especially valued.

However, while a lot can go well, with the aspects as they are, problems and tensions could still loom. Pressure, tiredness and busy lifestyles could give rise to some irritability, or a lack of communication could result in misunderstandings. If the Wood Goat becomes aware of this, he would do well to talk to others and spend more time sharing interests and activities. Watchfulness and input into family life can make so much difference.

In his social life, too, this is a year for the Wood Goat to be on his mettle. If he does find himself in a difficult or fraught situation or involved in a disagreement with a friend, he will need to be careful this does not escalate and spoil an otherwise good friendship. However, his social life will generally go well and through his work and interests he takes up or is already involved with he could find his social circle widening. May, July, September and December will be pleasing and active months socially.

Although the Dog year may have its pressures and awkward moments, by dealing with these as best he can, the Wood Goat will learn much from his experiences and his accomplishments will prepare the way for the encouraging progress that he is set to make next year.

TIP FOR THE YEAR
Use any chances to develop your work skills and interests. Also, keep your lifestyle in balance and set time aside for recreational pursuits.

The Fire Goat

This will be a demanding year for the Fire Goat and he will need to be clear in his aims and stay well organized, otherwise he could find he is spreading his energies too widely and not accomplishing as much as he would like.

In view of the prevailing trends, as the Dog year starts the Fire Goat would do well to give some careful thought to his plans for the year. These may concern his accommodation, activities and interests or work objectives, but whatever his ideas, by having some firm thoughts in mind, the Fire Goat will have something specific to aim for and can accomplish more as a result.

Also, throughout the year, the Fire Goat would find it helpful to be open rather than keep his thoughts and concerns to himself. That way others will be better able to support and advise and, in the case of problems, understand too.

As far as the Fire Goat's home life is concerned, this will often be a busy year, particularly in view of some of the projects and improvements he will be keen to carry out. If he discusses and tackles these with his loved ones, however, everyone involved will be pleased with how the plans take shape. Also, the Fire Goat should make sure that some time is set aside for simply spending together rather than the home being a continual whirl of activity.

It is also possible that both younger and more senior family members will have some important matters to deal with over the year and the support and advice the Fire Goat is able to give will be of value. However if he has any reservations about the actions or plans of those around him, he should let his views be known. It is better to be frank and to alert others to possible pitfalls than to say nothing for the sake of peace. And those concerned will not only value his honesty but also benefit from what he says.

The Fire Goat also needs to make sure his social life does not suffer due to the many demands on his time. Throughout the year he would do well to keep in regular contact with his friends and go to any events that appeal to him. Fire Goats who would welcome more companionship, could find that a new interest could turn out to be an excellent way to get to know others. Positive action on their part could bring them considerable pleasure.

The Fire Goat would also do well to give some thought to his well-being over the year and ensure that he takes sufficient exercise as well as eats a balanced diet. To remain on good form he does need to look after himself. Also, he should try to go away for a holiday at some time, as a break can do him a lot of good.

As far as the Fire Goat's work is concerned, a lot will be expected of him and in addition to an often heavy workload he could have some complex matters to deal with. However, while some of the year will be challenging, it will give the Fire Goat the chance to further his skills and to think more about the direction he would like his career to take. What he accomplishes and learns now will pave the way to some often significant developments in following years.

Although the Dog year is not one for major advances and many Fire Goats will decide to remain with their existing employer, there will be chances for the Fire Goat to extend his role, often by taking on or transferring to other responsibilities. By making the most of any opportunities to add to his skills, he can open up important possibilities for the future.

Those Fire Goats who are seeking work or are particularly anxious to change their position will need to remain persistent. Sometimes there will be considerable competition and opportunities may be limited, but with determination, many will find an opening which will provide an excellent platform for future development. Despite its challenging nature, the Dog year can leave a significant legacy. With aspects as they are, though, it is a case of making the most of opportunities as they arise. April, June and the period from late September to November will offer the most encouraging prospects.

In money matters this is very much a year for control and if at any time the Fire Goat has questions or uncertainties over any matter it is important that he checks the details, including any obligations he may be taking on, as well as seeks appropriate advice. This is *not* a year for taking risks, making assumptions or trusting his luck too far. Fire Goats, take note, and where financial matters are concerned, do be thorough.

Although the aspects may be mixed, provided the Fire Goat remains careful, manages his time well and liaises closely with others, he can do much to avoid or minimize some of the problem areas. The Dog year may not be the best of years for him, but the experience he gains will certainly prepare him for the important developments that await in the more favourable Pig year.

TIP FOR THE YEAR
Do set time aside for recreational pursuits. With the demands of the year, it is important that you have some respite from the activity as well as appreciate those who are dear to you and enjoy the fruits you work so hard for. Also, try to go away for a holiday over the year, as it can do you a lot of good.

The Earth Goat
There is a Chinese proverb which reminds us, 'Taste bitter before sweet and enjoy years of good fortune.' In 2006 it will be a case of tasting some of the bitter for the Earth Goat, but in its wake, *tremendous good can come.* This will be a demanding year for the Earth Goat, but by rising to the challenges, he will be preparing himself for the success he is soon to enjoy.

During the year the Earth Goat's workload and the pressures he is under will sometimes be great and, being conscientious, he will often worry about his situation and the expectations placed upon him. However, by concentrating on his duties and using his time and skills well, he will accomplish a great deal and in the process will often have the chance to extend his role in some way, go on courses or discover particular strengths that he would like to take further. While the year may be demanding, it will also be instructive, both in terms of providing experience and indicating possibilities to consider later on.

As he sets about his duties, the Earth Goat would do well to work closely with his colleagues. Not only will this help when dealing with certain pressures and problems, but he may also benefit from the advice and encouragement given by a more senior colleague. The Earth Goat would do well to listen closely to any suggestions. He should also make the most of any chances to build up his circle of contacts. This can help his situation and some of those he meets can become good friends.

However, while his relations with his colleagues will mostly be positive and helpful, with the aspects as they are, the Earth Goat does need to be wary about becoming embroiled in unhelpful situations or affected by the possible pettiness of other people. Fortunately, his perceptive nature and personal skills will help him deal well with any tricky moments, but this is something that he will need to watch out for during the year.

Although many Earth Goats will remain with their existing employer over the year, for those anxious to move to another position or seeking work, the Dog year can bring some significant developments. Those who may have been seeking work for some time or feeling disillusioned with what they are currently doing could benefit from retraining courses or advice from government or employment agencies. Their quest will not be easy, but by widening the scope of what they are prepared to consider and remaining persistent, many will secure a position which can set their career off on a more rewarding route. The events of 2006 can be far-reaching. April, June, October and November could see the best work opportunities.

The Earth Goat will need to be careful, however, in financial matters. With his many expenses and obligations, as well as possible home improvements, he will need to manage his situation well. Also, when entering into any new agreement or commitment, he needs to check the terms carefully and resolve any concerns before proceeding. Where finance is concerned, he will need to be both cautious and thorough.

As far as his relations with others are concerned, this will be an important year. For those Earth Goats with a partner there will often be plans and interests to share and these can make this a pleasing and rewarding year. Those Earth Goats who are parents or who become parents during the year will also enjoy watching their children develop. However, it is important that the Earth Goat is prepared to talk over any concerns, pressures or anxieties he may have. Earth Goats, do take note.

The Earth Goat will also value some of the excellent friendships he has and will particularly appreciate being able to share any matters on his mind. While he will often have much to do, he will find his social life a good way for him to relax and unwind. Those Earth Goats who may have let their social life lapse recently or have had some personal difficulties will find that becoming involved in new interests can lead to quite a transformation in their situation. For some, an important friendship or romance can be born. For socializing, May, July, September and December are particularly favourable months.

Overall, the Year of the Dog will not be the easiest of years for the Earth Goat. There will be pressures and sometimes problems to overcome, but by being careful and willing to learn as well as seeking the support and advice of others, he can learn a great deal. This is very much a time for laying the foundations and getting the experience necessary for the substantial improvement in fortunes that lies ahead, particularly in the following Pig year. In 2006 it *is* a case of experiencing the bitter before the sweet.

TIP FOR THE YEAR
Do draw on the support that those around you can give. Their assistance can make a considerable difference to what you are able to achieve this year.

FAMOUS GOATS

Pamela Anderson, W. H. Auden, Jane Austen, Anne Bancroft, Daniel Bedingfield, Cilla Black, Lord Byron, Leslie Caron, Coco Chanel, Mary Higgins Clark, Nat 'King' Cole, Robert de Niro, Catherine Deneuve, Charles Dickens, Ken Dodd, Sir Arthur Conan Doyle, Daphne du Maurier, Umberto Eco, Douglas Fairbanks, Dame Margot Fonteyn, Noel Gallagher, Bill Gates, Mel Gibson, Whoopi Goldberg, Mikhail Gorbachev, John Grisham, Larry Hagman, Oscar

Hammerstein, George Harrison, Sir Edmund Hillary, John Humphrys, Billy Idol, Julio Iglesias, Sir Mick Jagger, Norah Jones, Ulrika Jonsson, Nicole Kidman, Sir Ben Kingsley, John le Carré, Doris Lessing, Franz Liszt, John Major, Michelangelo, Joni Mitchell, Rupert Murdoch, Mussolini, Randy Newman, Des O'Connor, Sinead O'Connor, Michael Owen, Michael Palin, Eva Peron, Marcel Proust, Keith Richards, Julia Roberts, William Shatner, Gary Sinise, Jerry Springer, Lana Turner, Mark Twain, Rudolph Valentino, Vangelis, Barbara Walters, John Wayne, Fay Weldon, Bruce Willis.

2 FEBRUARY 1908 ⌣ 21 JANUARY 1909   *Earth Monkey*

20 FEBRUARY 1920 ⌣ 7 FEBRUARY 1921   *Metal Monkey*

6 FEBRUARY 1932 ⌣ 25 JANUARY 1933   *Water Monkey*

25 JANUARY 1944 ⌣ 12 FEBRUARY 1945   *Wood Monkey*

12 FEBRUARY 1956 ⌣ 30 JANUARY 1957   *Fire Monkey*

30 JANUARY 1968 ⌣ 16 FEBRUARY 1969   *Earth Monkey*

16 FEBRUARY 1980 ⌣ 4 FEBRUARY 1981   *Metal Monkey*

4 FEBRUARY 1992 ⌣ 22 JANUARY 1993   *Water Monkey*

22 JANUARY 2004 ⌣ 8 FEBRUARY 2005   *Wood Monkey*

THE
MONKEY

THE PERSONALITY OF
THE MONKEY

Anything you're good at contributes to happiness.
Bertrand Russell, a Monkey

The Monkey is born under the sign of fantasy. He is imaginative, inquisitive and loves to keep an eye on everything that is going on around him. He is never backward in offering advice or trying to sort out the problems of others. He likes to be helpful and his advice is invariably sensible and reliable.

The Monkey is intelligent, well read and always eager to learn. He has an extremely good memory and there are many Monkeys who have made particularly good linguists. The Monkey is also a convincing talker and enjoys taking part in discussions and debates. His friendly, self-assured manner can be very persuasive and he usually has little trouble in winning people round to his way of thinking. It is for this reason that the Monkey often excels in politics and public speaking. He is also particularly adept in PR work, teaching and any job which involves selling.

The Monkey can, however, be crafty, cunning and occasionally dishonest, and he will seize on any opportunity to make a quick gain or outsmart his opponents. He has so much charm and guile that people often don't realize what he is up to until it is too late. But despite his resourceful nature, the Monkey does run the risk of outsmarting even himself. He has so much confidence in his abilities that he rarely listens to advice or is prepared to accept help from anyone. He likes to help others but prefers to rely on his own judgement when dealing with his own affairs.

Another characteristic of the Monkey is that he is extremely good at solving problems and has a happy knack of extricating himself (and others) from the most hopeless of positions. He is the master of self-preservation.

With so many diverse talents the Monkey is able to make considerable sums of money, but he does like to enjoy life and will think nothing of spending his money on some exotic holiday or luxury which he has had his eye on. He can, however, become very envious if someone else has what he wants.

The Monkey is an original thinker and despite his love of company, he cherishes his independence. He has to have the freedom to act as he wants and any Monkey who feels hemmed in or bound by too many restrictions can soon become unhappy. Likewise, if anything becomes too boring or monotonous, the Monkey soon loses interest and turns his attention to something else. He lacks persistence and this can often hamper his progress. He is also easily distracted, a tendency which all Monkeys should try to overcome. By concentrating on one thing at a time, the Monkey will almost certainly achieve more in the long run.

The Monkey is a good organizer and even though he may behave slightly erratically at times, he will invariably have some plan at the back of his mind. On the odd occasion when his plans do not work out, he is usually quite happy to shrug his shoulders and put it down to experience. He will rarely make the same mistake twice and throughout his life he will try his hand at many different things.

The Monkey likes to impress and is rarely without followers or admirers. Many are attracted by his good looks, his sense of humour, or simply because he instils so much confidence.

Monkeys usually marry young and for it to be a success their partner must allow them time to pursue their many interests and indulge their love of travel. The Monkey has to have variety in his life and is especially well suited to those born under the sociable and outgoing signs of the Rat, Dragon, Pig and Goat. The Ox, Rabbit, Snake and Dog will also be enchanted by the Monkey's resourceful and outgoing nature, but he is likely to exasperate the Rooster and Horse, and the Tiger will have little patience with his tricks. A relationship between two Monkeys will work well – they will understand each other and be able to assist each other in their various enterprises.

The female Monkey is intelligent, extremely observant and a shrewd judge of character. Her opinions are often highly valued and, having such a persuasive nature, she invariably gets her own way. She has many interests and involves herself in a wide variety of activities. She pays great attention to her appearance, is an elegant dresser and likes to take particular care over her hair. She can be a doting parent and will have many good and loyal friends.

Provided the Monkey can curb his desire to take part in everything that is going on around him and concentrate on one thing at a time, he can usually achieve what he wants in life. Should he suffer any disappointment, he is bound to bounce back. He is a survivor and his life is usually both colourful and eventful.

THE FIVE DIFFERENT TYPES OF MONKEY

In addition to the 12 signs of the Chinese zodiac there are five elements and these have a strengthening or moderating influence on the sign. The effects of the five elements on the Monkey are described below, together with the years in which the elements were exercising their influence. Therefore those Monkeys born in 1920 and 1980 are Metal Monkeys, those born in 1932 and 1992 are Water Monkeys, and so on.

Metal Monkey: 1920, 1980

The Metal Monkey is very strong-willed. He sets about everything he does with a dogged determination and often prefers to work independently rather than with others. He is ambitious, wise and confident, and is certainly not afraid of hard work. He is very astute in financial matters and usually chooses his investments well. Despite his somewhat independent nature, he enjoys attending parties and social occasions and is particularly warm and caring towards his loved ones.

Water Monkey: 1932, 1992

The Water Monkey is versatile, determined and perceptive. He also has more discipline than some of the other Monkeys and is prepared to work towards a certain goal rather than be distracted by something else. He is not always open about his true intentions and when questioned can be particularly evasive. He can be sensitive to criticism but also very persuasive and usually has little trouble in getting others to fall in with his plans. He has a very good understanding of human nature and relates well to others.

Wood Monkey: 1944, 2004

This Monkey is efficient, methodical and extremely conscientious. He is also highly imaginative and is always trying to capitalize on new ideas or learn new skills. Occasionally his enthusiasm can get the better of him and he can get very agitated when things do not quite work out as he had hoped. He does, however, have a very adventurous streak and is not afraid of taking risks. He also loves travel. He is usually held in great esteem by his friends and colleagues.

Fire Monkey: 1956

The Fire Monkey is intelligent, full of vitality and has no trouble in commanding the respect of others. He is imaginative and has wide interests, although sometimes these can distract him from more useful and profitable work. He is very competitive and always likes to be involved in everything that is going on. He can be stubborn if he does not get his own way and he sometimes tries to indoctrinate those who are less strong-willed than himself. He is a lively character, attractive to others and most loyal to his partner.

Earth Monkey: 1908, 1968

The Earth Monkey tends to be studious and well read, and can become quite distinguished in his chosen line of work. He is less outgoing than some of the other types of Monkey and prefers quieter and more solid pursuits. He has high principles, a very caring nature and can be most generous to those less fortunate than himself. He is usually successful in handling financial matters and can become very wealthy in old age. He has a calming influence on those around him and is respected and well liked. He is, however, especially careful about whom he lets into his confidence.

PROSPECTS FOR THE MONKEY IN 2006

The Year of the Rooster (9 February 2005 to 28 January 2006) will have been a generally encouraging one for the Monkey, although as it draws to a close he will need keep his wits about him. As he will have discovered, this is a year for hard work and commitment, and should he become half-hearted or complacent, problems could loom. The closing months will require both effort *and* care.

In his work the Monkey's prospects are promising, but he will need to work hard and use his skills well. If he does, however, he may well find his efforts leading to other responsibilities as well as an increase in remuneration. Good work and application will be rewarded, with September and October containing some interesting opportunities.

The closing months of the year will, though, be an expensive time and the Monkey's outgoings will be considerable. In view of this it would be worth him making early provision for any increased spending and spreading out his purchases. This is a time when careful planning will help.

As the year draws to a close the Monkey will find himself in demand, with opportunities to go out and socialize as well as events to arrange with family and friends. With his outgoing nature, the Monkey will often revel in the activity. There could also be chances to travel.

The remaining months of the Rooster year will certainly be busy, but with good planning, the Monkey will find this an enjoyable (even if expensive) time. And the last quarter of the Rooster year could also contain some pleasing news.

The Year of the Dog starts on 29 January and while offering good prospects, it still requires a certain care. The Monkey should be particularly wary of taking risks or acting in haste. The Dog year can easily trip up the unwary and the Monkey does need to remain on his guard.

In his work there will be some excellent opportunities for him to further his position. However, throughout the year, the Monkey does need to remain alert to all that is happening and keep himself informed of developments. With changes under consideration, colleagues moving on or new schemes and initiatives being introduced, he could have some chances to adapt his role in some way. Over the year his resourceful nature will serve him well.

With the aspects as they are, however, the Monkey should aim to work closely with his colleagues rather than be too independent. He will benefit not only from the support that others can give but also from colleagues who can help keep him informed of new developments, which is so important this year.

As a result of their experience and the developments of the year, many Monkeys will be able to make good progress in their present place of work. For those who are eager to move elsewhere or are seeking work, the Dog year will also contain some fine opportunities. Rather than be too narrow in what they are prepared to consider, these Monkeys would do well to look at different types of work and other ways of using their skills. With persistence and their usual keenness, many will be successful in securing a position which can set their career off in an important and sometimes new direction. March, April, October and November could see some good work developments.

However, while his work prospects are promising, the Monkey will need to be careful when dealing with money matters. If he enters into any contractual agreement or conducts a large transaction, it is important that he checks the details and, if appropriate, obtains professional advice. The more thorough he is, the less likely it is that mistakes or misunderstandings will arise. He should also be careful if he is considering any risky speculation or lending any money. This is *not* a year for financial risks or for the Monkey to try his luck too far.

While there is this need for care, the Monkey can still use his money well. His interests and recreational pursuits can bring particular pleasure and he could also be pleased with certain acquisitions for his home. If he consults others about more sizeable purchases, he will be grateful for their suggestions. Again, care, attention and the avoidance of unnecessary rush can make a difference.

As far as the Monkey's domestic life is concerned, this will be a full and pleasing year with the Monkey again being grateful for the support and encouragement he receives from his loved ones. Throughout the year, he would do well to listen closely to any advice family members may give, even if it is cautionary. They do speak with his best interests at heart and will be keen to ensure that he makes the most of himself and takes the decisions that are right for him. This is a year when the Monkey can gain a great deal from the advice of others.

He will also derive much pleasure from his social life and, as a result of his work or interests, will find he is invited to an increasing number of social events. February, March, July and December could be especially active. However, while the Monkey will often thoroughly enjoy himself, he does need to be wary of getting too carried away and particularly of making remarks or acting in a way which could come to be misconstrued.

Despite this, the Dog year can still be special. A romance can become much more significant as the year progresses, while for the unattached, affairs of the heart are also well aspected, with a chance meeting often leading to new love. The Dog year may have its trickier aspects, but it does have its positive ones too!

One area which the Monkey should give some consideration to during the year is his own development. With his keen nature and desire to make the most of his talents, by putting some of his spare time to positive and constructive use, the Monkey will gain much personal satisfaction as a result.

Overall, during the Dog year the Monkey will certainly need keep his wits about him and remain alert to changing situations. By keeping himself informed, liaising closely with those around him and acting upon any opportunities that arise, he can make important progress. In addition, his domestic and social life will bring him considerable pleasure over the year, with the support, care and advice of his loved ones again being helpful as well as meaning a great deal to him.

The Metal Monkey

This will be an important although challenging year for the Metal Monkey. Not all his plans and ideas may work out the way he envisaged and in some cases he will have to look again at his situation. However, while the year will call for a certain flexibility, it will give the Metal Monkey the chance to add considerably to his experience and discover new strengths as well as set himself off on some important new paths. Indeed, problems and challenges often give rise to new opportunities, and so it will be for the Metal Monkey in 2006.

In his work this is very much a year for remaining aware of developments and being prepared to adapt to changing situations. If new procedures are introduced, by showing himself willing to learn, the Metal Monkey can do his prospects much good. Similarly, if he has a chance to extend his role in some way, including offering to do more at busy times or perhaps to train new colleagues, again he will find his efforts and commitment being noted. This is a year for putting himself forward and making the most of situations. Some of his duties could be demanding too, with problems to overcome or tight deadlines to meet, but by rising to the challenge, the Metal Monkey will discover more about his strengths, and he will be able to build on these in the future.

The Metal Monkey will also find his personal skills helpful. By maintaining good relations with his colleagues, he will not only benefit from their support but also be better informed of current developments.

Many Metal Monkeys will find their present duties will broaden out over the year and they will be well placed to take on a greater and often more specialist role. For those who are disillusioned with their present duties or seeking work, the Dog year can again bring important developments. By considering their options, making enquiries and following up any vacancies that interest them, many will be able to set their career off on a new and interesting path. The events of the Dog year may sometimes work out in surprising ways and not always as the Metal Monkey originally envisaged, but they can have considerable long-term benefit. Late February, March, April, October and November could see some interesting work opportunities.

Although many Metal Monkeys will enjoy an increase in income over the year, they will still need to manage their money carefully. If the Metal Monkey enters into any important agreement or loan it is important that he checks the small print. Similarly, if considering anything of a more speculative or risky nature, he would do well to study the claims and information given. Without such vigilance there is a risk that he could be misled or mistakes could be made. Metal Monkeys, do take note. This is a year for thoroughness and care.

Although the Metal Monkey will have a lot to do over the year, it is important he does not allow recreational pursuits to suffer as these can help balance his lifestyle. He will often find that they have other benefits too, including possibly getting him out of doors more, giving him additional exercise or bringing him into contact with others. Also, if he is intrigued by a new subject or feels a particular skill could be useful, he should follow it up. What is learned during the Dog year can give rise to interesting possibilities in the future.

The Metal Monkey will value the love and encouragement of those close to him over the year and for those Metal Monkeys with a partner, this can be a special time. There could be some good news to celebrate and the year will contain some happy moments. However, while so much can go well, a certain care is still needed. In view of the pressures on the Metal Monkey and those around him, there will be times when he will feel tired, tense and possibly irritable. When this occurs, he should be open about his feelings and encourage others to do the same. This way greater understanding can be shown, and tensions eased.

Also, if embarking on any domestic project, the Metal Monkey should allow plenty of time for it and should be wary of starting too many things at once. He may be enthusiastic (a typical Metal Monkey trait), but to avoid unnecessary pressure or too much disruption, it would be better for him to concentrate on one or just a few projects at a time. Again, good planning and communication will help.

Generally, though, this will be a positive and rewarding year as far as the Metal Monkey's domestic life is concerned.

This will also be an active year socially, with some of the changes that take place leading to some good social opportunities. Those Metal Monkeys who may have neglected their social life in recent years can forge some significant new friendships as well as enjoy an overall improvement in their situation. February, March, July and December 2006 and January 2007 could all see much social activity.

This will certainly be a full and active year for the Metal Monkey and while there will be pressures and a general need for care, by being adaptable, he can accomplish a great deal as well as learn a lot. And what he does now can pave the way to significant success in following years.

TIP FOR THE YEAR
Be flexible in outlook and prepared to make the most of changing situations. New possibilities can open up which, in time, can prove of great value. Also, do give time to those who are important to you.

The Water Monkey

This will be an important year for the Water Monkey and while a lot will go well, he will need to work hard to get the results he desires.

The Water Monkey born in 1992 will find a lot being asked of him. As he moves to more advanced work and studies new topics he will find himself with a great deal to learn. In addition, there will be course work to complete and important tests to prepare for and there will be times when the Water Monkey will be concerned about his workload and whether he is doing himself justice. However, by working consistently and being willing to learn, as well as not closing his mind to subjects he does not like, he will often be pleased with the progress he makes and *feels himself to be making*. Also, as he masters new skills and studies certain subjects in greater detail, he will discover more about his aptitudes and this will indicate areas it would be worth him concentrating on later. The Dog year will often ask a great deal of the Water Monkey, but he will learn a lot and add to his confidence.

During the year, should the Water Monkey find certain subjects difficult, he should not hold back from asking for help. Additional explanations really can help.

Away from his schoolwork, the Water Monkey will be pleased with how he is able to develop some of his interests. To help further these he should make the most of the opportunities available. Whether through after-school clubs or by joining a local group, he can certainly gain a great deal. Those Water Monkeys who may not have a particular interest or hobby at the moment would do well to find out more if they hear of one that appeals to them. Positive action could mark the start of an enjoyable new activity.

With his friendly and lively manner, the Water Monkey will enjoy his social life during the year and can look forward to a lot of fun with his close band of friends. In addition some out-of-school activities or interests can lead to a widening of his social circle. By getting to know others the Water Monkey will find many have similar concerns to his own, including possible difficulties over schoolwork, and knowing that he is not alone in his feelings can be reassuring. In 2006, the Water Monkey will certainly value his many friendships.

There will, however, be occasions when the Water Monkey will need to be on his guard. In some instances the mischief-making of others could hurt or mislead him and if he is concerned about anything he hears, he would do well to check it rather than accept it too readily. Also, if he does not wish to join in with the antics of others, he should stand firm and remain true to his principles. The Dog year can bring problems for the unwary and for those tempted to push their luck too far. Water Monkeys, take note.

This need for care also extends to money matters. Over the year the Water Monkey does need to make sure he is not misled over certain offers or claims he may hear about. If in doubt, it would be worth him seeking advice. Similarly, lending to others could lead to misunderstandings and problems. This is a year when the Water Monkey does need to be careful and alert. Also, as he will often want to do and buy a lot on often limited means, it would be worth him being disciplined in his spending.

Over the year the Water Monkey will appreciate the advice and support he is given by those close to him and when he is facing a decision, dilemma or problem, it would be worth him talking his situation over with those around him.

In addition, he will enjoy some of the domestic activities that take place and by being involved, he can often have a lot of fun as well as maintain the good rapport he has with others.

For those Water Monkeys born in 1932 this is also a year for being forthcoming over any matters that may be on their mind or any ideas they may have. That way there is more chance of receiving assistance as well as seeing many of their plans realized.

Also, as with all Monkeys during the Dog year, they will need to be vigilant when dealing with money matters and if entering into any large commitment, they would do well to obtain appropriate advice and make sure they are aware of *all* the implications involved.

More positively aspected, though, are personal interests and by spending time on pursuits they enjoy and taking up opportunities to meet other enthusiasts, the more senior Water Monkeys will find their interests – especially more creative ones – can bring many benefits too.

Overall, all Water Monkeys will certainly need to be aware of the trickier aspects of the year, but being careful, seeking advice when necessary and setting about their activities with willingness and commitment, they can accomplish a great deal. The Dog year will require care, but the long-term benefits can be considerable.

TIP FOR THE YEAR
Make the most of the opportunities available to you, particularly in developing your interests and skills. What is learned now can bring considerable satisfaction as well as provide a good base to build on.

The Wood Monkey

This will be a satisfying year for the Wood Monkey, although throughout he will need to set about his activities with care as well as remain mindful of others. This is not a year for risks or adopting too independent an approach.

One of the most positive aspects of the year concerns the Wood Monkey's interests and personal development. If there is a project that he has been considering this would be an excellent year to make a start, or if there is a skill he would like to learn or improve on, again he should follow this through. Over the year he can gain great pleasure from acting upon his ideas. Creative pursuits are particularly favoured.

The Wood Monkey would also do well to give some consideration to his well-being. If he does not tend to get much exercise or relies a lot on convenience foods he should seek advice on the best way to correct this. If he acts on what he is told and makes some changes, he can certainly benefit as a result. For some Wood Monkeys, enrolling on a keep-fit course with a friend could offer an additional incentive as well as make the activity more fun.

For those Wood Monkeys in work this will also be an excellent year to further their skills. As colleagues leave or new proposals and schemes are introduced, possibilities could open up for the Wood Monkey. However, he will still need to proceed carefully. Some new tasks and responsibilities could be challenging and the pressures considerable, and the Wood Monkey will need to remain well organized and focus on what is required. Work-wise, this can be a year of progress, but it is an exacting one too. It is a time for being involved, keeping informed *and* working well with others.

For those Wood Monkeys who are seeking work or considering changing the nature of their work, perhaps to a position involving less travel or fewer hours, the Dog year will also contain some interesting opportunities. Although persistence will be required, many Wood Monkeys will find that an unexpected turn of events can lead to a position which will give them the chance to develop new skills. While this may be initially daunting, by making the most of their opportunity, these Wood Monkeys will, in time, enjoy their new role. Again, the Dog year will often ask a great deal of the Wood Monkey, but by being willing to put in the effort, he will ultimately benefit. March, April, October and November could see the best work opportunities.

The Wood Monkey will need to be careful, however, when dealing with financial matters. If required to complete tax, benefit or other important forms, he does need to give these close and thorough attention. A mistake or delay could be to his detriment and if he has questions, it really would be worth him seeking advice rather making assumptions. Similarly, when entering into any major agreements, he should check the paperwork carefully as well as keep all the documentation safe. This is a year to be thorough and vigilant.

The Wood Monkey's domestic life will see much activity and with all the decisions that need making, it is important that there is good communication between family members. Should, at any time, any difference of opinion arise, a willingness to talk things over can often lead to a better understanding. However, mostly the Wood Monkey's domestic life will go smoothly and he will especially enjoy any activities that can be shared. In addition, any holidays or short breaks he can plan and take with loved ones can lead to some fine times away and do everyone good. However, to enjoy the year and the company of his loved ones, the key message for the Wood Monkey in the Dog year is to *communicate*.

The Wood Monkey's various interests and activities can also lead to some good social opportunities over the year. In addition to taking up invitations to go out and meet friends, if he sees any local events that appeal or has ideas about places to visit, he should follow these up. By acting upon his ideas, he can find the Dog year bringing some very pleasurable occasions. February, March, July and December could be active months socially and good months to meet others.

Overall, by being careful and consulting others, the Wood Monkey can do much to minimize some of the trickier aspects of the year. And by furthering his interests, he can make this a rewarding time.

TIP FOR THE YEAR
Try something new, whether learning a skill, taking up a different interest or trying out a certain activity. The change and challenge this can bring can often be enjoyable and satisfying.

The Fire Monkey

This year marks the Fire Monkey's fiftieth year and it will be an important one for him. As he enters a new decade of his life he will reflect back over all that he has done as well as consider his thoughts and hopes for the future. He will now be keen to act upon some of his ideas, feeling that if he does not make a start now some of what he is hoping for could elude him. As a result, he will make some important decisions over the year as well as see significant change. This is very much a year for action.

One area which the Fire Monkey will often consider changing will be his work. Many Fire Monkeys will feel they could be doing more or concerned about their limited prospects. While these Fire Monkeys may be anxious to make changes, the Dog year is not one for rash or impulsive actions. By remaining aware of the options available to them, however, when the right opportunity arises, these Fire Monkeys will feel ready to act and certain in their own mind that they are making the right decision. Career moves should not be rushed in 2006, but what the Fire Monkey decides on now can often give his career an exciting new impetus.

Those Fire Monkeys who do change their job over the year should also allow themselves the time to adjust to their new work pattern and familiarize themselves with their duties. For some, the changes in their role can be considerable and *will* take time to adjust to.

Other Fire Monkeys will, however, decide to remain where they are. While they will often be immersed in their duties, these Fire Monkeys do need to keep themselves informed about developments and possible changes, and be prepared to adapt if necessary. To do well this year it is very much a case of being aware and flexible. In addition, if problems arise, the Fire Monkey would do well to discuss these rather than keep them to himself. The input and support of others *can* make a difference.

For those Fire Monkeys seeking work this can be an important year too, and if they are eligible for retraining or can talk to advisers about the options available, they will often have new ideas to consider. While again they will need remain persistent, many will be successful in securing a position which suits their talents and personality well. The period from March to early May and October and November could see the best work opportunities.

As far as financial matters are concerned, this will be an expensive year for the Fire Monkey. In addition to his existing commitments, he will often have plans for his accommodation (with a few Fire Monkeys deciding to move altogether) as well as family expenses, including possibly helping younger relations in education. With the many demands on his resources, he will need to budget carefully. Also, when taking on new commitments, it is important that he checks the terms. This is not a year for risks or assumptions.

More positively, the Dog year will contain some particularly memorable occasions, including possibly a celebration to mark his fiftieth birthday, and he may also be able to carry out some of the plans he has often thought about. These could include visiting places he has long wanted to see, taking up invitations to visit family or friends living some distance away and spending time on interests and recreational pursuits that appeal to him. By acting upon his ideas, the Fire Monkey can enjoy many pleasurable times over the year.

He will also be encouraged by the support he receives from his loved ones and will value the close rapport he shares. If at any time he has any concerns and thoughts about his work situation, he should be prepared to discuss these so that his loved ones can better understand and support him. Although he may value a certain independence in some of his actions (a typical Monkey trait!) more openness on his part will certainly be to the benefit of all concerned.

The Fire Monkey will also enjoy his social life over the year, but with the aspects as they are, he should pay close attention to the views of his friends and be aware of any sensitivities, otherwise an inadvertent comment or moment of inattention could offend. This is a year in which the Fire Monkey will need to remain careful and tactful. February, March, July and December could see much social activity.

The Dog year certainly contains interesting prospects for the Fire Monkey and he should act upon his ideas and involve others in his plans. Although it will sometimes take time for some of these to get underway and for the results to filter through, with determination, good support and patience, this can be a satisfying and often significant year.

TIP FOR THE YEAR
Be patient but persevering. In time events and circumstances will start to move your way.

The Earth Monkey

The Earth Monkey has a very perceptive nature and is able to read situations well, and these abilities will serve him well during this interesting but sometimes challenging year.

In his work this will be a year of important develop-ments. Although many Earth Monkeys will decide to remain in their current position, they must not be resistant to change. If new procedures are introduced or they are asked to adapt or extend their role they should show will-ingness rather than hold back and possibly undermine both their position and prospects.

Also, while the Earth Monkey may feel competent in his role, he should make the most of any training opportuni-ties he may be offered or any chances to learn new duties. He will not only find this helpful now but it could also open up possibilities for later.

For those Earth Monkeys who are keen to change their work or are seeking a position, again the Dog year can give rise to significant developments. These Earth Monkeys *will*, however, need to remain persistent. Also, they should not be too narrow in outlook. By looking at a range of possibilities many will find themselves being offered some-thing which is a considerable change from what they have been doing but which has the potential for future develop-ment. The months from March to early May and October and November could see the best opportunities, but throughout the year persistence is the key.

Money matters need careful handling, however. With the Earth Monkey's many commitments, he will need to watch his spending. The more control he has, the better he will fare. Also, when entering into agreements or consid-ering major purchases, it is important that he checks the implications involved. This is very much a year for vigilance.

This need for care also extends to paperwork. The Earth Monkey needs to make sure important policies are kept up-to-date and are filed safely, otherwise problems could arise. Earth Monkeys, do take note and *do be thorough*.

More positively, the Earth Monkey will derive much satisfaction from his personal interests over the year and while he will have many demands on his time, he should make sure he sets some aside for his recreational pursuits. Not only will these offer the chance to relax and often have a pleasing social element too, but they can also bring an important balance to his lifestyle. Those Earth Monkeys who may have let their interests lapse really would do well to take up something new. Activities started in the Dog year can grow in significance.

The Earth Monkey will value his family life over the Dog year and again his perceptiveness and ability to relate so well to others will count for a great deal. With all his own commitments, though, and those around him often being equally busy, he will sometimes find family life becoming a fraught whirl of activity. By being aware of this and making sure time is set aside for talking and for helping out, he can do much to ease some of these tensions. Once again, his input and consideration can make a considerable difference. He would also do well to take a holiday with his loved ones over the year and the change will do everyone good.

The Earth Monkey's social life will be important too and his work and interests will often lead to opportunities to go out. Some firm friendships will be forged as a result. However, while the Earth Monkey will often enjoy himself and the good relations he has with so many, there is one word of warning that does need to be sounded. In view of the prevailing aspects, he does need to be wary of rumours, scandal mongering or even petty jealousy. His perceptiveness and ability to sense the truth will help, but this is a year to remain aware as well as be prepared to check anything he considers wrong or doubtful.

Although in general the Dog year does call for care, by being prepared to adapt and to make the most of the opportunities that arise the Earth Monkey will fare well and learn a great deal, and his accomplishments will prove significant in following years.

TIP FOR THE YEAR
Over the year your relations with others will be important to many of your activities. Do liaise closely with those around you and make the most of any chances to get to know others. New work contacts and friendships made as a result of shared interests can prove of great value both now and in the future.

FAMOUS MONKEYS

Gillian Anderson, Jennifer Aniston, Francesca Annis, Christina Aguilera, Michael Aspel, J. M. Barrie, Johnny Cash, Jacques Chirac, Joe Cocker, Colette, John Constable, David Copperfield, Patricia Cornwell, Joan Crawford, Leonardo da Vinci, Timothy Dalton, Bette Davis, Danny De Vito, Celine Dion, Michael Douglas, Mia Farrow, Carrie Fisher, F. Scott Fitzgerald, Ian Fleming, Dick Francis, Fiona Fullerton, Paul Gauguin, Jerry Hall, Tom Hanks, Martina Hingis, Harry Houdini, P. D. James, Pope John Paul II, Lyndon B. Johnson, Julius Caesar, Buster Keaton, Edward

Kennedy, Alicia Keys, Don King, Gladys Knight, Bob Marley, Walter Matthau, Kylie Minogue, V. S. Naipaul, Peter O'Toole, Anthony Perkins, Lisa Marie Presley, Lou Reed, Debbie Reynolds, Little Richard, Anne Robinson, Mary Robinson, Mickey Rooney, Diana Ross, Donald Rumsfeld, Boz Scaggs, Gerhard Schröder, Michael Schumacher, Tom Selleck, Omar Sharif, Wilbur Smith, Rod Stewart, Jacques Tati, Elizabeth Taylor, Dame Kiri Te Kanawa, Justin Timberlake, Harry Truman, Venus Williams.

22 JANUARY 1909 〜 9 FEBRUARY 1910   *Earth Rooster*

8 FEBRUARY 1921 〜 27 JANUARY 1922   *Metal Rooster*

26 JANUARY 1933 〜 13 FEBRUARY 1934   *Water Rooster*

13 FEBRUARY 1945 〜 1 FEBRUARY 1946   *Wood Rooster*

31 JANUARY 1957 〜 17 FEBRUARY 1958   *Fire Rooster*

17 FEBRUARY 1969 〜 5 FEBRUARY 1970   *Earth Rooster*

5 FEBRUARY 1981 〜 24 JANUARY 1982   *Metal Rooster*

23 JANUARY 1993 〜 9 FEBRUARY 1994   *Water Rooster*

9 FEBRUARY 2005 〜 28 JANUARY 2006   *Wood Rooster*

THE
ROOSTER

THE PERSONALITY OF
THE ROOSTER

If you create an act, you create a habit. If you create a
habit, you create a character. If you create a character, you
create destiny.

André Maurois, a Rooster

The Rooster is born under the sign of candour. He has a
flamboyant and colourful personality and is meticulous in
all that he does. He is an excellent organizer and wherever
possible likes to plan his various activities well in advance.

The Rooster is highly intelligent and usually very well
read. He has a good sense of humour and is an effective
and persuasive speaker. He loves discussion and enjoys
taking part in any sort of debate. He has no hesitation in
speaking his mind and is forthright in his views. He does,
however, lack tact and can easily damage his reputation or
cause offence by some thoughtless remark or action. He
has a very volatile nature and should always try to avoid
acting on the spur of the moment.

The Rooster is usually very dignified in his manner
and conducts himself with an air of confidence and
authority. He is adept at handling financial matters and
organizes his financial affairs with considerable skill. He
chooses his investments well and is capable of achieving
great wealth. Most Roosters save or use their money
wisely, but there are a few who are the reverse and are
notorious spendthrifts. Fortunately, the Rooster has great

earning capacity and is rarely without sufficient funds to tide himself over.

Another characteristic of the Rooster is that he invariably carries a notebook or scraps of paper around with him. He is constantly writing himself reminders or noting down important facts lest he forgets – the Rooster cannot abide inefficiency and conducts all his activities in an orderly, precise and methodical manner.

The Rooster is usually very ambitious, but can be unrealistic in some of what he hopes to achieve. He occasionally lets his imagination run away with him and while he does not like any interference from others, it would be in his own interests to listen to their views a little more often. He also does not like criticism, and if he feels anybody is doubting his judgement or prying too closely into his affairs, he is certain to let his feelings be known. He can also be rather self-centred and stubborn over relatively trivial matters, but to compensate for this he is reliable, honest and trustworthy, and this is appreciated by all who come into contact with him.

Roosters born between the hours of five and seven, both at dawn and sundown, tend to be the most extrovert of their sign, but all Roosters like to lead an active social life and enjoy attending parties and big functions. The Rooster usually has a wide circle of friends and is able to build up influential contacts with remarkable ease. He often belongs to several clubs and societies and involves himself in a variety of different activities. He is particularly interested in the environment, humanitarian affairs and anything affecting the welfare of others. He has a very caring nature and will do much to help those less fortunate than himself.

He also gets much pleasure from gardening and while he may not always spend as much time in the garden as he would like, his garden is invariably well kept and productive.

The Rooster is generally very distinguished in his appearance and if his job permits he will wear an official uniform with great pride and dignity. He is not averse to publicity and takes great delight in being the centre of attention. He often does well at PR work or any job which brings him into contact with the media. He also makes a very good teacher.

The female Rooster leads a varied and interesting life. She involves herself in many different activities and there are some who wonder how she can achieve so much. She often holds very strong views and, like her male counterpart, has no hesitation in speaking her mind or telling others how she thinks things should be done. She is supremely efficient and well organized and her home is usually very neat and tidy. She has good taste in clothes and usually wears smart but very practical outfits.

The Rooster usually has a large family and takes a particularly active interest in the education of his children. He is very loyal to his partner and will find that he is especially well suited to those born under the signs of the Snake, Horse, Ox and Dragon. Provided they do not interfere too much in the Rooster's various activities, the Rat, Tiger, Goat and Pig can also establish a good relationship with him, but two Roosters together are likely to squabble and irritate each other. The rather sensitive Rabbit will find the Rooster a bit too blunt for his liking, and the Rooster will quickly become exasperated by the ever-inquisitive and artful Monkey. He will also find it difficult to get on with the anxious Dog.

If the Rooster can overcome his volatile nature and exercise more tact, he will go far in life. He is capable and talented and will make a lasting – and usually favourable – impression almost everywhere he goes.

THE FIVE DIFFERENT TYPES OF ROOSTER

In addition to the 12 signs of the Chinese zodiac there are five elements and these have a strengthening or moderating influence on the sign. The effects of the five elements on the Rooster are described below, together with the years in which the elements were exercising their influence. Therefore those Roosters born in 1921 and 1981 are Metal Roosters, those born in 1933 and 1993 are Water Roosters, and so on.

Metal Rooster: 1921, 1981
The Metal Rooster is a hard and conscientious worker. He knows exactly what he wants in life and sets about everything in a positive and determined manner. He can at times appear abrasive and he would almost certainly do better if he were more willing to reach a compromise with others rather than hold so rigidly to his beliefs. He is very articulate and most astute when dealing with financial matters. He is loyal to his friends and often devotes much energy to working for the common good.

Water Rooster: 1933, 1993

This Rooster has a very persuasive manner and can easily gain the co-operation of others. He is intelligent, well read and enjoys taking part in discussions and debates. He has a seemingly inexhaustible amount of energy and is prepared to work long hours in order to secure what he wants. He can, however, waste a lot of valuable time worrying over minor and inconsequential details. He is approachable, has a good sense of humour and is highly regarded by others.

Wood Rooster: 1945, 2005

The Wood Rooster is honest, reliable and often sets himself high standards. He is ambitious, but he is also more prepared to work in a team than some of the other types of Rooster. He usually succeeds in life but does have a tendency to get caught up in bureaucratic matters and attempt too many things at the same time. He has wide interests, likes to travel and is very caring and considerate towards his family and friends.

Fire Rooster: 1957

This Rooster is extremely strong-willed. He has many leadership qualities, is an excellent organizer and is most efficient in his work. Through sheer force of character he often secures his objectives, but he does have a tendency to be very forthright and not always consider the feelings of others. If he can learn to be more tactful he can often succeed beyond his wildest dreams.

Earth Rooster: 1909, 1969

This Rooster has a deep and penetrating mind. He is efficient, perceptive and particularly astute in business and financial matters. He is also persistent and once he has set himself an objective, he will rarely allow himself to be deflected from achieving his aim. He works hard and is held in great esteem by his friends and colleagues. He usually enjoys the arts and takes a keen interest in the activities of the various members of his family.

PROSPECTS FOR THE ROOSTER IN 2006

The Year of the Rooster (9 February 2005 to 28 January 2006) is always a significant one for those born under the Rooster sign and in what remains of their year, they can accomplish a great deal.

In his work the Rooster can make positive headway. August and November could see some good possibilities. This is also an excellent time to put forward any work-related ideas.

The closing months will, though, be an expensive time and, with strong possibilities of travel and an often active social life, the Rooster does need to manage his money carefully. Good budgeting and planning could help.

The Rooster will also find himself in demand on a personal level at this time. In his domestic life he will play a key role in organizing activities as well as in assisting loved ones. While often busy, his home life will contain many rewarding occasions as well as chances to meet up with relations he does not often get to see.

The closing months of the year could also bring many social opportunities and for the unattached it can be an active and often exciting time.

One of the key features of the Rooster's personality is that he likes to plan ahead and set about his activities in a careful and orderly way. However, in the Dog year, he will need to show flexibility. The Dog year, which begins on 29 January, can be a reasonable one for the Rooster, but it does call for care and watchfulness.

In his work the Rooster would do well to regard this more as a year to add to his experience than to make major advances. For the many Roosters who have changed their duties over the last year, this year will give them the chance to immerse themselves in their new role and familiarize themselves with different aspects of their work. By being willing to learn, they will acquire useful skills.

The Rooster should also make the most of any chances he has to meet colleagues. With his good personal skills, he will often be able to impress as well as building up some useful contacts.

However, while the Dog year will give the Rooster excellent chances to add to his skills and consolidate his position, it also requires a certain care. There will be times during the year when he could have a particularly heavy workload and complex matters to deal with. And when the pressures are great, the Rooster needs to be careful that his high standards do not slip. Although usually so meticulous, he could find that an oversight could cause problems and possibly rebound on him later. Roosters, take note and *do* be your thorough and vigilant selves.

Roosters who are anxious to change their position or are seeking work would also do well to show some flexibility. With sometimes fierce competition, these Roosters would do well to widen the range of positions they are prepared to consider. By making the most of advice and chances available, many will be given an important opportunity. This is, though, a year when the Rooster will need to make the most of situations *as they are*. March, June, September and October could see some interesting career developments.

The Dog year can also be an expensive one for the Rooster and he would do well to budget carefully. He should also be wary of rushing into expensive purchases or agreements. More time spent comparing his options as well as waiting for favourable buying opportunities could save him considerable outlay. It would also benefit him to study the terms of any new agreement carefully. Without vigilance, problems could arise.

A more positive area concerns the way in which the Rooster will be able to develop his personal interests over the year. If there is a skill he feels it could be helpful to acquire or a recreational pursuit that particularly intrigues him, he should find out more. His actions could have a surprising and pleasing outcome.

Travel is also favourably aspected and the Rooster should aim to go away at some time during the year. A holiday will do him good. Some Roosters will also find their travelling can have a great social element.

The Rooster invariably plays a central role in his home life and this year will be no exception. His ability to keep tabs on everything will certainly be appreciated. In addition, his skills at relating and empathizing will be important and his honest opinions greatly valued. If he himself has any matters concerning him, he should be prepared to seek advice. Good communication will be to the advantage of everyone.

Also, while the Rooster likes to be a great organizer, he would do well to show some flexibility over the year. If he intends to carry out any home improvements, he should allow plenty of time for these rather than set tight deadlines for their completion. The year will be busy enough without adding to the pressure by rushing jobs or being involved in too much at any one time.

With so much hectic activity, the Rooster should also aim to ensure some time is spent just enjoying various pursuits with his loved ones.

The Rooster's social life will also see considerable activity. With his fine conversational skills and outgoing personality, the Rooster will often find himself in demand. However, in some situations he should be careful not to be unguarded in his comments or act in a way he may later regret. The Dog year can be hard on those who lower their guard. However, provided the Rooster is mindful of this, from a social point of view this can be a full and pleasing year. April, June, July and November will be active months.

The Rooster will certainly see a lot of activity over the year and any knowledge and skills he acquires will serve him well both now and in the future. However, in all matters, the Rooster needs to be careful and to remain mindful of others. This is not a year for risks, for lowering his standards or for acting without consideration and the support of those around. Provided he remains aware of this, he will fare well and often reap a long-term benefit from what he does and achieves.

The Metal Rooster

The Metal Rooster possesses a keen and determined nature and acts with considerable firmness and resolve. He is certainly not one to hold back and, particularly over the last few years, will have accomplished a great deal. And although his achievements in the Dog year may not always meet his expectations, he will continue to make useful headway as well as gain invaluable experience. The key message for this year is to make the most of situations.

As far as his work is concerned, the Dog year will bring some marvellous learning opportunities. Metal Roosters who are relatively new in their position will find that by showing commitment and a willingness to master the different aspects of their work, their efforts will be recognized and often rewarded with the chance to progress to other duties. Also, when pressures arise, these too will be a good opportunity for the Metal Rooster to show his worth.

In addition all Metal Roosters, whether new in their role or more established, should make the most of any chances that come their way. These could include deputizing for colleagues, offering to do more at busy times or putting forward ideas, but by being active and willing to contribute, the Metal Rooster can again help his prospects. He would also do well to take advantage of any training opportunities. The long-term benefits of the Dog year can be considerable.

Although many Metal Roosters will remain with their present employer over the year and will often benefit from in-house opportunities, for those who feel their prospects could be bettered by moving elsewhere or who are seeking work, again events in the Dog year can have long-term significance. As many will find, though, their quest will not be easy. In some cases competition will be considerable and opportunities limited. However, this is when the Metal Rooster's fortitude and resourcefulness will prove so useful. When applying for a position, if he finds out more about the company and duties involved, he will find his extra knowledge can often tip the balance in his favour. Also, by being prepared to talk to those who might be able to help him, he could find himself being alerted to new possibilities. The Metal Rooster will need to work hard to make progress, but his tenacity *will* pay off. March, June and the period from September to early November could bring some important work developments.

Although the Metal Rooster can look forward to a rise in income over the year and may be able to supplement this through possible overtime or extra work, this is still a year to be careful in money matters. With his many outgoings, the Metal Rooster will need to keep a watchful eye on his situation. Should he have uncertainties about any financial matter, it is important that he checks his position thoroughly and, if necessary, seeks advice. This is not a year for risks or for paying insufficient attention to paperwork. Metal Roosters, take note.

The Dog year will, though, bring some good travel opportunities and whether going on holiday or taking up invitations to visit others, the Metal Rooster will enjoy the chance to see different areas and some often impressive sights. Some Roosters will be tempted by a travel offer that they see at the last minute and the spontaneity could lead to some memorable times. Travel-wise, this is a positive year.

This will also be a busy and often eventful year as far as the Metal Rooster's personal life is concerned. For those with a partner, there will be many plans to share. These may include home improvements as well as more personal interests. Many Metal Roosters will have splendid cause for a personal celebration over the year, with some seeing an addition to their family.

The Metal Rooster will also be grateful for the support of other family members, especially more senior relations. Whether seeking advice about important decisions or accepting offers of assistance, he will find the love and support of others can really make a difference.

The Dog year will also bring many social opportunities. In some cases these will be connected with the Metal Rooster's work and will be a good way for him to meet other colleagues. However, the Metal Rooster does need to be careful not to act in a way that he could later come to regret. Any personal lapse or indiscretion could bring problems. Metal Roosters, do take note. This warning apart, the Metal Rooster will often enjoy his social life. Any Metal Roosters who may be lonely, perhaps as a result of moving to a new area or some recent difficulty in their personal life, will find that by immersing themselves in new activities they will soon get to build up what can be a more fulfilling social circle. For some, romance will also beckon. Some Metal Roosters could also find their travels leading to new friendships. April, the months from June to mid-August and November could all be active socially.

The Metal Rooster can certainly fare well in the Dog year and by furthering his experience and skills, he will prepare the way for the progress he will make in following years. He will also be grateful for the support and help he is given. However, throughout the Dog year, he will need to be thorough and avoid risks. This is a year for care, for liaising well with others and for making the most of situations.

TIP FOR THE YEAR
As a Metal Rooster you possess a keen and ambitious nature, but in order to realize your aims, you do need to build up your experience. What you achieve during the Dog year will often have considerable long-term value.

The Water Rooster

Attitude is going to be a key factor in how the Water Rooster fares this year. He will find a lot being asked of him, but provided he is prepared to give his best and make the most of his situation, then he will learn a great deal and emerge from the year with a lot to his credit. If, however, he remains inflexible and is unwilling to adapt, then problems could loom. This is very much a year for being adaptable and *making the most of current situations.*

For those Water Roosters born in 1993 this will be an important year. In their schoolwork they will have a lot to learn and while the Water Rooster will have his favourite subject areas, it is important that he does not ignore those he finds more challenging. By being prepared to put in the effort he *will* make headway. He will also find those around him willing to help and, if he feels he needs advice or is uncertain over any matter, he should ask. Again, attitude is key. With a willing approach, the young Water Rooster can do well and lay firm foundations for some of the more advanced work he will have in following years.

The Water Rooster should also make the most of the facilities available to him and if there is an after-school club or activity that appeals or a skill he wants to develop, he should follow this up. Again this is a year for being willing and being prepared to try.

The young Water Rooster will also be in demand on a personal level and will enjoy the company of his close circle of friends as well as get to know others as he becomes involved in different activities. His social life will often be fun and rewarding. However, the Water Rooster should not allow himself to be misled by rumours or dubious pieces of information. If at any time he is doubtful over what he has heard, it would be worth checking.

Another area which requires care is sport or other physical activities. Here the Water Rooster does need to listen closely to instructions. To ignore these could result in a strain or mishap. This is not a year for foolhardiness or paying insufficient attention. Water Roosters, do take note.

Those Water Roosters born in 1933 will also find this is a year for remaining mindful of others. Although the more senior Water Rooster may be keen to set about certain plans and activities, it is important that he talks these over with others and listens closely to their advice. They could be aware of pitfalls he may not have foreseen. In the Dog year discussion can really make a difference to how the Water Rooster fares.

Also, in setting about his activities the more senior Water Rooster should allow plenty of time. Although he may be enthusiastic, delays can sometimes occur and he *will* need to show patience. In addition, if any of his plans involve more physical activities, whether in the home or garden, it is important that he follows the recommended procedures (especially if lifting) or asks for help if necessary. This is not a year to take risks with his well-being.

Another area which requires close attention is finance, particularly any forms and paperwork the Water Rooster may have to complete. Although he may regard some of these as unnecessary or too detailed, to delay a return or provide insufficient details could be to his disadvantage as well as lead to a lengthier and sometimes more costly correspondence. Should the Water Rooster have questions or concerns about any bureaucratic matter, he should seek advice rather than take risks or make assumptions. This is very much a year for vigilance and thoroughness. Also, if considering any large and expensive purchase, he would do well to seek the opinion of loved ones as well as consider all the implications involved. Again, too much haste could lead to mistakes.

However, while it requires patience and care, the Dog year also has some particularly positive features. One of these is travel and the Water Rooster should make the most of his opportunities to go away as he will enjoy the change of scene and socializing that his travels will so often bring.

His social life too is well aspected and he will again enjoy meeting up with his friends. Local activities, societies or even some charitable work will also be good ways for him to meet others. For those Water Roosters who would welcome a more active social life, this is a year for becoming more involved in any activities that appeal.

The Water Rooster can also look forward to some fine family occasions over the year and for some the progress of a younger relation will be the source of much joy.

Although the Water Rooster will need to be careful over the year, provided he is prepared to make the most of situations and is flexible in outlook, then he can accomplish a great deal. He will often benefit from the assistance he receives and with a willing attitude, he can make this a positive and personally satisfying year.

TIP FOR THE YEAR
Two tips! If anything is troubling you or you need help with any matter, do seek advice. Support *is* available. Also, spend time developing your personal interests. These can benefit you in a great many ways.

The Wood Rooster

This will be a generally rewarding year for the Wood Rooster, although to benefit he will need to proceed carefully and thoughtfully and also liaise well with others.

For those Wood Roosters in work this will be a year of important developments. As colleagues move on and new procedures and initiatives are introduced, there will be important decisions for the Wood Rooster to make. In some cases there will be the chance to move to a more specialist role, often one that he has been hankering after for some time. However, there will also be some Wood Roosters who will decide to make other changes, possibly moving to a position nearer to their home or one involving fewer hours. The Dog year will present the Wood Rooster with some important possibilities which can mean significant change.

In view of some of the decisions the Wood Rooster will need to take, he would do well to talk his options over. If he is uncertain of his rights or the implication of any decision, obtaining the relevant information can help him make the right choice. This is a year to be alert, aware *and* thorough.

Work-wise, the Dog year can certainly be a significant one, with the Wood Rooster's decisions helping to shape the next few years. March, June, September and October could see important developments, but throughout the Dog year, the Wood Rooster should act in a way that he feels is right for him.

For those Wood Roosters seeking work the Dog year can also bring some interesting opportunities and although these Wood Roosters will need to be flexible in what they are prepared to consider, many will be successful in securing an opening which will develop their talents.

Money matters will, though, need care. Although many Wood Roosters will receive something extra over the year, possibly a bonus payment, a gift or the fruition of a policy, this is not a year for risks or for proceeding on an ad hoc basis. If the Wood Rooster is able to manage his situation carefully and keep a watchful eye on his outgoings, he will find he is able to make better use of his resources and do far more as a result.

` He also needs to be careful in handling important paper-work. The Dog year can be unforgiving of mistakes and without sufficient attention, the Wood Rooster could find himself involved in some protracted correspondence. Again, this is a year to be thorough *and* vigilant.

The Dog year is, though, favourably aspected for travel and the Wood Rooster would do well to take up any chances to go away. His travels could be great fun.

Another positive area is the Wood Rooster's personal interests, especially the way he is able to develop these over the year. With his enquiring nature, if there is a new interest or subject that appeals to him, he should aim to find out more. He will also derive much satisfaction from some of the projects he decides to tackle over the year, even though some may take longer than anticipated. And with his liking for the outdoors, time spent in the garden can also bring much pleasure.

Although the Wood Rooster usually keeps himself active, many Wood Roosters will also decide to give more attention to their well-being over the year. For some this will be by improving their diet while others will decide to take more exercise and perhaps enrol on a fitness programme. By following medical guidance, the Wood Rooster will often be pleased with the benefits that result.

The Wood Rooster will also be grateful for the support of those around him and by talking to loved ones, he will not only gain encouragement and good advice, but may also find important wheels set in motion with regards to some of his ideas. He can also look forward to many fine occasions in his domestic life. Shared activities can bring particular pleasure.

The Dog year will also bring many social opportunities. In addition to regularly meeting up with his friends, the

Wood Rooster could also get to know others while travelling, at a local group or society he belongs to (or joins) or through changes in his work and some of those he meets will, in time, become firm friends. April, June, July, November and December could all see much social activity.

Overall, although the Dog year does call for care, by remaining aware, acting on opportunities and ideas and drawing on the support and advice of others, the Wood Rooster can fare well and enjoy himself.

TIP FOR THE YEAR
Aim to further your interests over the year and, if possible, meet other enthusiasts. Also, if any complex or worrying matter arises, do draw on the advice of those with experience.

The Fire Rooster

This will be an important year for the Fire Rooster and although not all his activities may go smoothly, it will often have long-term significance. In particular certain events will cause many Fire Roosters to look closely at their present situation and consider their future. As a result, many will make decisions which can have long-term implications. In many ways the Dog year will be one for taking stock, planning and preparing the way ahead.

In his work the Fire Rooster will need to proceed carefully. As he will find, pressures and problems will arise which will test his skills as well as require a lot of effort to deal with. As a result, the Fire Rooster will need to remain focused on his duties and be his thorough and vigilant self.

In the Dog year inattention or too much rush can lead to mistakes and this is something the Fire Rooster will need to watch. Also, although he may like to be involved in a great many things, he should be wary of spreading his attention too widely. This is very much a year for prioritizing and focusing on his specific responsibilities.

The events of the year will often cause the Fire Rooster to consider how he would like his future to develop. Some Fire Roosters may be keen to move to more senior positions in their current organization while others will consider other ideas. Whatever his plans, the Fire Rooster would find it helpful to talk to close contacts and colleagues. Also, if he feels it could be helpful to improve his skills in certain areas, he should look at ways in which he can do this. The decisions he takes now can have an important bearing on his future.

Those Fire Roosters seeking work will also find this a significant year. Although their quest will require much determination, a position they are offered can turn out to be an important platform from which to progress. March, June and the period from September to early November could see some interesting developments.

The Fire Rooster will also benefit from developing his personal interests over the year. If there is an activity which he is keen to learn, a project he wants to tackle or a recreational pursuit that appeals, he should look to take this further. The activities and events of the Dog year can teach the Fire Rooster a great deal and often alert him to strengths and possibilities he can build on.

The Fire Rooster would also do well to give some consideration to his well-being over the year, especially if he does not tend to get much exercise or eat a particularly balanced diet. He may find additional walking, cycling, swimming or a discipline such as yoga or tai chi not only physically beneficial but also enjoyable.

The Fire Rooster will, though, need to be careful when dealing with money matters. This is a year to be thorough and meticulous. If entering into new agreements or conducting important transactions, he does need to study the small print and, if appropriate, obtain professional advice. Similarly, if tempted by something of a speculative nature, he should seek guidance. This is *not* a year for risks. He would also find it helpful to keep a close watch on his purse-strings.

The Fire Rooster also needs to keep his paperwork in order, including keeping receipts and guarantees safely as well as making sure important policies are kept up to date. His efficient Rooster nature will help, but this *is* a year for care.

Throughout, the Fire Rooster will, though, be grateful for the advice and support given by both family and friends. In his home life he will find that by being prepared to talk over any changes he may be considering, particularly regarding his work and his interests, he will benefit from a helpful and encouraging response.

He will also enjoy some of the household activities and projects he tackles with those around him. By pooling ideas and talents, everyone will be proud of what they are able to achieve. However, where practical projects are concerned, the Fire Rooster will need to allow plenty of time.

In view of the Fire Rooster's often busy lifestyle, he may decide to reduce his social commitments over the year.

However, his social life is an excellent way for him to relax and enjoy himself and can help to keep his lifestyle in balance. Fire Roosters, do bear this in mind. Also, any Fire Roosters who would welcome more companionship will find that an interest they decide to take up can turn out to be an excellent way to meet others. Again, the events of the Dog year can be far-reaching.

The Dog year will certainly be an active one for the Fire Rooster and throughout he will need to keep his wits about him. However, by proceeding carefully, being willing to share his thoughts and ideas with those around him and developing his skills, he can make this a year of great value. It may demand a lot of the Fire Rooster, but it can teach him a lot too and prepare the way for the exciting times that await in following years.

TIP FOR THE YEAR
Be thorough and determined. What you accomplish now, even if it is the result of some difficult moments, can prove highly significant in the near future.

The Earth Rooster

The Earth Rooster is a realist. When conditions are right and he is satisfied with his plans, he will proceed with fortitude and often much success. However, when he has reservations or feels conditions are not in his favour, he is prepared to hold back and be patient. The Dog year will be one of those years when he will do a fair amount of holding back. In 2006 he will sometimes find progress difficult and have some challenging situations to deal with.

However, while the year will be demanding at times, it will give the Earth Rooster an excellent chance to add to his experience, learn new skills and prepare for the future. This may not be an easy year, but its effects can be far-reaching.

In his work the Earth Rooster would do well to regard this as a year for consolidating his position and furthering his experience, particularly if he is relatively new in his position. In addition, all Earth Roosters, regardless of their position, should take advantage of any training opportunities. 'Diligence leads to riches', as the Chinese proverb states, and in the Dog year, this very much applies to the Earth Rooster's personal development.

Many Earth Roosters will decide to remain in their present position over the year, but for those eager to move or seeking work, the Dog year can bring some interesting opportunities. Their quest will not be easy, but by remaining persistent and widening the scope of what they are prepared to consider, many Earth Roosters will be offered what can turn out to be an excellent position. Although their new duties may be different from those they have done before, by learning the skills required, they can start an exciting new phase in their career. March, June, September and October will contain the most interesting work developments.

The work contacts the Earth Rooster is able to build up will also be important and in view of his future ambitions, he should make the most of his chances to meet others.

The Earth Rooster will, though, need to be careful in money matters and would do well to keep close control over his purse-strings. This is very much a year for vigilance.

Also, if he takes on any new financial obligations, he needs to check the details and get any questions answered before proceeding. This is very much a year for the Earth Rooster to be his thorough and cautious self.

A more positive area is travel and the Earth Rooster would do well to make provision for going away at some time over the year. It will often do him a lot of good.

The Earth Rooster will also take pleasure in his recreational interests. Those Earth Roosters who enjoy outdoor activities will find them a good way to take additional exercise and get away from everyday pressures. Those who are sedentary for much of the day or who do not tend to get much exercise should consider taking up some physical activity too. By obtaining medical guidance on the best way to proceed, these Earth Roosters could feel much better as a result. Also Earth Roosters may find a new activity or course they enrol on quickly turning into a key interest and often having a social element as well. Any time the Earth Rooster can give to his recreational activities and well-being over the year will certainly be worthwhile.

This will be a busy year as far as the Earth Rooster's domestic life is concerned and those dear to him will often seek out his views or ask for his assistance. However, in view of all he does around the home as well as his other commitments, it is important that the Earth Rooster does not shoulder too much on his own and makes sure that everyone does their fair share. Similarly, if there is any matter on his mind, he should seek advice. For family life to go well, good communication is important.

For those Earth Roosters who are alone and may be feeling dispirited, this is a year of interesting developments. The Earth Rooster's work, travelling or recreational activities can all help to bring him into contact with others, with some new and sometimes special friendships being made. April, June, July and November could be good times for meeting others.

The Year of the Dog will demand a lot of the Earth Rooster and his progress may not always meet his expectations. However, to offset this, the experience he gains, the difficulties he surmounts and the ways in which he develops himself and his interests *will* serve him well in following years. This is very much a year of preparation for the upturn in fortune that awaits in the future, particularly in the following Pig year.

TIP FOR THE YEAR
Do make the most of any chances to further your skills and talents. This is truly an excellent year for personal development.

FAMOUS ROOSTERS

Mohamed al Fayed, Dame Janet Baker, Natasha Bedingfield, Beyonce, Enid Blyton, Cate Blanchett, Sir Michael Caine, Enrico Caruso, Christopher Cazenove, Jean Chrétien, Eric Clapton, Joan Collins, Rita Coolidge, Craig David, Daniel Day Lewis, Minnie Driver, the Duke of Edinburgh, Gloria Estefan, Roger Federer, Bryan Ferry, Errol Flynn, Benjamin Franklin, Dawn French, Stephen Fry, Melanie Griffith, Deborah Harry, Goldie Hawn, Katherine Hepburn, Lleyton Hewitt, Catherine Zeta Jones,

Quincy Jones, Diane Keaton, Søren Kierkegaard, D. H. Lawrence, David Livingstone, Ken Livingstone, Jayne Mansfield, Steve Martin, James Mason, W. Somerset Maugham, Paul Merton, Bette Midler, Van Morrison, Willie Nelson, Kim Novak, Yoko Ono, Dolly Parton, Matthew Perry, Michelle Pfeiffer, Priscilla Presley, Mary Quant, Joan Rivers, Kelly Rowland, Jenny Seagrove, George Segal, Carly Simon, Britney Spears, Johann Strauss, Barbara Taylor Bradford, Verdi, Richard Wagner, Serena Williams, Renée Zellweger.

10 FEBRUARY 1910 〜 29 JANUARY 1911	*Metal Dog*
28 JANUARY 1922 〜 15 FEBRUARY 1923	*Water Dog*
14 FEBRUARY 1934 〜 3 FEBRUARY 1935	*Wood Dog*
2 FEBRUARY 1946 〜 21 JANUARY 1947	*Fire Dog*
18 FEBRUARY 1958 〜 7 FEBRUARY 1959	*Earth Dog*
6 FEBRUARY 1970 〜 26 JANUARY 1971	*Metal Dog*
25 JANUARY 1982 〜 12 FEBRUARY 1983	*Water Dog*
10 FEBRUARY 1994 〜 30 JANUARY 1995	*Wood Dog*
29 JANUARY 2006 〜 17 FEBRUARY 2007	*Fire Dog*

THE
DOG

THE PERSONALITY OF THE DOG

Each player must accept the cards life deals him. But once they are in hand, he alone must decide how to play the cards in order to win the game.

Voltaire, a Dog

The Dog is born under the signs of loyalty and anxiety. He usually holds very firm views and beliefs and is the champion of good causes. He hates any sort of injustice or unfair treatment and will do all in his power to help those less fortunate than himself. He has a strong sense of fair play and will be honourable and open in all his dealings.

The Dog is very direct and straightforward. He is never one to skirt round issues and speaks frankly and to the point. He can be stubborn, but he is more than prepared to listen to the views of others and will try to be as fair as possible in coming to his decisions. He will readily give advice where it is needed and will be the first to offer assistance when things go wrong.

The Dog instils confidence wherever he goes and there are many who admire him for his integrity and resolute manner. He is a very good judge of character and can often form an accurate impression of someone very shortly after meeting them. He is also very intuitive and can frequently sense how things are going to work out long in advance.

Despite his friendly and amiable manner, the Dog is not a big socializer. He dislikes having to attend large functions or parties and much prefers a quiet meal with friends or a chat by the fire. He is an excellent conversationalist and is often a marvellous raconteur of amusing stories and anecdotes.

The Dog is also quick-witted and his mind is always alert. He can keep calm in a crisis and although he does have a temper, his outbursts tend to be short-lived. He is loyal and trustworthy, but if he ever feels badly let down or rejected by someone, he will rarely forgive or forget.

The Dog usually has very set interests. He prefers to specialize and become an expert in a chosen area rather than dabble in a variety of different activities. He usually does well in jobs where he feels that he is being of service to others and is often suited to careers in the social services, the medical and legal professions and teaching. He does, however, need to feel motivated in his work. He has to have a sense of purpose and if ever this is lacking he can quite often drift through life without ever achieving very much. Once he has the motivation, however, very little can prevent him from securing his objective.

Another characteristic of the Dog is his tendency to worry and to view things rather pessimistically. Quite often his worries are totally unnecessary and are of his own making. Although it may be difficult, worrying is a habit which all Dogs should try to overcome.

The Dog is not materialistic or particularly bothered about accumulating great wealth. As long as he has the money necessary to support his family and to spend on the occasional luxury, he is more than happy. However, when he does have any spare money he tends to be rather a spendthrift and does not always put his money to its best use. He is also not a very good speculator and would be advised to get professional advice before entering into any major long-term investment.

The Dog will rarely be short of admirers, but he is not an easy person to live with. His moods are changeable and his standards high, but he will be loyal and protective to his partner and will do all in his power to provide a good and comfortable home. He can get on extremely well with those born under the signs of the Horse, Pig, Tiger and Monkey, and can also establish a sound and stable relationship with the Rat, Ox, Rabbit, Snake and another Dog, but will find the Dragon a bit too flamboyant for his liking. He will also find it difficult to understand the imaginative Goat and is likely to be highly irritated by the candid Rooster.

The female Dog is renowned for her beauty. She has a warm and caring nature, although until she knows someone well she can be both secretive and very guarded. She is highly intelligent and despite her calm and tranquil appearance she can be extremely ambitious. She enjoys sport and other outdoor activities and has a happy knack of finding bargains in the most unlikely of places. She can also get rather impatient when things do not work out as she would like.

The Dog usually has a very good way with children and can be a doting parent. He will rarely be happier than when he is helping someone or doing something that will benefit others. Providing he can cure himself of his tendency to worry, he will lead a very full and active life – and in that life he will make many friends and do a tremendous amount of good.

THE FIVE DIFFERENT TYPES OF DOG

In addition to the 12 signs of the Chinese zodiac there are five elements and these have a strengthening or moderating influence on the sign. The effects of the five elements on the Dog are described below, together with the years in which the elements were exercising their influence. Therefore those Dogs born in 1910 and 1970 are Metal Dogs, those born in 1922 and 1982 are Water Dogs, and so on.

Metal Dog: 1910, 1970

The Metal Dog is bold, confident and forthright and sets about everything he does in a resolute and determined manner. He has a great belief in his abilities and has no hesitation about speaking his mind or devoting himself to some just cause. He can be rather serious at times and can become anxious and irritable when things are not going according to plan. He tends to have very specific interests and it would certainly help him if he were to broaden his outlook and become more involved in group activities. He is extremely loyal and faithful to his friends.

Water Dog: 1922, 1982

The Water Dog has a very direct and outgoing personality. He is an excellent communicator and has little trouble in persuading others to fall in with his plans. He does, however, have a somewhat carefree nature and is not as disciplined or as thorough as he should be in certain matters. Neither does he keep as much control over his finances as he should, but he can be most generous to his family and friends and will make sure that they want for nothing. The Water Dog is usually very good with children and has a wide circle of friends.

Wood Dog: 1934, 1994

This Dog is a hard and conscientious worker and will usually make a favourable impression wherever he goes. He is less independent than some of the other types of Dog and prefers to work in a group rather than on his own. He is popular, has a good sense of humour and takes a keen interest in the activities of the various members of his family. He is often attracted to the finer things in life and can obtain much pleasure from collecting stamps, coins, pictures or antiques. He prefers to live in the country rather than the town.

Fire Dog: 1946, 2006

This Dog has a lively, outgoing personality and is able to establish friendships with remarkable ease. He is an honest and conscientious worker and likes to take an active part in all that is going on around him. He also likes to explore new ideas and providing he can get the necessary support and advice, he can often succeed where others have failed. He does, however, have a tendency to be stubborn.

Providing he can overcome this, he can often achieve considerable fame and fortune.

Earth Dog: 1958

The Earth Dog is very talented and astute. He is methodical and efficient and is capable of going far in his chosen profession. He tends to be rather quiet and reserved but has a very persuasive manner and usually secures his objectives without too much opposition. He is generous and kind and is always ready to lend a helping hand when it is needed. He is also held in very high esteem by his friends and colleagues and is usually most dignified in his appearance.

PROSPECTS FOR THE DOG IN 2006

The Year of the Rooster (9 February 2005 to 28 January 2006) will have been a variable one for the Dog and in the remaining months he will need to proceed with care. However, with the approach of his own year, his prospects are about to enjoy a major upturn and what he is able to do in the closing months of the Rooster year can often have a positive bearing on the year ahead.

In his work the Dog would do well to work closely with others and use any chances to get to know other colleagues and extend his experience. The more active he is, the more he can help his prospects. Effort and good work in the closing months of the year can pay sizeable dividends.

The Dog will also benefit from the support of those close to him and if he is concerned about any matter, talking to loved ones can be a real help. Planning activities together can also lead to some special occasions.

The Dog will, though, need to be careful in money matters at this time and should check the terms of any new agreement he enters into and watch his general level of spending. He should also be wary of anything potentially risky or of lending to others. Without vigilance, problems could easily arise. Dogs, do take note.

The Year of the Rooster may not have been the easiest for the Dog but his accomplishments and the experience he has gained can often be useful to him in the more favourable times that await in his own year.

The Year of the Dog begins on 29 January and holds excellent prospects for the Dog. This is *his* year and one for him to enjoy.

As the year starts the Dog would do well to regard this as a time for moving forward. As Virgil once wrote, 'Fortune favours the bold,' and this will certainly hold true for the Dog in his own year.

In his work his prospects are especially encouraging and he will find himself ideally placed to make headway. For some Dogs this will mean promotion with their current employer, but those who feel there are greater possibilities elsewhere can also be successful in advancing their career. Even if certain applications do not go their way, events in the Dog year can work in curious ways and a rejection could prove a blessing in disguise as a more suitable position becomes available.

The aspects are also favourable for those Dogs seeking work. Although some will have become disillusioned, with determination many will be successful in setting their career off on an exciting new path. March, April, September and October could see some interesting career developments.

All Dogs can also help their position by taking advantage of any opportunities to further their experience. Those Dogs who have been seeking work for some time or are considering a career change will find that refresher or retraining courses can open up some important possibilities. Positive action in his own year really will reward the Dog well.

The progress the Dog makes in his work will also lead to an increase in his income and some Dogs may be able to supplement this through extra work or an enterprising idea. The Dog's earning abilities will certainly be on good form over the year. As a result, many Dogs will decide to carry out some ideas they have for their home as well as take up more recreational pursuits or go travelling. The Dog could also find it helpful to spend time looking at his overall financial situation and if he is able to reduce any borrowings or set money aside for specific plans or a savings policy this too could be to his advantage.

Another rewarding aspect of the year is the way the Dog will be able to develop his interests. In addition, if he has any travel ideas, he should discuss these with those close to him. He will often find his ideas leading to some memorable times away. The second half of the year could see some particularly fine travel opportunities.

This will also be an active year as far as the Dog's home life is concerned. Many Dogs will decide to tackle some often substantial improvements to their home, with some even moving. Often the Dog will have had these ideas in mind for some time and will feel that now is the right time to go ahead. By carefully considering the options and getting a range of costs, the Dog will be pleased with what he is able to accomplish. However, while the aspects indicate a lot of practical activity, important decisions should not be rushed. Also, the Dog will find that certain projects will give rise to a considerable amount of disruption and he does need to allow for this.

Similarly, for those Dogs who decide to move, the whole process will be time-consuming, but with persistence, they will find their efforts well rewarded. In this respect, too, the Dog year will often mark the start of a new chapter.

The Dog will value the support of his loved ones over the year, but he does need be forthcoming and talk over his ideas and any concerns. That way others will be better able to advise as well as help him to realize certain aims. There will also be some family events that will mean much.

The Dog's social life is also well aspected. Over the course of the year he will get to meet many new people, with some becoming particularly good friends. For the unattached Dog, a chance meeting could be important. Romantically, the Dog year is splendidly aspected. For any Dogs who may have had some sadness or problems in their personal life, this is very much a year for a new start. February, March, July and August are especially good months for socializing and meeting others.

The Dog year does hold considerable potential for the Dog, but to benefit he does need to act. This is no year for reticence or holding back. It really is a time to draw a line under past disappointments and look to the future. So much is possible in 2006. For the determined Dog, his own year is one of the best.

The Metal Dog

The Metal Dog is blessed with an active and determined nature and over the year his personal qualities and considerable experience can serve him well. This is a year for progress and some pleasing achievements.

The aspects are especially promising as far as the Metal Dog's work is concerned and during the year he will have the chance to advance his position and enjoy some notable successes. In many cases he will find the experience and in-house knowledge he has built up will make him a strong candidate for promotion. By putting himself forward, he will often be successful. And with the aspects as they are, one advance could quickly lead on to another. This is very much a year for remaining alert and acting on the possibilities that can suddenly open up.

Those Metal Dogs who feel they can best further their career by moving to another employer should also actively follow up any openings that interest them. With persistence, many will be successful in securing a position which can be a useful stepping-stone in their professional life.

This also applies to those Metal Dogs seeking work. While some will have understandably become disillusioned in recent times, they should regard this as a year for fresh starts. If they are eligible for training or refresher courses, they would do well to make the most of these. Information and guidance from employment agencies and professional organizations can also alert them to new possibilities. By doing all they can to help their prospects, many of these Metal Dogs will be successful in their quest. March, April and the period from September to early November could see particularly interesting work developments, but overall this is very much a year for growth.

The progress the Metal Dog makes in his work will also have a positive bearing on his finances and most Metal Dogs will enjoy an increase in income over the year. Some will also be able to supplement this by additional work or an enterprising idea. However, the Metal Dog does still need to manage his finances well. With some Metal Dogs deciding to move or going ahead with major purchases for their home, accommodation costs will be high, and with existing commitments as well, the Metal Dog would do well to keep track of his outgoings and make early provision for some of his more expensive purchases. Financially, this can be an improved year, but it does require good management.

This will be a busy and meaningful year as far as the Metal Dog's home life is concerned. A lot of time will be spent on accommodation matters, especially by those who move. However, the Metal Dog and his loved ones will feel that any disruption and pressure will be worthwhile. Also, tackling plans and activities together will help to ease certain pressures as well as lead to better decisions and results.

There will also be many domestic occasions that the Metal Dog will not only enjoy but also help arrange. These could range from a possible house-warming party to other get-togethers and trips out. Domestically, the Dog year will be busy but often rewarding.

Although the Metal Dog will have many demands on his time, he should still set aside time for his personal interests and social life. Both can be an excellent way for him to unwind and have a break from his usual activities. And if there is a subject that has been intriguing him, this would be a good year to find out more. What is started during the Dog year can often have long-term value.

The Metal Dog should also keep in regular contact with his friends and, despite other commitments, take up any invitations he receives as well as go to any social events that appeal to him, as he can make some good friends over the year. For Metal Dogs who have had difficulties in their personal life, this *is* a time to move forward. By becoming involved in different activities and going out more, these Metal Dogs will find their social life undergoing quite a transformation, with a chance meeting quickly becoming significant. The Dog year is very promising as far as the Metal Dog's relations with others are concerned and for the unattached, affairs of the heart are favourably aspected. February, March and the period from mid-June to August are good times for socializing and meeting others.

The Year of the Dog certainly holds many possibilities for the Metal Dog, but to benefit he does need to seize the initiative and make the most of his ideas and opportunities. This is a year to advance and it can bring pleasing and often far-reaching developments.

TIP FOR THE YEAR

Look to move ahead. This is not a year to feel hampered by past disappointments or current frustrations. By making the decision to do something positive, you can achieve a great deal.

The Water Dog

This is a year of great potential for the Water Dog and by following through his ideas and acting upon his opportunities, he can look forward to some important successes.

The Water Dog's personal life is especially well aspected. For those Water Dogs with a partner, there will be many plans and ideas to pursue together. Attention will be particularly focused on the home, with quite a few Water Dogs deciding to move. For many, getting their home as they want it will make this an exciting time.

There may also be several causes for celebration over the year, with some Water Dogs becoming engaged or married or seeing an addition to their family. From a personal point of view, the Dog year will certainly be marked by some memorable occasions.

This also applies to those Water Dogs who may have had recent disappointments in their personal life. This is a year for drawing a firm line under the past and looking to move forward. As a result of activities they become involved in or changes in their work, these Water Dogs could see quite a transformation in their situation and could not only make some wonderful new friends but also meet their future partner. Affairs of the heart are superbly aspected. The first quarter of the year and July and August will be good times for meeting others and socializing.

Also, throughout the year, it is important that the Water Dog does not forget that he does have support should he need it. More senior relations in particular will often be keen to assist and if at any time the Water Dog is about to make a major decision or take on a large commitment, it could be worth him talking this over with them and obtaining their advice. More senior relations not only have valuable experience but also have the Water Dog's best interests at heart and their input could be useful.

The excellent aspects also extend to the Water Dog's work and in this respect, too, this will be a significant year. For those Water Dogs who are establishing themselves in a particular career, this is a time of opportunity and growth. By showing commitment and a willingness to learn, these Water Dogs will often find themselves with the chance to move to greater responsibilities, with many being promoted. The emphasis of the year is on progress and throughout the Water Dog should make the most of any opportunities that arise. With the reputation he has built up and his keen nature, he already has much in his favour.

For those Water Dogs who are dissatisfied with their current position, who feel perhaps that they have not yet found the right type of work or who are seeking work, this will also be an important year. With determination and a keenness to learn, many will be given an opportunity that can set their career off on a more fulfilling path. This is a year when initiative will be rewarded. The months from February to April and September to early November could see some interesting work developments.

In addition to the progress the Water Dog makes in the course of his duties, he should take full advantage of any training he may be offered. Adding to his skills and knowledge will help his prospects as well as widen his choices for the future. Also, if there is a particular quali-fication he has been advised to obtain, he should look at ways of doing so. Even if this involves studying in his own time, it is an investment in his future and can, in time, be well rewarded.

The Water Dog will also derive much satisfaction from his interests over the year, whether these are of an outdoor nature or allow him to draw on his more creative talents. And if he can encourage loved ones to join him in his interests or can meet other enthusiasts, this can add to his enjoyment.

There will also be some interesting travel opportunities for the Water Dog and in some cases he could get to visit some quite distant places. To make the most of his travels he would do well to read up on his destination beforehand and make sure he goes fully prepared. That way he will get far more out of his trips.

The one area in which he will need to exercise care is finance. Although many Water Dogs will enjoy a rise in income over the year, with accommodation costs, the chance to travel and all their other plans, they will need to keep a close watch on their outgoings and budget accordingly. It would also be worth the Water Dog thinking twice if tempted by impulse buys or what could be costly undertakings. Also, if entering into any long-term agreement or taking on any loans, he needs to check the details and implications and, if appropriate, seek advice. Certain agreements will remain in place for many years and it is important that the Water Dog chooses wisely.

However, while there is this need for care, the Dog year will contain an element of luck and the Water Dog could do well in a competition he enters or have an enterprising idea which can add to his income. Several times over the year he will benefit from a stroke of good fortune.

The Year of the Dog certainly holds excellent prospects for the Water Dog. In his work this is a year to advance as well as develop his skills and further his experience. His personal life is also splendidly aspected. With so much in his favour, this is a time when the Water Dog should seize the initiative and the many good opportunities that the year will bring.

TIP FOR THE YEAR

As a Water Dog you have a keen and resolute nature and like to set about your activities in your own way. However, do not let this prevent you from seeking the views of those who have the experience to guide you. Good advice and support can really make a difference.

The Wood Dog

This will be a year of opportunity for the Wood Dog, with much going in his favour.

For those Wood Dogs born in 1994 the year will bring some important developments. In their education many will start a new range of subjects and some will also change their school. While some of the changes may seem daunting at first, by making the most of their situation, these Wood Dogs will soon settle down and enjoy the challenges before them. Also, as the year progresses, the young Wood Dog will often discover that he has an aptitude for some of the new subjects he has to study and will not only make encouraging progress in these but often find this will help in other areas of his schoolwork as well. The Wood Dog certainly possesses a keen and enquiring mind and his curiosity will be often aroused by new work given him.

In addition to the progress he makes in his studies, the Wood Dog will be pleased with the way he is able to develop certain of his interests. Those Wood Dogs who are keen on sport, dance, drama, art or music will again be able to further their knowledge and skills and take great satisfaction in what they are able to do. This is an excellent year for developing talents and those Wood Dogs who do not have a particular hobby or interest at the moment really can gain a lot by taking one up over the year.

The Wood Dog will also find that some of the changes that take place and activities he becomes involved in will lead to some strong friendships being made. On a social level this will be an often busy and rewarding year.

Although so much will go well, if at any time the young Wood Dog has any concerns or is worried over any matter, it is important that he tells either his tutors or those at home. By being forthcoming, he will find others often sympathetic and able to do much to ease any problems. Throughout the year the young Wood Dog should remember that support is there should he need it.

For those Wood Dogs born in 1934 this will also be an important year. As with so many Dogs this year, accommodation matters will feature prominently and some of the more senior Wood Dogs will decide to move to accommodation more suitable for their present needs. Although this will, for some, be a considerable upheaval, by drawing on the support of those around them, they will often feel that the benefits are well worth all the effort involved. Again the events of the Dog year can be significant.

Money matters will, however, need care. The Wood Dog will need to check the terms and implications of any large transaction and when completing forms relating to finance, pension or benefits, he should give them his full attention.

However, while paperwork and financial matters do need to be handled with care, the Wood Dog will enjoy some good fortune as well. For the many Wood Dogs who enjoy collecting or appreciate more aesthetic items, some purchases or finds can bring much delight. Also, during the year, the Wood Dog could decide to give himself and his loved ones some special treats and these will bring considerable pleasure.

The Wood Dog will also enjoy spending time on his personal interests over the year, especially any that are creative. Also, if there is a subject or skill the Wood Dog feels it could be useful to learn, for instance adding to internet or computer skills, he would do well to follow this up. Whatever he does, by spending time in pleasurable and often purposeful pursuits, the Wood Dog will enjoy himself over the year.

As always, he will also take a keen and fond interest in the progress and activities of other family members and several times over the year there will be some pleasing news to celebrate. This could include a family wedding or the birth of a grandchild or great-grandchild. The Wood Dog will also value the advice and support he is given and will be pleased to reciprocate, often helping younger relations in particular. As far as his family life is concerned, this will be an often rewarding and special year.

The Year of the Dog certainly holds encouraging prospects for the Wood Dog and for many there will be some important changes in store. For the younger Wood

Dog these are likely to concern their education and for more senior Wood Dog their accommodation. By making the most of their situation and opportunities, both younger and more senior Wood Dogs will take pleasure in what they are able to achieve over the year. And they will be supported and encouraged well by those around them, with the year again holding many personally pleasing times.

TIP FOR THE YEAR

The aspects are very much on your side this year and by following up your ideas and acting upon the chances you are given, you can accomplish a lot. This is a year when positive action and determination *will* be rewarded.

The Fire Dog

This is the year of Fire Dog and his prospects during his own year are especially encouraging.

For those Fire Dogs in work this will be a year of important change. Some will retire or decide to reduce their working hours in order to give time to other interests. However, for those who remain in employment, it will be a time of considerable opportunity. As a result of their background and knowledge many will find themselves well placed for promotion or will have the chance to become involved in more specialist duties. These Fire Dogs will often revel in the challenges. Also in many cases the developments of the year can provide a new impetus to their career and reward them for the loyalty and commitment they have shown for so long. March, April, September and October could see important developments.

In view of their seniority, some Fire Dogs will also find that part of their role will involve training and mentoring others and this is something that many will enjoy doing. The Fire Dog's considerable knowledge will prove a real asset and will be something he is pleased to share.

For those Fire Dogs who retire or decide to reduce their working hours, again the year offers considerable scope. With more time at their disposal, these Fire Dogs will often enjoy setting about activities and projects they have long had in mind.

One area which will feature prominently will be accommodation. Some Fire Dogs will decide to move and while this will often involve considerable upheaval, they will regard it as the start of a new chapter in their lives and will enjoy settling into their new area. Fire Dogs who remain where they are will also often decide to go ahead with certain alterations to their home, perhaps redecorating or buying new furnishings. In addition, many Fire Dogs will decide to mount an efficiency drive, and get rid of clutter. The year will see much practical activity around the home and many benefits as a result.

Throughout the year the Fire Dog will also be grateful for the support of those close to him. Their advice will lead to him achieving far more. And in addition to the assistance he receives, he will find that openness and good discussion can help with the rapport and understanding he so values.

While the Fire Dog's domestic life will see much practical activity and also moments of disruption as certain plans go ahead, it will also be a source of much pleasure. In addition to the possible marking of his own sixtieth birthday, there will be some family events that will mean a great deal to him, including the achievements of a younger relation. Throughout the year the Fire Dog will be glad to help those who are dear to him and it will be much appreciated.

The Fire Dog's social life is also pleasingly aspected and is set to become busier as the year progresses. In addition to regularly meeting up with his friends, he will often find his interests and other activities leading to invitations to go out and his social circle widening as a result. Those Fire Dogs whose social life may have lapsed in recent years or who move house will find that by immersing themselves in local activities and interest groups they can see quite a transformation in their situation. February, March and late June to August will be busy times.

The year will also bring some good travel opportunities and some Fire Dogs will choose to mark their sixtieth year by taking a special holiday, perhaps to a place they have long wanted to see. If they plan their itinerary carefully, such a holiday could surpass expectations. Also, with the positive social aspects of the year, the Fire Dog's travels could bring many opportunities to make new friends.

The Fire Dog's good fortune will also extend to his financial situation and many Fire Dogs can look forward to receiving some extra money over the year, possibly in the form of a gift, the fruition of a policy or some form of bonus. This will often encourage the Fire Dog to go ahead with some of the ideas he has in mind. However, when embarking on anything involving considerable expense, it would be worth him comparing prices and checking the terms and obligations beforehand. Although this may be a positive year, it is still not a time to take risks or make assumptions. Again, the Fire Dog should remember that help is available should he need it.

The Fire Dog will, however, be blessed with a certain amount of luck during the year and if he sees a competition that appeals to him, especially one related to an interest of his, he would do well to enter it. With the aspects so favourable, he could emerge a winner.

The Year of the Fire Dog certainly offers excellent prospects for the Fire Dog and by acting on his ideas and making the most of his opportunities, he will accomplish a great deal. This is a time for setting his plans in motion.

TIP FOR THE YEAR
Do not let ideas and opportunities come to nothing. This is a year to seize the initiative. With good support and determination, your efforts will often be well rewarded.

The Earth Dog

There is a Chinese proverb which is very apt for the Earth Dog this year: 'Hoist your sail when the wind is fair. Seize the opportunity.' The wind will be fair for the Earth Dog this year, bringing him excellent chances to make progress.

The aspects are especially encouraging as far as his work is concerned. With the considerable experience he has behind him and his desire to make the most of his situation, he will often be in an excellent position for promotion or more specialist duties. When the chance arises, the Earth Dog should put himself forward. Some Earth Dogs could have waited quite some time for such an opportunity and this is the year when their patience and hard work will be rewarded.

Many Earth Dogs will be able to advance within their current organization and will find their reputation and in-house knowledge an asset. However, for those who feel there is better scope elsewhere, making enquiries and remaining alert for opportunities will in many cases lead to what will be an ideal opening. This also applies to those Earth Dogs who consider they are not making the most of their talents. By resolving to take action, these Earth Dogs will find important possibilities opening up and will be able to set their career on a more rewarding track.

The aspects are also encouraging for those Earth Dogs seeking work, either as the Dog year begins or during it. Again the Dog year will often give these Earth Dogs the chance to take on a different type of work and provide them with experience in new areas – experience that they can build on in the future. As so many will find, the events of the year can be far-reaching. March, April and the months from September to early November could see some good opportunities and even if certain applications do not go his way, the Earth Dog should not lose heart. Perseverance in the Dog year *will* be rewarded.

All Earth Dogs should also take advantage of any training opportunities they are offered or any chances to add to their qualifications. This will not only be useful in their current duties but also of value when they look to move on. And for those who feel unfulfilled in their present position or consider themselves in a rut, training and additional skills can give their prospects an important boost. Earth Dogs, do take note.

The progress the Earth Dog makes in his work will also lead to an increase in income and many Earth Dogs could have the chance to supplement this with some additional work or an idea they have. The Earth Dog's earning abilities will certainly be in good form over the year. In view of this, he would do well to look closely at his financial situation and if he is able to reduce any borrowings or make savings for the future, he could find this to his advantage. Also, with the many ideas he has for his accommodation (and accommodation matters do feature prominently for many Dogs over the year), as well as his other plans and commitments, good management can make a noticeable difference.

The Earth Dog's domestic life is favourably aspected and will again see much activity. Some Earth Dogs will see members of their household move for the purposes of education, work or marriage and the support and help they can give to those experiencing change will often be of more value than they may realize. In addition many Earth Dogs will give important assistance to more senior relations and once again their thoughtfulness can make a lot of difference.

The Earth Dog will also enjoy many of the family activities that take place and will often instigate or help arrange them. By playing such a central role, he can make his domestic life both rich and personally rewarding.

The year will also contain many fine social opportunities, often arising from the Earth Dog's personal interests or his work. By taking up invitations and getting to know his colleagues and those who share similar interests to his own, he will find his social life becoming much more fulfilling. For those Earth Dogs who would welcome a more active social life, the year is splendidly aspected, with February, March and late June to August being busy and favourable months. For the unattached Earth Dog, a significant romance could be born. Personally, too, this is a year of important events.

The aspects are certainly on the Earth Dog's side in 2006, but to benefit, he does need to act, otherwise chances could slip by and opportunities be lost. Even though some of what he initiates will bring change and uncertainty, these are inevitable on the path of progress and the events of the year will allow the Earth Dog to develop and grow. Overall, a good and constructive year.

TIP FOR THE YEAR
Act upon your ideas and hopes and make the most of your considerable Earth Dog strengths. This is a year for action and moving forward.

FAMOUS DOGS

André Agassi, King Albert II of Belgium, Jane Asher, Brigitte Bardot, Gary Barlow, Candice Bergen, David Bowie, Bertolt Brecht, George W. Bush, Laura Bush, Naomi Campbell, Mariah Carey, King Carl XVI Gustaf of Sweden, José Carreras, Paul Cézanne, Cher, Sir Winston Churchill, Bill Clinton, Leonard Cohen, Jamie Lee Curtis, Matt Damon, Charles Dance, Claude Debussy, Dame Judi Dench, Sally Field, Joseph Fiennes, Robert Frost, Ali G, Ava Gardner, Judy Garland, George Gershwin, Lenny Henry, O.

Henry, Victor Hugo, Barry Humphries, Holly Hunter, Michael Jackson, Al Jolson, Felicity Kendal, Jennifer Lopez, Sophia Loren, Joanna Lumley, Shirley MacLaine, Madonna, Norman Mailer, Barry Manilow, Freddie Mercury, Liza Minelli, David Niven, Sydney Pollack, Elvis Presley, Tim Robbins, Lord George Robertson, Paul Robeson, Andy Roddick, Linda Ronstadt, Susan Sarandon, Jennifer Saunders, Claudia Schiffer, Dr Albert Schweitzer, Sylvester Stallone, Robert Louis Stevenson, Sharon Stone, Jack Straw, David Suchet, Donald Sutherland, Chris Tarrant, Mother Teresa, Uma Thurman, Donald Trump, Voltaire, Prince William, Shelley Winters.

30 JANUARY 1911 ～ 17 FEBRUARY 1912	*Metal Pig*
16 FEBRUARY 1923 ～ 4 FEBRUARY 1924	*Water Pig*
4 FEBRUARY 1935 ～ 23 JANUARY 1936	*Wood Pig*
22 JANUARY 1947 ～ 9 FEBRUARY 1948	*Fire Pig*
8 FEBRUARY 1959 ～ 27 JANUARY 1960	*Earth Pig*
27 JANUARY 1971 ～ 14 FEBRUARY 1972	*Metal Pig*
13 FEBRUARY 1983 ～ 1 FEBRUARY 1984	*Water Pig*
31 JANUARY 1995 ～ 18 FEBRUARY 1996	*Wood Pig*

THE
PIG

THE PERSONALITY OF THE PIG

> To laugh often and much, to win the respect of intelligent
> people and the affection of children, to earn the
> appreciation of honest critics and endure the betrayal of
> false friends, to appreciate beauty, to find the best in others,
> to leave the world a bit better, whether by a healthy child, a
> garden patch, or a redeemed social condition, to know even
> one life has breathed easier because you have lived, this is
> to have succeeded.
>
> *Ralph Waldo Emerson, a Pig*

The Pig is born under the sign of honesty. He has a kind
and understanding nature and is well known for his abilities
as a peacemaker. He hates any sort of discord or unpleasantness and will do everything in his power to sort out differences of opinion or bring opposing factions together.

He is also an excellent conversationalist and speaks
truthfully and to the point. He dislikes any form of falsehood or hypocrisy and is a firm believer in justice and the
maintenance of law and order. In spite of these beliefs,
however, the Pig is reasonably tolerant and often prepared
to forgive others for their wrongdoings. He rarely
harbours grudges and is never vindictive.

The Pig is usually very popular. He enjoys other
people's company and likes to be involved in joint or group
activities. He will be a loyal member of any club or society
and can be relied upon to lend a helping hand at functions.
He is also an excellent fundraiser for charities and is often
a great supporter of humanitarian causes.

The Pig is a hard and conscientious worker and is particularly respected for his reliability and integrity. In his early years he will try his hand at several different jobs, but he is usually happiest where he feels that he is being of service to others. He will unselfishly give up his time for the common good and is highly valued by his colleagues and employers.

The Pig has a good sense of humour and invariably has a smile, joke or some whimsical remark at the ready. He loves to entertain and to please others, and there are many Pigs who have been attracted to careers in show business or who enjoy following the careers of famous stars and personalities.

There are, unfortunately, some who take advantage of the Pig's good nature and impose upon his generosity. The Pig has great difficulty in saying 'no' and, although he may dislike being firm, it would be in his own interests to say occasionally, 'Enough is enough.' The Pig can also be rather naïve and gullible; however, if at any stage in his life he feels that he has been badly let down, he will try to become self-reliant. There are many Pigs who have become entrepreneurs or forged a successful career on their own after some early disappointment in life. Although the Pig tends to spend his money quite freely, he is usually very astute in financial matters and there are many Pigs who have become wealthy.

Another characteristic of the Pig is his ability to recover from setbacks reasonably quickly. His faith and his strength of character keep him going. If he thinks that there is a job he can do or he has something that he wants to achieve, he will pursue it with a dogged determination.

He can also be stubborn and, no matter how many may plead with him, once he has made his mind up he will rarely change his views.

Although the Pig may work hard, he also knows how to enjoy himself. He is a great pleasure-seeker and will quite happily spend his hard-earned money on a lavish holiday or an expensive meal – for the Pig is a connoisseur of good food and wine – or taking part in a variety of recreational activities. He also enjoys small social gatherings and if he is in company he likes he can very easily become the life and soul of the party. He does, however, tend to become rather withdrawn at larger functions or when among strangers.

The Pig is a creature of comfort and his home will usually be fitted with all the latest in luxury appliances. Where possible, he will prefer to live in the country rather than the town and will opt to have a big garden, for the Pig is usually a keen and successful gardener.

The Pig is very popular with others and will often have numerous romances before he settles down. Once settled, however, he will be loyal to his partner and he will find that he is especially well suited to those born under the signs of the Goat, Rabbit, Dog and Tiger and also to another Pig. Due to his affable and easygoing nature he can also establish a satisfactory relationship with all the remaining signs of the Chinese zodiac, with the exception of the Snake. The Snake tends to be wily, secretive and very guarded, and this can be intensely irritating to the honest and open-hearted Pig.

The female Pig will devote all her energies to the needs of her children and her partner. She tries to ensure that they want for nothing and their pleasure is very much her pleasure. She can be a caring and conscientious parent and has very good taste in clothes. Her home will either be very clean and orderly or hopelessly untidy. Strangely, there seems to be no in between with Pigs – they either love housework or detest it! The female Pig does, however, have considerable talents as an organizer and this, combined with her friendly and open manner, enables her to secure many of her objectives.

The Pig is usually lucky in life and will rarely want for anything. Provided he does not let others take advantage of his good nature and is not afraid of asserting himself, he will go through life making friends, helping others and winning the admiration of many.

THE FIVE DIFFERENT TYPES OF PIG

In addition to the 12 signs of the Chinese zodiac there are five elements and these have a strengthening or moderating influence on the sign. The effects of the five elements on the Pig are described below, together with the years in which the elements were exercising their influence. Therefore those Pigs born in 1911 and 1971 are Metal Pigs, those born in 1923 and 1983 are Water Pigs, and so on.

Metal Pig: 1911, 1971
The Metal Pig is more ambitious and determined than some of the other types of Pig. He is strong, energetic and likes to be involved in a wide variety of different activities. He is very open and forthright in his views, although he

can be a little too trusting at times and has a tendency to accept things at face value. He has a good sense of humour and loves to attend parties and other social gatherings. He has a warm, outgoing nature and usually has a large circle of friends.

Water Pig: 1923, 1983

The Water Pig has a heart of gold. He is generous and loyal and tries to remain on good terms with everyone. He will do his utmost to help others, but sadly there are some who will take advantage of his kind nature and he should, in his own interests, be a little more discriminating and be prepared to stand firm against anything that he does not like. Although he prefers the quieter things in life, he has a wide range of interests. He particularly enjoys outdoor pursuits and attending parties and social occasions. He is a hard and conscientious worker and invariably does well in his chosen profession. He is also gifted in the art of communication.

Wood Pig: 1935, 1995

This Pig has a friendly, persuasive manner and is easily able to gain the confidence of others. He likes to be involved in all that is going on around him but can sometimes take on more responsibility than he can properly handle. He is loyal to his family and friends and derives much pleasure from helping those less fortunate than himself. He is usually an optimist and leads a very full, enjoyable and satisfying life. He also has a good sense of humour.

Fire Pig: 1947

The Fire Pig is both energetic and adventurous and he sets about everything he does in a confident and resolute manner. He is very forthright in his views and does not mind taking risks in order to achieve his objectives. He can, however, get carried away by the excitement of the moment and ought to exercise more caution in some of the enterprises in which he gets involved. He is usually lucky in money matters and is well known for his generosity. He is also very caring towards the members of his family.

Earth Pig: 1959

This Pig has a kindly nature. He is sensible and realistic and will go to great lengths in order to please his employers and to secure his aims and ambitions. He is an excellent organizer and is particularly astute in business and financial matters. He has a good sense of humour and a wide circle of friends. He also likes to lead an active social life, although he does sometimes have a tendency to eat and drink more than is good for him.

PROSPECTS FOR THE PIG IN 2006

The Year of the Rooster (9 February 2005 to 28 January 2006) will have been a rewarding one for the Pig, with the closing months being an active and encouraging time.

One of the Pig's greatest strengths is his ability to get on well with others and in what remains of the Rooster year he will be in demand. There will be plenty of opportunities to go out and meet others and for the unattached or those Pigs enjoying romance, this can be an exciting time. August and December could be especially active socially.

The Pig will also see a lot happening in his domestic life, including a possible family celebration or get-together. Once more he will play a large part in all that goes on, although he does need to consult others rather than try to deal with too much on his own.

The Pig's considerable personal skills will also be useful in his work and in the closing months of the Rooster year he will again get to meet and impress many as well as be able to make good headway in many of his activities. In the last quarter of the year there could also be chances for him to take on greater responsibilities, with November being a particularly encouraging month.

Overall, the closing months of the Rooster year will be a busy time for the Pig and, with his genial and outgoing nature, he will often enjoy himself.

The Year of the Dog starts on 29 January and will be a reasonably good one for the Pig. Although he may not always accomplish as much as he would like, the experience he gains can be of considerable long-term value.

In his work the Pig will find his greatest gains will come from adding to his skills. Furthering his knowledge can be particularly helpful to his prospects. Also, there will be plenty of chances for him to do more in his present position, including possibly training new colleagues or becoming involved in new projects. By showing his usual enthusiasm and commitment, he can do much to help his standing.

The Pig should also take advantage of any training he may be offered and if there are specific skills he feels could help him progress, he should look at ways of obtaining them, even if this involves studying in his own time. He will be investing in his future.

Those Pigs who are dissatisfied in their current role or seeking work should aim to make enquiries and follow up openings that interest them. In some cases it could be worth contacting professional organizations for advice and information. By remaining determined and persistent, many Pigs will secure a position and experience gained during the Dog year can often be significant in the advances the Pig will make towards the end of the year and particularly in the more progressive Pig year that follows.

However, while there will be chances for the Pig to make progress, the year will also contain some salutary lessons. In some cases applications will not go the Pig's way or certain ideas or hopes will be more difficult to realize than he anticipated. Although this may hurt the sensitive Pig, by looking at reasons why events went the way they did he can learn a great deal. In some cases he could find that his approach and manner were wrong, that he needed more experience or that the situation was not right for him. Whatever the reasons for his disappointment, by learning from any mistakes (and the Pig *is* a good learner), he will emerge wiser and better prepared for next time.

As far as his work prospects are concerned, late February, March and the period from October to early December could contain some interesting opportunities, but generally the second half of the year will be more productive than the first.

As far as the Pig's finances are concerned, this will be a generally favourable year. Although the Pig likes to enjoy the fruits of his labours, he is also astute when it comes to money matters. He could also benefit from some financial good fortune over the year, perhaps through additional work or a gift or bonus. In view of this, if the Pig is able to add to his savings or to reduce any borrowings, he could find this to his advantage. Also, when considering any large purchase or costly undertaking, it would be worth him spending time considering his various options. The greater the care he takes with his finances, the better.

With his outgoing and amiable nature the Pig attaches considerable importance to his relations with others and over the year both his domestic and social life will bring him considerable pleasure.

As far as his home life is concerned, the Pig will play an important part and his organizational abilities and good nature will be valued. His talents for averting problems or smoothing out possible differences of opinion will also be much appreciated. Domestically, the Dog year will contain many happy moments. Also, if the Pig has any ideas for treats he thinks everyone would enjoy, he should put these forward. In the Dog year input into family life really can make a difference.

However, while the Pig is willing to do so much, it is also important that if at any time he feels under strain, he talks to others and, if necessary, asks for help. Those around him will often be glad to reciprocate his kindnesses, but occasionally they may need prompting into action. Pigs, do take note. Be forthcoming and do not forgo the help that others can give.

The positive aspects of the year extend to the Pig's social life and in many cases personal interests or activities can lead to some fine social opportunities. For those Pigs who are unattached, the Dog year has good romantic possibilities and someone met purely by chance could quickly become special. For those who would welcome new friendships and perhaps romance, the year is certainly well aspected. March, April, July and September are good months for socializing and meeting others.

The Pig will also derive much pleasure from his personal interests over the year and despite his many commitments, he should set a regular time aside for them. Not only can they be a good way for him to relax but they can also keep his lifestyle in balance. If there are skills or techniques that can help him with his interests, he should follow them up. This is a superb year for self-development.

In many ways the Dog year will be a valuable one for the Pig and while it may not be a time for rapid or substantial progress, he will often derive much pleasure from his activities and, importantly, will be preparing the way for the considerable success that awaits in his own year.

The Metal Pig

This will be an important year for the Metal Pig and can have far-reaching effects.

This will be an especially significant year as far as the Metal Pig's work is concerned. Although many Metal Pigs will be content in their current position, with their ambitions for the future they should make the most of any chance to extend their experience, perhaps by taking on greater responsibilities, becoming involved in other duties or seeking a transfer or promotion. Also, all Metal Pigs, regardless of whether they are relatively new in their position or well established, should make the most of any training opportunities. Adding to their skills can help their prospects considerably.

Although many Metal Pigs will remain with their present employer over the year and often benefit from internal opportunities, those who feel they could advance their career better elsewhere should keep alert for suitable openings as well as contact those in a position to help. By putting in the effort, many will be successful in securing a position which will be a springboard to greater things in the future. As so many Metal Pigs will discover, this is not a year to expect major advances, but what is accomplished now can have considerable long-term value.

This also applies to those Metal Pigs seeking work. Although their quest will demand considerable time and effort and there will be disappointments along the way, once in a position these Metal Pigs will have an excellent platform to build on. In some cases what they are offered will be different from what they have been doing, but by being willing to learn, they can often widen their scope for the future. Late February, March and the months from October to December could see some good opportunities, but the main benefits of the year will come from the experience the Metal Pig is able to gain and the skills he can develop.

With the year's emphasis so firmly placed on personal development, the Metal Pig should also look at ways he can make more of his personal interests. If he sets himself a particular challenge or activity to tackle over the year, this can bring him a good deal of satisfaction. By using his spare time to advantage, he will find his interests going well and often bringing personal benefits.

The Dog year is a generally positive one as far as the Metal Pig's financial prospects are concerned. In addition to an increase in income, he could benefit from a financial gift or find an interest or enterprising idea he has bringing him something extra. However, the Metal Pig does need to manage his money well. With his many commitments and some of the more expensive plans he has in mind, he does need to keep track of his outgoings and budget carefully. At times it would be worth him thinking twice if tempted by impulse purchases. To do all he wants over the year, the Metal Pig does need to remain disciplined in financial matters and plan ahead.

This will be a busy year as far as the Metal Pig's domestic life is concerned. Over the year those dear to him will often look to him for support. While the Metal Pig will be willing to do his best for others, there will be occasions when he will despair of all that is being asked of him. However, by keeping well organized and prioritizing his various tasks, he will find himself able do a great deal. In addition, if he feels others could help more with certain activities, including some household chores, he should ask. Metal Pigs, take note and do accept help.

While the Metal Pig's home life will be busy, it will also often be rewarding. In particular, time set aside for shared interests and home projects will be appreciated by all concerned. Some other family activities will also be good fun – perhaps trips out, a family holiday or other special treats. The Dog year will certainly contain many happy moments.

The Dog year is also favourably aspected for social matters and some new friends and contacts could turn out to be important in the near future. For Metal Pigs who are unattached, someone met almost in a fortuitous way can quickly become special. In this respect, too, what happens during the Dog year can often be far-reaching. March, April, July and September will be busy and favourable months socially.

The Year of the Dog certainly holds encouraging prospects for the Metal Pig and by furthering his experience and making the most of his opportunities, he can pave the way to the success he will enjoy in following years.

TIP FOR THE YEAR
Although there will be considerable demands on your time, do not allow your personal interests or recreational pursuits to suffer. They are an excellent way to keep your lifestyle in balance and in such a full year this is important.

The Water Pig

This will be a year of pleasing developments for the Water Pig with most aspects of his life going well.

The Water Pig's personal life is especially well aspected. There will often be excellent cause for celebration as some Water Pigs become engaged, marry, see an addition to their family or carry out some exciting accommodation plans. Also, with the love and support of another and the responsibilities they now have, these Water Pigs will often feel determined to make more of themselves and will set about their activities with greater resolve and enthusiasm. For many, the Dog year will not only be personally significant but also mark a positive change in their outlook *and* confidence.

For unattached Water Pigs the Dog year can also see quite a transformation. Over the year many will meet someone who will quickly become important. Often a romance will start in an almost fortuitous way, as if fate were playing a part.

In addition to the favourable aspects in the Water Pig's personal life, this will also be an active year socially and the Water Pig will find his work and interests leading to a widening of his social circle. Though he will often thoroughly enjoy himself, one word of warning does need to be sounded. If he is tempted to have a succession of particularly late nights as well as face a demanding schedule during the day, there will be times when tiredness will begin to take its toll, with the Water Pig not feeling his best as well as becoming prone to colds and other niggling complaints. In view of his generally active lifestyle, he does need to make sure he gets sufficient rest and has a balanced diet. Water Pigs, do take note.

March, April and July to September could be the busiest months socially as well as often marking the start of a new friendship or romance.

This will also be an important year as far as the Water Pig's work prospects are concerned. With his keen and ambitious nature, and aware of responsibilities he may now have, he will be eager to improve on his position. While he will be able to make encouraging progress over the year, his greatest gains will often be in the form of the experience and skills he is able to acquire. Whenever he has the chance to go on training courses or to extend his role in some way, he really should make the most of it. By showing enthusiasm and commitment, he will not only be learning a great deal but also helping both his reputation and his future prospects.

For those Water Pigs who are seeking work or feeling disillusioned with their present position, this can also be a year of significant developments. Sometimes agencies or professional organizations can provide helpful leads and following up vacancies that interest them, these Water Pigs will find important doors opening. Even if the position some are given is of a routine nature, it will be a platform they can build on. Again, what is achieved in the Dog year can be of considerable long-term value. Late February, March and the period from October to December could see some interesting career developments.

In addition to the experience and training the Water Pig gets through his work, if he feels it would be useful to acquire a further qualification or skill, this would be an excellent year to try and secure this. Any studying he can do can be helpful to his prospects.

Also, for those Water Pigs currently involved in further education or studying for particular qualifications, the discipline and effort they put into their work will be well rewarded, with their results opening up some important possibilities. Again the Water Pig's achievements during the Dog year can be important and far-reaching.

The Water Pig's financial prospects are also encouraging, with many Water Pigs enjoying a rise in income over the year. Some might also be able to supplement this through some additional work or an idea they have. The Water Pig will often find his willingness and enterprise helping to improve his financial position. However, with accommodation costs, personal plans, an often active social life and in many cases travelling too, this is very much a year for good control and planning. Also, if the Water Pig enters into any major commitment, he needs to check the implications and obtain sound advice. Again, care taken now can prevent problems later.

In view of the general activity of the year, it is also important for the Water Pig to remember that if at any time he would welcome assistance or advice, he should ask. Water Pigs, do bear this in mind at busy times or when facing important decisions.

Overall the Dog year holds encouraging prospects for the Water Pig, with his personal life bringing some memorable times, while as far as his work is concerned, the experience he gains will be of great value as he enjoys greater successes in following years.

TIP FOR THE YEAR
Do make the most of your chances, especially any that will enable you to add to your experience and skills. You have an exciting future ahead of you and what you do this year can prepare you for the success you are soon to enjoy.

The Wood Pig
This will be a pleasing year for the Wood Pig with most of his activities going well. He will be well supported

throughout the year and if there are any ideas he wishes to pursue, he really would find it of value to talk to others. This can make a real difference to how he fares.

One important feature of 2006 is that it is a good year for trying out new things and if the Wood Pig sees an interest or subject that appeals to him, he would do well to find out more, perhaps by reading about it, enrolling on a course or joining an activity group. This will often bring him much personal satisfaction as well as sometimes having a pleasing social element.

The Wood Pig will also get much pleasure from outdoor pursuits. For those born in 1935, this could often be through gardening, with their 'green fingers' serving them well. In addition, visits to places of interest or beauty can lead to many enjoyable occasions. The young Wood Pig too will often be drawn out of doors, with many taking a lively interest in sporting activities. Playing games and adding to their skills can again bring them a lot of enjoyment. The one word of caution that does need to be sounded for all Wood Pigs is that whenever gardening or taking part in sport or other strenuous activities, they do need to follow recommended procedures. If not, a strain could cause considerable discomfort and curtail the Wood Pig's activities for some while. Wood Pigs, do take care.

There will be good opportunities for the Wood Pig to travel over the year and those born in 1935 would do well to take up any invitations to visit family and friends living some distance away. Also, if these Wood Pigs see a travel offer that particularly appeals to them, perhaps at short notice, they would do well to follow this up. Travel is well aspected and many Wood Pigs can look forward to seeing some interesting sights as the year progresses. In addition, their travels can often bring some good social opportunities.

The Wood Pig's home life will also be rewarding and he will take a fond interest in the activities of loved ones as well as assist those who may be busy or under pressure. His thoughtfulness will often be greatly appreciated. However if at any time he has concerns over any actions or decisions being considered by others, it is important that he makes his views known. His insights will often be timely and helpful. In general, though, domestic life will go well and with excellent possibilities of travel and other family activities, there will be much for the Wood Pig to enjoy.

In addition to being so willing to help family members, the Wood Pig has a caring and humanitarian side to his nature and some Wood Pigs will decide to give support to charitable causes over the year or to assist someone in need. Again, what they do will be greatly appreciated.

The Wood Pig will also fare well in money matters and may receive additional funds over the year. However, the Wood Pig should be wary of spending anything extra all too readily. By giving careful thought to possible plans and purchases, he will find himself getting more pleasure and often better value as a result. Also, when conducting any transaction or completing any financial forms, he does need to check the small print. Carelessness could prove costly. Wood Pigs, take note and take care.

For those Wood Pigs born in 1995 the year can herald some changes, particularly as many will move school and/or start a range of new subjects. However, with a willing attitude, good support and the comradeship of others, the young Wood Pig will soon get into his stride and make the most of the opportunities and challenges before him. For many, this will be a year for trying things out and discovering more about their capabilities and strengths. The skills and interests they develop now can prove particularly helpful in the longer term.

The Dog year certainly holds encouraging prospects for the Wood Pig and by following up his ideas and making the most of his opportunities, he will find this a satisfying and pleasing time. However, to benefit, it is important that he is forthcoming and tells others of his hopes and ideas. That way he can accomplish that much more.

TIP FOR THE YEAR
Remember the proverb, 'There is no time like the present'. This is very much a year for positive action and for making the most of your chances.

The Fire Pig

This will be a pleasant year for the Fire Pig with most of his activities going well and bringing him satisfaction.

In his work this will be a significant time. Although many Fire Pigs will be content to remain in their present position, as more senior colleagues leave or other changes take place there will often be the chance to take on greater responsibilities, secure promotion or become involved in more specialist areas. By making most of these, the Fire Pig can experience some interesting new challenges. Also, with the following Pig year being so favourable, progress made now can lead to further advances in the near future.

Those Fire Pigs seeking work will also find this a year of interesting developments. Although their quest may not be easy, by being flexible in the type of work they are prepared to consider, many will be given an opportunity that will add to their experience and have the potential for future development. Late February, March and mid-September to early December could see some interesting possibilities.

Another positive feature of the year is the way in which the Fire Pig will be able to add to his skills. Often this will come as a result of changes in his duties, but if he is given the chance of additional training, he will often find this helping his present position as well as opening up possibilities for later.

However, while the aspects are encouraging work-wise, there will be some Fire Pigs who will decide to retire or to reduce their working commitments. For those who do, the Dog year can again provide some significant opportunities, particularly as it will give them the chance to follow up ideas they may have had for some time. With some carefully thought out plans, these Fire Pigs will be satisfied with how they spend their extra time.

All Fire Pigs will derive much satisfaction from the way they are able to develop their interests over the year. In many cases these will have a good social element too. Many Fire Pigs will also give some thought to their well-being and if they feel they are lacking exercise or that their diet could be improved, by obtaining medical advice on how best to proceed, they will again be pleased with what they are able to do and with the benefits that follow.

The Fire Pig's home life will mean much to him over the year and he will follow the progress of loved ones with fond interest as well as often being able to help relations who may be busy or under pressure, including those with young families. As always, he will play a central and valued role in family life and his willingness to be involved will prove a real asset.

The Fire Pig's social life is also favourably aspected and with his wide interests and many friends, he will rarely be short of things to do or people to see. Those Fire Pigs who may have let their social life lapse will find that taking up new interests can lead to valuable friendships. March, April, July and September will see the most social activity.

The Fire Pig can also look forward to some strokes of good fortune over the year. This could include a competition win or a bonus payment or gift. The Dog year will certainly have a lucky element to it and many Fire Pigs will enjoy an improvement in their financial situation. While welcome, the Fire Pig should still manage his finances carefully and, if possible, make early provision for forthcoming expenses as well as consider reducing borrowings or making savings.

In most respects this will be a positive and satisfying year for the Fire Pig, but as with every year, problems will sometimes raise their head. When they do, the Fire Pig would do well to tackle them early rather than ignore them If not dealt with, they could escalate and become an unwelcome distraction. At the first sign of difficulties, the Fire Pig should talk to others. If he should have a bureaucratic problem, it would also be worth seeking guidance rather than trying to tackle what could be a complex matter on his own. Fire Pigs, do take note.

The Dog year will, though, be a generally satisfying one for the Fire Pig and he will be pleased with how many of his plans develop. With his prospects being so favourable in his own year, which follows, his achievements now can lead to considerable success in the near future.

TIP FOR THE YEAR
Make the most of learning opportunities. Whether they involve acquiring new work skills or furthering personal interests, the knowledge you gain really can serve you well and bring great personal satisfaction too.

The Earth Pig

This will be a satisfying year for the Earth Pig and though it may lack the activity of some, his accomplishments during it can pave the way to future success.

In his work the Earth Pig will have good opportunities to use his skills and talents and by concentrating on the areas he knows best, he will often obtain some encouraging results. As the year progresses, many Earth Pigs will have the chance to take on greater responsibilities and show some of their potential and strengths. What the Earth Pig can do over the year can be significant both now and in the auspicious Pig year that follows.

The Earth Pig will also be helped by his ability to work well with others and by making the most of his chances to meet new people he can make some important contacts. With his personable nature and good reputation, the Earth Pig will certainly impress many.

Also, with his future in mind, the Earth Pig should take

advantage of any training opportunities he may be offered. Similarly, if there is a particular skill or qualification he feels would be useful, this would be an excellent year to see if he can obtain it. The Dog year is very much a time for preparing the way for future progress.

Many Earth Pigs will remain with their present employer over the year but for those who are eager to move on or seeking work, the Dog year will contain some important opportunities. Admittedly, their quest will not always be easy but by making an extra effort and emphasizing their experience, many Earth Pigs will be able to set their career off on an interesting new track. Late February, March and the period from mid-September to early December could see some interesting work developments.

This is an encouraging year as far as the Earth Pig's finances are concerned and in addition to enjoying an increase in income, he could have chances to supplement this through overtime or an idea he has. However, too many spending sprees or indulgences could quickly eat into anything extra that he earns. Over the year the Earth Pig would do well to watch his general level of spending as well as budget for forthcoming expenses. Money matters can go well for him, but good control is required.

The Dog year is well aspected for travel and the Earth Pig should aim to go away for a break or holiday at some time. The change of scene will not only do him good but can often be fun and interesting as well.

The Earth Pig will also derive much satisfaction from his personal interests and although there will often be many demands on his time, it is important that he does not neglect them. Those that give him the chance of additional exercise could be especially beneficial. Also, if he is able to meet other enthusiasts, he will enjoy the social element that this will bring.

As far as the Earth Pig's domestic life is concerned, this will contain many pleasing occasions, with the success of a close relation often meaning a great deal. However, with his busy lifestyle, it is important that the Earth Pig sets aside time to talk to those around him, especially if he has reservations about plans being considered by both younger and more senior relations. With a readiness to talk, concerns can be better addressed and good relationships maintained.

Socially, this will be a busy and pleasing year. For some Earth Pigs, new acquaintances will soon become firm friends. March, April, July and September will see much social activity.

The Earth Pig will certainly fare well over the Dog year and the events and lessons of the year will serve him well, particularly with his prospects looking so promising in the following Year of the Pig.

TIP FOR THE YEAR

Two tips. Make the most of your chances to meet others. Some can become good friends and helpful contacts. Also, allow time for your personal interests. These will not only bring you pleasure but also be a good way to relax and enjoy yourself.

FAMOUS PIGS

Bryan Adams, Woody Allen, Julie Andrews, Marie Antoinette, Fred Astaire, Hector Berlioz, Humphrey Bogart, James Cagney, Maria Callas, Richard Chamberlain, Hillary Rodham Clinton, Glenn Close, the Duchess of Cornwall, David Coulthard, Noël Coward, Oliver Cromwell, Billy Crystal, the Dalai Lama, Ted Danson, Dido, Richard Dreyfuss, Ben Elton, Ralph Waldo Emerson, Sven-Goran Eriksson, Henry Ford, Emmylou Harris, William Randolph Hearst, Ernest Hemingway, Henry VIII, Conrad Hilton, Alfred Hitchcock, Sir Elton John, Tommy Lee Jones, Carl Gustav Jung, Boris Karloff, Charles Kennedy, Stephen King, Kevin Kline, Hugh Laurie, Nigella Lawson, David Letterman, Jerry Lee Lewis, Ewan McGregor, Marcel Marceau, Ricky Martin, Johnny Mathis, Abu Mazen, Meat Loaf, Wolfgang Amadeus Mozart, Camilla Parker Bowles, Michael Parkinson, James Patterson, Luciano Pavarotti, Iggy Pop, Prince Rainier of Monaco, Maurice Ravel, Ronald Reagan, Ginger Rogers, Françoise Sagan, Carlos Santana, Arnold Schwarzenegger, Kevin Spacey, Steven Spielberg, Emma Thompson, Holly Valance, Jules Verne, Michael Winner, the Duchess of York.

APPENDIX

———•◆•———

The relationships between the 12 animal signs, both on a personal level and business level, are an important aspect of Chinese horoscopes and in this appendix the compatibility between the signs is shown in the two tables that follow.

Also included are the names of the signs ruling the hours of the day and from this it is possible to find your ascendant and discover yet another aspect of your personality.

Finally, to supplement the earlier chapters on the personality and horoscope of the signs, I have included a guide on how you can get the best out of your sign and the year.

RELATIONSHIPS BETWEEN THE SIGNS

Personal Relationships

KEY

1 Excellent. Great rapport.
2 A successful relationship. Many interests in common.
3 Mutual respect and understanding. A good relationship.
4 Fair. Needs care and some willingness to compromise in order for the relationship to work.
5 Awkward. Possible difficulties in communication with few interests in common.
6 A clash of personalities. Very difficult.

	Rat	Ox	Tiger	Rabbit	Dragon	Snake	Horse	Goat	Monkey	Rooster	Dog	Pig
Rat	1											
Ox	1	3										
Tiger	4	6	5									
Rabbit	5	2	3	2								
Dragon	1	5	4	3	2							
Snake	3	1	6	2	1	5						
Horse	6	5	1	5	3	4	2					
Goat	5	5	3	1	4	3	2	2				
Monkey	1	3	6	3	1	3	5	3	1			
Rooster	5	1	5	6	2	1	2	5	5	5		
Dog	3	4	1	2	6	3	1	5	3	5	2	
Pig	2	3	2	2	2	6	3	2	2	3	1	2

Business Relationships

KEY
1 Excellent. Marvellous understanding and rapport.
2 Very good. Complement each other well.
3 A good working relationship and understanding can be developed.
4 Fair, but compromise and a common objective are often needed to make this relationship work.
5 Awkward. Unlikely to work, either through lack of trust, understanding or the competitiveness of the signs.
6 Mistrust. Difficult. To be avoided.

	Rat	Ox	Tiger	Rabbit	Dragon	Snake	Horse	Goat	Monkey	Rooster	Dog	Pig
Rat	2											
Ox	1	3										
Tiger	3	6	5									
Rabbit	4	3	3	3								
Dragon	1	4	3	3	3							
Snake	3	2	6	4	1	5						
Horse	6	5	1	5	3	4	4					
Goat	5	5	3	1	4	3	3	2				
Monkey	2	3	4	5	1	5	4	4	3			
Rooster	5	1	5	5	2	1	2	5	5	6		
Dog	4	5	2	3	6	4	2	5	3	5	4	
Pig	3	3	3	2	3	5	4	2	3	4	3	1

YOUR ASCENDANT

The ascendant has a very strong influence on your personality and, together with the information already given about your sign and the effects of the element on your sign, it will help you gain an even greater insight into your true personality according to Chinese horoscopes.

The hours of the day are named after the 12 animal signs and the sign governing the time you were born is your ascendant. To find your ascendant, look up the time of your birth in the table below, bearing in mind any local time differences in the place you were born.

11 p.m.	to	1 a.m.	The hours of the Rat
1 a.m.	to	3 a.m.	The hours of the Ox
3 a.m.	to	5 a.m.	The hours of the Tiger
5 a.m.	to	7 a.m.	The hours of the Rabbit
7 a.m.	to	9 a.m.	The hours of the Dragon
9 a.m.	to	11 a.m.	The hours of the Snake
11 a.m.	to	1 p.m.	The hours of the Horse
1 p.m.	to	3 p.m.	The hours of the Goat
3 p.m.	to	5 p.m.	The hours of the Monkey
5 p.m.	to	7 p.m.	The hours of the Rooster
7 p.m.	to	9 p.m.	The hours of the Dog
9 p.m.	to	11 p.m.	The hours of the Pig

RAT

The Rat ascendant is likely to make the sign more outgoing, sociable and careful with money. A particularly beneficial influence for those born under the signs of the Rabbit, Horse, Monkey and Pig.

OX

The Ox ascendant has a restraining, cautionary and steadying influence which many signs will benefit from. This ascendant also promotes self-confidence and willpower and is especially good for those born under the signs of the Tiger, Rabbit and Goat.

TIGER

The Tiger ascendant is a dynamic and stirring influence which makes the sign more outgoing, action-orientated and impulsive. A generally favourable ascendant for the Ox, Tiger, Snake and Horse.

RABBIT

The Rabbit ascendant has a moderating influence, making the sign more reflective, serene and discreet. A particularly beneficial influence for the Rat, Dragon, Monkey and Rooster.

DRAGON

The Dragon ascendant gives strength, determination and ambition to the sign. A favourable influence for those born under the signs of the Rabbit, Goat, Monkey and Dog.

SNAKE

The Snake ascendant can make the sign more reflective, intuitive and self-reliant. A good influence for the Tiger, Goat and Pig.

HORSE

The Horse ascendant will make the sign more adventurous, daring and on some occasions fickle. Generally a beneficial influence for the Rabbit, Snake, Dog and Pig.

GOAT

The Goat ascendant will make the sign more tolerant, easygoing and receptive. It could also impart some creative and artistic qualities. An especially good influence for the Ox, Dragon, Snake and Rooster.

MONKEY

The Monkey ascendant is likely to impart a delicious sense of humour and fun to the sign. It will make the sign more enterprising and outgoing – a particularly good influence for the Rat, Ox, Snake and Goat.

ROOSTER

The Rooster ascendant helps to give the sign a lively, outgoing and very methodical manner. Its influence will increase efficiency and is good for the Ox, Tiger, Rabbit and Horse.

DOG

The Dog ascendant makes the sign more reasonable and fair-minded as well as giving an added sense of loyalty. A very good ascendant for the Tiger, Dragon and Goat.

PIG

The Pig ascendant can make the sign more sociable and self-indulgent. It is also a caring influence and one which can make the sign want to help others. A good ascendant for the Dragon and Monkey.

HOW TO GET THE BEST FROM YOUR CHINESE SIGN AND THE YEAR

Each of the 12 Chinese signs possesses its own unique strengths and by identifying them you can use them to your advantage. Similarly, by becoming aware of possible weaknesses you can do much to rectify them and in this respect I hope the following sections will be useful. Also included are some tips on how you can get the best from the Year of the Dog.

The Rat
The Rat is blessed with many fine talents, but his undoubted strength lies in his ability to get on with others. He is sociable, charming and a good judge of character. He also possesses a shrewd mind and is good at spotting opportunities.

However, to make the most of himself and his abilities, the Rat does need to impose some discipline upon himself. He should resist the (sometimes very great) temptation of getting involved in too many activities all at the same time.

By concentrating his energies on specific matters he will fare much better as a result. Also, given his personable manner, he should seek out positions where he can use his personal relations skills to good effect. For a career, sales and marketing could prove ideal.

The Rat is also astute in dealing with finance, but while often thrifty, he can sometimes give way to moments of indulgence. It may be in his interests to exercise restraint when tempted to satisfy expensive whims!

The Rat's family and friends are important to him and while he is loyal and protective towards them, he does tend to keep his worries to himself and would be helped if he were more willing to discuss his anxieties. Others are prepared to help him, but for them to do so the Rat does need to be less secretive and guarded.

With his sharp mind, keen imagination and sociable manner, the Rat does, however, have much in his favour. When he has commitment, he can be irrepressible and, given his considerable charm, often irresistible as well! Provided he channels his energies wisely, he can make much of his life.

Advice for the Rat's Year Ahead

GENERAL PROSPECTS

Throughout the year the Rat will need to keep his wits about him, be thorough and liaise closely with others. His abilities to read situations and relate well to others will help, but this is not a year for pushing his luck too far.

CAREER PROSPECTS

This will be a busy and often demanding year, and the Rat will need to remain disciplined and well organized, but he will be supported by his colleagues and what he achieves now can be particularly helpful in the longer term.

FINANCE

With a rise in income and good chances of receiving something extra from other sources, the Rat's financial prospects are encouraging. By putting his money to good use, he can improve his position over the year.

RELATIONS WITH OTHERS

With his outgoing and sociable nature, the Rat really values his relations with others. However, the Dog year requires great care. Despite his often considerable other commitments, it is important that the Rat spends time with others and shares his concerns.

The Ox

Strong-willed, determined and resolute, the Ox certainly has a mind of his own! He is persistent and sets about achieving his objectives with a dogged determination. In addition he is reliable and tenacious and is often a source of inspiration to others. He is an achiever, and he often achieves a great deal. However, for him to really excel, he would do well to try and correct some of his weaknesses.

Being so resolute and having such a strong sense of purpose, the Ox can be inflexible and narrow-minded. He can be resistant to change and if he were prepared to be more adaptable and adventurous he would find his progress easier.

The Ox would also be helped if he were to broaden his range of interests and become more relaxed in his approach. At times he can be so preoccupied with his own activities that he is not always as mindful of others as he should be and his demeanour can sometimes be studious and serious. There are times when he would benefit from a lighter touch.

However, the Ox is true to his word and loyal to his family and friends. He is admired and respected by others and his tremendous willpower usually enables him to achieve a great deal in life.

Advice for the Ox's Year Ahead

GENERAL PROSPECTS

This year will be a good test of the Ox's redoubtable nature. There will be pressures, challenges and problems to deal with, but by doing his best, the Ox will add considerably to his experience. This may not be an easy year for him, but it can bring many long-term benefits.

CAREER PROSPECTS

There will be some good opportunities for the Ox to take on new responsibilities over the year. However, a lot will be expected of him and he will need to remain focused and disciplined. He should make the most of any chances to meet others. The contacts, skills and experience he can gain now can be to his future benefit.

FINANCE

A year for care and vigilance. With many outgoings as well as good travel possibilities, the Ox does need to manage his money well and, whenever possible, make early provision for his costlier purchases and plans.

RELATIONS WITH OTHERS

The Ox's domestic life can go well, but in view of the busy nature of the Dog year, it is important that he regularly consults those close to him. His social life will be active, with excellent prospects for new friendships and romance.

The Tiger

Lively, innovative and enterprising, the Tiger enjoys an active lifestyle. He has a wide range of interests, an alert mind and a genuine liking of others. He likes to live life to the full. However, he does not always make the most of his considerable potential.

By being so versatile, the Tiger does have a tendency to jump from one activity to another or dissipate his energies by trying to do too much at the same time. To make the most of himself he should try to exercise a certain amount of self-discipline. If he can overcome his restless tendencies, he will accomplish much more as a result.

Also, in spite of his sociable manner, the Tiger likes to retain a certain independence in his actions and would sometimes find life easier if he were more prepared to work in conjunction with others. His reliance upon his own judgement does sometimes mean that he excludes the views and advice of those around him, and this can be to his detriment. The Tiger may possess an independent spirit, but he must not let it go too far!

The Tiger does, however, have much in his favour. He is bold, original and quick-witted. If he can keep his restless nature in check, he can enjoy considerable success. In addition, he is well liked and much admired.

Advice for the Tiger's Year Ahead

GENERAL PROSPECTS

With clear objectives and careful consideration of the prevailing situations and the advice of others, the Tiger can achieve a great deal. This is very much a time for action, with effort and initiative being well rewarded.

CAREER PROSPECTS

There will be some excellent opportunities for the Tiger to make headway, although he will need to act quickly and remain fairly flexible. This is not a year for being too restrictive in what he is prepared to consider, otherwise some good opportunities could be lost.

FINANCE

A promising year, but the Tiger would do well to plan ahead as well as watch his outgoings. This is a year when a disciplined approach will pay off.

RELATIONS WITH OTHERS

The Tiger will value the support he is given by his family, friends and colleagues, and whenever he has important decisions to take or would welcome advice or assistance, he should ask. Domestically and socially, this will be an active and rewarding year and new friendships and romance can add a definite sparkle.

The Rabbit

The Rabbit is certainly one who appreciates the finer things in life. With his good taste, companionable nature and wide range of interests, he knows how to live well – and usually does!

However, for all his finesse and style, the Rabbit does possess traits he would do well to watch. His desire for a settled lifestyle makes him err on the side of caution. He dislikes change and as a consequence can miss out on opportunities. Also, there are many Rabbits who will go to great lengths to avoid difficult and fraught situations, and again, while few may relish these, sometimes in life it is necessary to take risks or stand your ground.

The Rabbit also attaches great importance to his relations with others and while he has a happy knack of getting on with most people, he can be sensitive to criticism. Difficult though it may be, he should really try to develop a thicker skin and recognize that criticism can provide valuable learning opportunities, as can some of the problems he strives so hard to avoid.

However, with his agreeable manner, keen intellect and shrewd judgement, the Rabbit does have a lot in his favour and invariably makes much of his life – and enjoys it too!

Advice for the Rabbit's Year Ahead

GENERAL PROSPECTS

A much improved year, but the Rabbit will need to seize the initiative and be bold. For the active, keen and enterprising, the Dog year holds great potential.

CAREER PROSPECTS

Over the year the Rabbit should make the most of his experience and move his career forward. By acting upon the opportunities that arise, he can make important headway. Work-wise, this is a significant year.

FINANCE

A positive year and by managing his money well, the Rabbit will be pleased with what he is able to acquire, especially for his home. Making early provision for some of his larger expenses, including travel plans, could be helpful.

RELATIONS WITH OTHERS

There will be excellent chances for the Rabbit to add to his social circle, often as a result of new personal interests or changes at work. His relations with others will go well over the year and mean a great deal to him.

The Dragon

Enthusiastic, enterprising and honourable, the Dragon possesses many admirable qualities and his life is often full and varied. He always gives his best and even though not all his endeavours may meet with success, he is nonetheless resilient and hardy, and is much admired and respected.

However, the Dragon can be blunt and forthright and, through sheer strength of character, sometimes domineering. It would certainly be in his interests to listen more closely to others rather than be so self-reliant. Also, his enthusiasm can sometimes get the better of him and he can be impulsive. To make the most of his abilities, he should give himself priorities and set about his activities in a disciplined way. More tact might not come amiss either!

However, with his lively and outgoing manner, the Dragon is well liked. With good fortune, his life is almost certain to be eventful and fulfilling. He has many talents and if he uses them wisely he will enjoy much success.

Advice for the Dragon's Year Ahead

GENERAL PROSPECTS

The Dragon may be keen and eager, but this is not a year for risks or hurried or impulsive action. Planning carefully and acting with the support of others will lead to more being accomplished.

CAREER PROSPECTS

The main benefits of the year will be the experience the Dragon is able to gain. Making the most of his chances to develop his skills or acquire new ones can prove *very* significant in the near future.

FINANCE

The Dragon will generally fare well in money matters, but with often considerable accommodation expenses and opportunities to travel, he does need to manage his situation well.

RELATIONS WITH OTHERS

Socially, this will be a promising year and with his outgoing nature and wide interests, the Dragon will often see his social circle widening. However, domestically he does need to make sure he spends quality time with those who are special to him. Travel is favourably aspected and a family holiday or trip with friends could be especially appreciated.

The Snake

The Snake is blessed with a keen intellect. He has wide interests, an enquiring mind and good judgement. He tends to be quiet and thoughtful and plans his activities with considerable care. With his fine abilities he often does well in life, but he does possess traits which can undermine his progress.

The Snake is often guarded in his actions and sometimes loses out to those who are more assertive. He can also be a loner and likes to retain a certain independence, and this too can hamper his progress. It would be in his interests to involve others more readily in his plans. The Snake has many talents and possesses a warm and rich personality, but there is a danger that this can remain concealed behind his often quiet and reserved manner. He would fare better if he were more outgoing and showed others his true worth.

However, the Snake is very much his own master. He invariably knows what he wants in life and is often prepared to journey long and hard to achieve his objectives. He does, though, have it in his power to make that journey easier. Lose some of that reticence, Snake, be more open and assertive, and do not be afraid of the occasional risk!

Advice for the Snake's Year Ahead

GENERAL PROSPECTS
The Snake is generally cautious and likes to take his time in setting about his various activities. However, this is a year to be bold and move forward. With the aspects on his side, a lot can happen.

CAREER PROSPECTS
In the Dog year the Snake's talents, experience and ideas can lead to him making excellent and often well-deserved progress. To benefit, though, he will need to act positively and show some flexibility. The headway he makes now can have important long-term value.

FINANCE
A favourable year for money matters with a possible rise in income and good chances of something extra from other sources. To benefit, though, the Snake does need to manage his finances well and be thorough when considering any major purchase.

RELATIONS WITH OTHERS

The Snake will have good reason to value the support he receives over the year, although to benefit fully he does need to be willing to share his thoughts and plans. It is also important that he spends time with those who are special to him as well as on socializing and recreational pursuits. With this being such a constructive year, any attention he can give to his well-being can make a difference.

The Horse

Versatile, hardworking and sociable, the Horse makes his mark wherever he goes. He has an eloquent and engaging manner and makes friends with ease. He is quick-witted, has an alert mind and is certainly not averse to taking risks or experimenting with new ideas.

The Horse possesses a strong and likeable personality, but he does also have his weaknesses. With his wide interests he does not always finish everything he starts and he would do well to be more persevering and to overcome his restless tendencies. When he has made his plans he should stick with them.

The Horse loves company and values both his family and friends. However, throughout his life, he needs to keep his temper in check and be diplomatic in tense situations. If not, he could risk jeopardizing the respect and good relations he so values.

However, the Horse has a multitude of talents and a lively and outgoing personality. If he can overcome his restless and volatile nature, he can lead a rich and highly fulfilling life.

Advice for the Horse's Year Ahead

GENERAL PROSPECTS

This will be a busy and eventful year for the Horse, but throughout he does need to draw on the support and advice of others rather than do too much on his own.

CAREER PROSPECTS

The Horse will be able to make considerable and well-deserved progress over the year although he does need to be swift in following up opportunities and putting himself forward. He should also aim to work closely with others. With good support and backing, so much more can be accomplished.

FINANCE

This will be an expensive year, especially as many Horses will move. As a result the Horse would do well to keep a close watch on his level of spending. Good management and some prudence will help.

RELATIONS WITH OTHERS

The Horse's relations with others will be important over the year, and by involving others in his plans he will find far more can be accomplished as a result. Affairs of the heart are well aspected and the Horse can also look forward to a full and active social life.

The Goat

The Goat has a warm, friendly and understanding manner and gets on well with most people. He is generally easy-going, has a fond appreciation of the finer things in life and possesses a rich imagination. He is often artistic and enjoys the creative arts and outdoor activities.

However, despite his engaging manner, there lurks beneath his skin a sometimes tense and pessimistic nature. The Goat can be a worrier and without the support and encouragement of others can feel insecure and be hesitant in his actions.

To make the most of himself the Goat should aim to become more assertive and decisive as well as more at ease with himself. He has much in his favour, but he really does need to promote himself more and be bolder. He would also be helped if he were to sort out his priorities and set about his activities in an organized and disciplined manner. There are some Goats who tend to be haphazard in the way they go about things and this can hamper their progress.

Although the Goat will always value the support of others, it would also be in his interests to become more independent and not be so reticent about striking out on his own. He does, after all, possess many talents, as well as a likeable personality, and by always giving his best he can make his life rich, rewarding and enjoyable.

Advice for the Goat's Year Ahead

GENERAL PROSPECTS

This will be a demanding year for the Goat and he will face both pressures and problems. However, by rising to the challenges and drawing on the support of others, he will discover a lot about himself and prepare the way for the success that awaits in following years.

CAREER PROSPECTS

This is a year that will test the Goat. He should pay careful attention to his relations with his colleagues, heed the advice of more senior colleagues and aim to add to his circle of contacts. He needs to be wary of being drawn into unhelpful squabbles or being distracted by the pettiness of others too. However, what he achieves and gains in experience can be significant in his future advance.

FINANCE

A year for vigilance and control. With his current obligations and some of his more expensive plans, the Goat would find it helpful to keep a close watch on his financial situation and to plan ahead.

RELATIONS WITH OTHERS

In view of the tricky aspects prevailing this year it is important that the Goat is forthcoming about any problems and concerns he may have and draws on the help that others can give. Spending time with loved ones will also help to maintain a good rapport. The Goat should also aim to get in contact with those who share similar interests. Some important new friendships can be made as a result. He does need to be aware of possible problem areas and the sensitivities of others, but his perceptive nature will often guide him well.

The Monkey

Lively, enterprising and innovative, the Monkey certainly knows how to impress. He has wide interests, a good sense of fun and relates well to others. He also possesses a shrewd mind and often has a happy knack of turning events to his advantage.

However, despite his versatility and considerable gifts, the Monkey does have his weaknesses. He often lacks persistence, can get distracted easily and also places tremendous reliance upon his own judgement. While his self-belief is commendable, it would certainly be in his interests to be more mindful of the views of others. Also, while he likes to keep tabs on all that is going on around him, he can be evasive and secretive with regard to his own feelings and activities, and again a more forthcoming attitude would be to his advantage.

In his desire to succeed the Monkey can also be tempted to cut corners or be crafty and he should recognize that such actions can rebound on him!

However, the Monkey is resourceful and his sheer strength of character will ensure he has an interesting and varied life. If he can channel his considerable energies wisely and overcome his restless tendencies, his life can be crowned with success. And with his amiable personality, he will enjoy the friendship of many.

Advice for the Monkey's Year Ahead

GENERAL PROSPECTS

This can be a year of change and opportunity, but the Monkey will need to liaise closely with others as well as keep himself informed of developments. He may like to be his own master, but in 2006 he will fare much better by doing things with others.

CAREER PROSPECTS

Some important changes are in the offing, but the Monkey will need to keep a close watch on unfolding situations and be prepared to adjust as necessary. However, there will be some excellent chances for those Monkeys who want to change the nature of their work or broaden their experience, and the Monkey's resourceful nature will serve him well.

FINANCE

This is a year for care and caution. If entering into important agreements the Monkey does need to check the terms and obligations as well as avoid unnecessary risks. He should also be wary of lending to others.

RELATIONS WITH OTHERS

The support the Monkey receives over the year can make a considerable difference to how he fares. However, to benefit, he does need to talk *and listen*. Also, despite an often busy lifestyle, he should make sure time is set aside for sharing with others. If he does so, his domestic and social life can add a richness to his life and year.

The Rooster

With his considerable bearing and incisive and resolute manner, the Rooster cuts an impressive figure. He has a sharp mind, is well informed on many matters and expresses himself clearly and convincingly. He is meticulous and efficient and commands a great deal of respect. He also has a genuine interest in others.

The Rooster has much in his favour, but there are some aspects of his character that can tell against him. He can be candid in his views and overzealous in his actions, and sometimes he can say or do things he later regrets. His high standards also make him fussy, even pedantic, and he can get diverted into relatively minor matters when in truth he could be occupying his time more profitably. Also, while the Rooster is a great planner, he can sometimes be unrealistic in his expectations. In making plans – indeed, in most of his activities – he would do well to consult others. By doing so, he would greatly benefit from their input.

The Rooster has considerable talents as well as commendable drive and commitment, but to make the most of himself he does need to channel his energies wisely and watch his candid and sometimes volatile nature. With care, however, he can make a success of his life, and with his wide interests and outgoing personality, he will enjoy the friendship and respect of many.

Advice for the Rooster's Year Ahead

GENERAL PROSPECTS

This will be a challenging year for the Rooster and he will need to remain mindful of prevailing situations and show some flexibility in approach. Throughout the year, he will gain a lot from talking to and consulting with others.

CAREER PROSPECTS

The Dog year will be a testing time for the Rooster. He will face pressures and have sometimes complex matters to deal with, but by rising to the challenges and maintaining his high standards, he will not only learn a great deal but also add to his reputation. The lessons of the year can prove positive and far-reaching.

FINANCE

A year for vigilance. Transactions, new agreements and paperwork all need to be handled carefully and risks should be avoided. The Rooster's efficient nature will help, but the year can be unforgiving of lapses and mistakes.

RELATIONS WITH OTHERS

The Rooster has always recognized the value of good communication and this is very much a year for dialogue, particularly in view of all that it might bring and the decisions that may need taking. There will be excellent opportunities for the Rooster to widen his social circle.

The Dog

Loyal, dependable and with a good understanding of human nature, the Dog is well placed to win the respect and admiration of many. He is a no-nonsense sort of person and hates any sort of hypocrisy and falsehood. With the Dog you know where you stand and, given his direct manner, where he stands on any issue. He also has a strong humanitarian nature and often champions good and just causes.

The Dog has many fine attributes, although there are certain traits that can prevent him from either enjoying or making the most of his life. He is a great worrier and can get anxious over all manner of things. Whenever he is tense or concerned, he should be prepared to speak to others rather than shoulder his worries all by himself. In some cases, they could even be of his own making! Also, the Dog has a tendency to look on the pessimistic side and he would certainly be helped if he were to view his undertakings more optimistically. He does, after all, possess many skills and should justifiably have faith in his abilities. Another weakness is his tendency to be stubborn over certain issues.

If the Dog can reduce the anxious and pessimistic side of his nature, then he will not only enjoy life more but also find he is achieving more. He possesses a truly admirable character and his loyalty, reliability and sincerity are appreciated by all he meets. In his life he will do much good and befriend many – and he owes it to himself to enjoy life too. Sometimes it might help him to recall the words of another Dog, Sir Winston Churchill: 'When I look back on all these worries I remember the story of the old man who said on his deathbed that he had had a lot of trouble in his life, most of which never happened.'

Advice for the Dog's Year Ahead

GENERAL PROSPECTS

This is a year of considerable potential for the Dog, but to benefit he really does need to seize the initiative, draw a line under any past disappointments and move ahead. Fortune will certainly favour the bold and the willing.

CAREER PROSPECTS

The Dog's work prospects are excellent. To benefit, though, he will need to pursue any openings that interest him as well as further his skills. For those Dogs who are unfulfilled in their present position, this is a year to consider other possibilities. Positive action *will* be rewarded.

FINANCE

The Dog's earning abilities will be in good form over the year. However, with some Dogs moving and many spending a great deal on their accommodation, the Dog does need to manage his finances well. Good control can make an important difference.

RELATIONS WITH OTHERS

By sharing thoughts, plans and activities, the Dog can make this a rich and rewarding year. There will be excellent opportunities for him to add to his social circle, and for the unattached a romance started during the year can make this a special time.

The Pig

Genial, sincere and trusting, the Pig gets on well with most people. He has a kind and caring nature, a dislike of discord and often a good sense of humour. In addition, he has a fondness for socializing and enjoying the good life!

The Pig possesses a shrewd mind, is particularly adept at dealing with business and financial matters, and has a robust and resilient nature. Although not all his plans may work out as he would like, he is tenacious and will often rise up and succeed after experiencing setbacks and difficulties. In his often active and varied life he can accomplish a great deal, although there are certain aspects of his character that can tell against him. If he can modify these or keep them in check then his life will certainly be easier and possibly even more successful.

In his activities the Pig can sometimes overcommit himself and while he does not want to disappoint, he would certainly be helped if he were to set about his activities in an organized and systematic manner and give himself priorities at busy times. He should also not allow others to take advantage of his good nature and it would be in his interests to be more discerning. There will have been times when he has been gullible and naïve; fortunately, though, he quickly learns from his mistakes. However, he possesses a stubborn streak and if new situations do not fit in with his line of thinking, he can be inflexible. Such an attitude may not always be to his advantage.

The Pig is a great pleasure-seeker and while he should enjoy the fruits of his labours, he can sometimes be self-indulgent and extravagant. This again is something he would do well to watch.

However, though the Pig may possess some faults, those who come into contact with him are invariably impressed by his integrity, amiable manner and intelligence. If he uses his talents wisely, his life can be crowned with considerable achievement and he will also be loved and respected by many.

Advice for the Pig's Year Ahead

GENERAL PROSPECTS
The Pig can fare well this year, although he does need to keep his expectations modest. He should aim to build steadily on his present position and to add to his experience. What is accomplished now can lead to success in the following and more auspicious Pig year.

CAREER PROSPECTS
The Pig should take full advantage of any chances to add to his skills and experience, including going on training courses and gaining additional qualifications. What he achieves now can turn out to be an important stepping-stone to future success.

FINANCE
A positive year with the Pig often enjoying some good fortune. However, with his many expenses, plans and travel possibilities, he does need to manage his finances carefully.

RELATIONS WITH OTHERS
The good-natured Pig really values his relations with others and will be encouraged by the support he is given. When he has ideas he wants to take further or decisions he has to make, he really would do well to discuss these. Socially, some good friendships will be formed over the year, while for the unattached, romance can blossom.